FIRE IN THE REED
Intimations Regarding Thelemic Priestcraft

M. Dionysius Rogers
(e.k.a. T Polyphilus, *Ep. Gn.*)

Dedicated to those clergy
who have elected
to educate me
by serving the Church
under my formal supervision.

Heavy is the labor, but great indeed is the reward.

QUID VOLES ILLUD FAC

INITIUM SAPIENTIAE AMOR DOMINI

OFFERIMUS TIBI DONUM CORPUS DEI

DEUS EST HOMO

0. Greeting

Peace, Tolerance, Truth:
Salutation on all Points of the Triangle.

Do what thou wilt shall be the whole of the Law.

This volume is intended primarily as a resource for clergy of the Gnostic Catholic Church (*Ecclesia Gnostica Catholica*, or E.G.C.) in our work as ministers of the Law of Thelema. Along with the initiatory degree system of *Mysteria Mystica Maxima,* E.G.C. is one of the outer rites of *Ordo Templi Orientis* (O.T.O.), a religious body dedicated to the Law of Thelema. The ceremonial details of *Mysteria Mystica Maxima* are private and confidential, whereas the Gnostic Catholic Church conducts most services publicly. Our central sacrament, the Gnostic Mass, is intended to serve as the "broad base of public association" in a wider Thelemic culture and community.[*] Although *Fire in the Reed* is aimed at the formation of aspirants to knowledgeable and puissant Thelemic priesthood within the particular institution of E.G.C., it is my hope that it will also serve to inform our inquisitive laity and reflective Thelemites who are not connected with the Church, as well as those who may simply be curious about the Law and our rite.

In common with O.T.O. which provides our leadership and spiritual sanction, the Gnostic Catholic Church accepts the prophetic work of Aleister Crowley (1875–1947 EV) generally, and *The Book of the Law* more especially, as the indispensible cornerstone of the Law of Thelema. O.T.O. is the "Caliphate" of Thelema, in the sense that we strive to embody the social system advocated by the Prophet of the Æon (a.k.a. Baphomet, the Master Therion, 666, Perdurabo, etc.), perpetuating his religious authority in a direct, exoteric transmission of recognized global heads. From the vantage-

---

[*] Aleister Crowley to Karl Germer, 12-14 March, 1942.

1

point of E.G.C., these heads are considered to be the universal Patriarchs (or potentially, Matriarchs) of the Church. The Church's hierarchy is a topic examined in the body of this book.

I was baptized into E.G.C. in East Chicago in 1993 EV, and confirmed in Austin, Texas later that same year. At the time, I had already considered myself a Thelemite for a few years, and I immediately applied myself to a novitiate in aspiration to the Church's holy orders. After two years, I was admitted to the diaconate, and I became a priest another two years after that. For nearly all of my first decade in the Church, I was a member of Circle of Stars Sanctuary, the E.G.C. congregation hosted by Scarlet Woman Lodge O.T.O. in Austin. During this period I was also active as the choragus of the Unknown Rivers choir, assembled for the purpose of Thelemic sacred song.

My episcopal consecration took place on 22 July 2006 EV, and as a function of my new office I also adopted the name T Polyphilus. This name stems from Poliphilo, the bereaved dreamer-protagonist of the fifteenth-century *Hypnerotomachia*, an enigmatic tome with themes of erotic supremacy, hermetic magic, and pagan pageantry that anticipate Thelema. In fact, the nymph *Thelemia* who serves as a counselor to Poliphilo was in all likelihood the proximate source for Rabelais' use of the name *Thélème* for his literary abbey of "Do what thou wilt."

As a bishop, I train novices for service in the diaconate and the priesthood, and I supervise clergy in the diaconal and sacerdotal orders as well as the novitiate. I continue to be active as a ritualist, administering the full range of the Church's sacraments, and constantly at work on the development of new ceremonies. In addition, I work with fellow clergy in seeking more effective ways to promulgate the Law and to bring Thelema to the attention of a wider public.

Although I have tried to make the contents of this book as accessible as possible to novices, it is intended as an intermediate text and manual of reference, rather than a complete primer. I presume a basic acquaintance with Liber XV, the ritual of the Gnostic Mass which is the central ceremony of the Church. Readers may want to have a copy at hand; see the bibliography for editions that have "approved" status for official use. With all of the other materials that I was anxious to include here, I have elected *not* to create yet another unapproved edition of that widely-available text. In addition, I do not balk at the use of some rather specialized terminology in discussing the operations of the priesthood, and these preliminary remarks are probably a good time to alert readers to the fact that a glossary is available at the end of the book to address the more recondite terms and special usages.

Discussion of the church hierarchy and the cardinal sacraments in this book is consistently focused on the implementation of E.G.C. in the United States of America. In the other Grand Lodges and National Sections of O.T.O., as well as those areas not under any such jurisdiction, institutional features of the E.G.C. rite vary from the ones which supply the grounds for *Fire in the Reed*. While I hope that this book still contains much of interest to E.G.C. clergy and members in other countries, they should be aware that their ecclesiastical circumstances may differ from mine.

Much of the material included here has been previously published at my website *Vigorous Food & Divine Madness*. My thanks go out to Al Billings and John G. Bell as the managers of the hermetic.com domain which has played host to my earlier efforts to share this sort of information with a global audience. Earlier versions of individual rituals and essays have also appeared in various O.T.O. publications, including the U.S. Grand Lodge newsletter *Agapé*, *The Scarlet Letter* of Scarlet Woman Lodge, *Doomsayer's Digest* of Subtlety or Force Encampment, and *The Current* of

Aum. Ha. Lodge. Finally, some of this material originally took the form of talks and presentations given at national O.T.O. conferences in the United States, the London conference for the centennial of M∴M∴M∴.. and various synaxes for E.G.C. clergy. Thanks to Clay and Valerie, who have been in the front line of readers and supplied corrections to the book in proof.

Love is the law, love under will.

T Polyphilus
Centennial, Colorado
A.L. V v
Sol in Gemini, Luna in Scorpio

1. Thelema, Magick, and Worship

In electing to use the word *priestcraft* in the title of this book, I deliberately court notoriety. Although the term at one time had a more neutral valuation of "sacerdotal business," it was seized upon and promoted by anti-clerical parties in the European Enlightenment specifically to imply the culpability of church hierarchies in deluding and oppressing the people.[*] Even so, the raw denotations of its components *priest* and *craft* speak directly to my purpose here.

Thelema demands a priesthood. The word *priest* appears more than a dozen times in our Holy Books, and one of the Prophet's descriptions of an adept of Thelema is "a magician, and a priest of the Holy One."[†] While we certainly recognize the moral and metaphysical bankruptcy of the slave-religions of the old æon, we also perceive the need for healthy expressions of spiritual authority. Our Prophet wrote against the misunderstanding of "Do what thou wilt" as vulgar political anarchism, in a chapter of *The Book of Lies* entitled "Louis Lingg." I have presumed to riff on that text in the following epigram which I call "Louie Lingam":

> I am not an Atheist in your sense of the word:
> > your doctrine is too coarse for any known blasphemy to shame it.
>
> I am not an Atheist in your sense of the word:
> > fancy a Priest let loose on Society!
>
> As long as men and women shall bury their
> > own perfect natures in fear, guilt, and shame—I am against Atheism, and for the Mysteries.
>
> Every "rational enlightenment" has engendered
> > new superstitions.

---

[*] And yet, consider *Liber Legis* II:25!
[†] Crowley, *Magick,* p. 476.

Crowley himself claimed to be both an atheist and the "truest of all Christians."*

Effective, constructive priesthood—especially of the sort elicited by the Law of Thelema—requires *craft* in nearly every sense. In its most basic, original capacity, the word means *power*: the personal power of knowledge and charisma, the social power of cultures and institutions, the conceptual power of symbols and discourses, and the material power of resources and action. Additionally, *craft* evokes the skills involved in making objects, the trades organized to authenticate and vend those skills, and the mysteries founded to train aspirants to those trades. Whichever traditions we consult, whether it is the craft of writing or weaving, of masonry or witchery, the full gist of the manifold term *craft* turns out to be little different than that of *magick*: the art and science of producing change in accordance with will.

In the Master Therion's eighteenth theorem of magick, he declares that the magician "may attract to himself any force of the Universe by making himself a fit receptacle for it, establishing a connection with it, and arranging conditions so that its nature compels it to flow toward him."† In his reforms of O.T.O. and his agenda for the liturgy of E.G.C., the Prophet's concern was to establish connections with the great religious movements of history, and to arrange conditions so that the emergent human nature of the New Æon would compel groups and social agents to embrace the Law. In turn, when individual Thelemites recognize in themselves a desire to serve humanity with the force of the Crowned and Conquering Child who is the animating spirit of the Æon, those Thelemites can become fit receptacles through training, establish a connection to the Church through the sacrament of holy orders, and arrange conditions so that the sacerdotal power flows to and through them.

---

* *Crowley on Christ,* pp. 116 & 196.
† Crowley, *Magick,* p. 130.

6

Finally, it is worth attending to that activity which priests and priestesses conduct, and which is typically thought to be at the core of the generic practice of religion: **worship**. Etymologically, the word is free of metaphysical baggage. It is simply "worth-ship," or *value*. Worship is nothing other than the expression of value. To those whose worship consists of equating objects to quantities of metal, estimating rates of return on bloodless speculations, or appraising the extent to which markets of exchange may be exploited to advantage, I say to those: your rites are furnished elsewhere. Likewise, to those whose worship is grounded in the supposed dictates of a persnickety Most High, or the deontological postulates of texts from past millenia, I bid them pass on to their musty rewards. But to any for whom *value* can still signify the longing of a gaze, the tenderness of a caress, the richness of a memory, or the heat of a breath, to these I extend this exploration of our mystery. For, "Love is the law, love under will."

"The world needs religion."

Aleister Crowley and his early occult pupil J.F.C. Fuller were frequently at odds on the subject of religion. They were of one mind regarding their opposition to popular Christianity; but Fuller condemned religion wholesale, while Crowley intended to recuperate it under the heading of Magick. The Beast maintained that his teachings could only function in the context of a proper appreciation for metaphysical conditions including the existence of a "spiritual hierarchy."[*] In this respect, Crowley was keeping to a course set in the works of his immediate prior incarnation Eliphas Levi (✠Alphonse Louis Constant), who rigorously identified true occult magic with the power expressed in the sacerdotal acts of the Roman Catholic Church.

Later, Crowley wrote the following as the opening of his Editorial in the Blue *Equinox* of 1919 EV:

> The world needs religion.
>
> Religion must represent Truth, and celebrate it.
>
> This truth is of two orders: one, concerning Nature external to Man; two, concerning Nature internal to Man.
>
> Existing religions, especially Christianity, are based on primitive ignorance of the facts, particularly of external Nature.
>
> Celebrations must conform to the custom and nature of the people.
>
> The Law of Thelema offers a religion which fulfils all necessary conditions.
>
> The philosophy and metaphysics of Thelema are sound, and offer a solution of the deepest problems of humanity.

---

[*] Crowley, *Confessions,* pp. 540-1.

The science of Thelema is orthodox; it has no false
theories of Nature, no false fables of the origin
of things.
The psychology and ethics of Thelema are perfect.
It has destroyed the damnable delusion of
Original Sin, making every one unique,
independent, supreme, and sufficient.
The Law of Thelema is given in the Book of
the Law.

Nearly thirty years later, Louis Wilkinson IX° wrote:

The gain that the reader will get from this book
[*The Book of the Law*] will be primarily religious. For
the "Law" is in its essence a religious Law; its
sanctions, its injunctions, and its prohibitions are
religious. At the same time it is not a dogmatic
religion in the sense in which most religions are
dogmatic; it is a faith for the individualist, as is
clearly shown by its central text, "Do what thou
wilt shall be the whole of the Law."*

O.T.O. is a religious organization which promulgates and
demonstrates this Law. The religious features of O.T.O. are
in no way limited to the rite of the Gnostic Catholic Church
which depends from it. The initiations of *Mysteria Mystica
Maxima* express a sacramental intention through religious
mechanisms, and the ultimate teachings of the higher
degrees of O.T.O. unlock the genuine esoteric spiritual
legacies of religions throughout history and around the
world. But *Ecclesia Gnostica Catholica* has been singled out by
the Prophet of Thelema as a means of addressing an
inherent religious appetite and need of the common range of
healthy people who might aspire to Thelema. In his
Confessions, he wrote:

---

* Introduction to *The Law Is for All,* p. 17.

Human nature demands (in the case of most people) the satisfaction of the religious instinct, and, to very many, this may best be done by ceremonial means. I wished therefore to construct a ritual through which people might enter into ecstasy as they have always done under the influence of appropriate ritual.[*]

The ambition to "enter into ecstasy" is addressed in much greater detail in Crowley's essay "Energized Enthusiasm," which provides some ideas about what he may have intended by the phrase "appropriate ritual." "Energized Enthusiasm" opens with an invocation of the divine by the name IAO, just as the Gnostic Mass does, and goes on to express a theory of three methods by which individuals or groups may connect with and draw upon the energies that reside in the great spiritual battery of the divine.[†] He attributes this theory to the ancient Greeks, and uses three Greek gods to characterize the methods.[‡] These are Dionysus for the pharmaceutical method, Apollo for the musical, and Aphrodite for the sexual. At the end of the essay (written prior to the composition of the Gnostic Mass), there is a purported exposé of a secret congregational ritual in which "By the use of the three methods in one the whole being of man may thus be stimulated."[§] While admittedly less radical in its application of the methods than the ceremony described in "Energized Enthusiasm," the Gnostic Mass does indeed employ all three of these devices for the production of ecstasy.

---

[*] Crowley, *Confessions,* p. 714.
[†] Crowley, "Energized Enthusiasm," *The Equinox* I:9, p. 23. He actually writes of "discharging the Lyden Jar of Genius."
[‡] It seems relatively certain to me that he had in mind the frenzies or *furores* of Plato's *Phaedrus,* which have been perpetuated and interpreted throughout the Western esoteric tradition, figuring in the works of Ficino, Agrippa, and others.
[§] Crowley, "Energized Enthusiasm," p. 28.

The pharmaceutical method in the ceremony of "Energized Enthusiasm" involves a mysterious elixir with evidently powerful psychedelic properties. The Gnostic Mass resorts to the more pedestrian but highly traditional alternative of cakes and wine. The intention that the wine should have a drug effect is indicated by the facts that each communicant is to be provided with their own goblet, and that fasting prior to communication is recommended.*

For the method of Aphrodite, the presiding officers of the "Energized Enthusiasm" rite, a High Priest and Priestess, decorously copulate on a platform painted with a large cross, while the chapel fills with perfumed purple smoke. The ritual of the Gnostic Mass contains an assortment of barely less direct erotic elements, including the stroking of the lance, the disrobing and unveiling of the priestess, the priest's kisses to the knees and between the breasts of the priestess, and finally the climactic "marriage" in which the lance transmits the particle to the graal.

The musical method is evident in both ceremonies also. While the Gnostic Mass doesn't include liturgical elements as ambitious as Sappho's hymn to Aphrodite (which figured in its original Greek in the ritual of "Energized Enthusiasm"), it does frequently and explicitly call for music. The anthem of the Mass, which was the germ of its original composition, is to be "set to music, which may be as elaborate as art can devise."

Having thus brought into the Gnostic Mass the full range of techniques that he had earlier classed as methods of "theurgy," 666 could later claim:

> In this ceremony we have every opportunity for the enjoyment of those states of consciousness which will alleviate the pain of the realization of the

---

* The individual goblets are prescribed in Liber XV. For fasting, see "Conditions for Eucharistic Magic" later in this volume.

futility of material existence. But there is nothing in the ritual which is not scientifically accurate. And the element which produces fanaticism and other socially dangerous states of mind is eliminated.[*]

The feature "eliminated" from our liturgy is what he elsewhere characterized as "this awful fear of nature and of God ... twisted into an engine of oppression and torture against any one who declines to grovel and cringe before their filthy fetish."[†] We demand no penance for the human condition; we offer no condemnations of individuality or carnality. The pervasiveness of these features in Christianity has only set down deeper roots in the most active of both Protestant and Catholic cults since the Reformation. Such "morality" testifies to the loss of true wisdom that once resided in an institution which had even so "maintained well enough the traditions of the true Gnostic Church in whose keeping the secrets are," with respect to sacramental discipline.[‡]

In "Energized Enthusiasm," Crowley opined that "A special and Secret Mass, a Mass of the Holy Ghost, a Mass of the Mystery of the Incarnation, to be performed at stated intervals, might have saved both monks and nuns, and given the Church eternal dominion of the world."[§] But the monks and nuns were not saved. Our Gnostic Mass may adumbrate the Secret Mass of Crowley's conjecture more than actually realize it. Still, it is the central ceremony by which we seek to slake that widespread *need* in our world for a vital religion that provides an ecstatic path to peace, tolerance, and truth, and a conscientious rejection of fear, guilt, and shame. Do what thou wilt shall be the whole of the Law.

---

[*] Crowley, letter to Walter Duranty, 14 Nov. 1929. (Thanks to Richard Kaczynksi for this reference.)
[†] Crowley, *The World's Tragedy,* p. xxxi.
[‡] Crowley, *Magick,* p. 269.
[§] Crowley, "Energized Enthusiasm," p. 32.

Theology is the Enemy of Ecstasy

Our Prophet once declared:

> A Protestant is one to whom all things sacred are
> profane, whose mind being all filth can see
> nothing in the sexual act but a crime or a jest,
> whose only facial gestures are the sneer and the
> leer. Protestantism is the excrement of human
> thought, and accordingly in Protestant countries
> art, if it exists at all, only exists to revolt.*

And he should know! He was himself, after all, raised among
the ultra-Protestant Plymouth Brethren.

For better or for worse, though, the intellectual and
institutional consequences of the Protestant Reformation
have served for centuries to condition the sense of the word
religion, and it may well have been just this consideration
which later caused Crowley to remark that "a great deal of
misunderstanding, and ... a rather stupid kind of mischief"
might follow from calling Thelema "a new religion."† It is a
strange twist of history that even Buddhism has taken its
modern form in response to influences from Protestantism,
chiefly through the avenue of the Buddhist catechism constructed in the nineteenth century by Theosophical Society
founder Henry Steele Olcott. Much of the nascent science of
cultural anthropology in that same period was based on data
from Protestant missionaries, and their biases have infected
not only that discipline but the entire scholarly enterprise of
comparative religion from its root.‡

---

* Crowley, "Energized Enthusiasm," *The Equinox* I:9, p. 24.
† Crowley, *Magick Without Tears,* p. 219.
‡ See discussion in J.Z. Smith's *Drudgery Divine*, and a more hopeful
continuation of the topic in the "Comparative Mystics" chapter of
J. Kripal, *The Serpent's Gift.*

Our Saint Friedrich Nietzsche called Protestantism the "original sin" that contaminates German philosophy. He further wrote for his "Definition of Protestantism: the partial paralysis of Christianity—*and* of reason."* The confessional conflicts occasioned by the Protestant Reformation elevated theology to the defining attribute of religious identity. Orthodoxy, or "right belief," was prized and contested, to the frequent neglect of *orthopraxy,* or "right practice." The Protestant derogation of "works" was certainly to blame in part for this emphasis, but it was complemented by the Catholic policing of consciences and the tendency of both religious and secular academies to reduce religion to a psychological epiphenomenon of a series of texts.

In the early years of the New Æon, the classicist Jane Ellen Harrison cut to the heart of the matter, when she wrote:

> Until recent times definitions of religion have usually included some notion of a relation of the human soul to a god; they have been in some sense theological. ... [I]t is important to note that theology is in all ... religions not essential and integral, but rather a phase, a stage in marking a particular moment in development.†

Note that Harrison came to this understanding in the course of her efforts to clarify the popular religious life of ancient Greece, prior to and apart from Christianity, and that she also marks out **magic** as a necessary prerequisite for religion, far more essential than the later accretions of theology.‡ In these positions, she was influenced by the sociological concepts of Émile Durkheim, who also viewed theology as a late and superficial accretion to basic religious functions. I

---

* *The Anti-Christ,* trans. J. Norman, aphorism 10.
† Jane Ellen Harrison, *Themis,* p. 488.
‡ *Ibid., op. cit.,* pp. 215-6.

14

strongly concur with these views about the contingency of the theological enterprise.

Further, I assert that the religious manifestations characteristic of Thelema are properly *post-theological*. In particular, I wish to identify two general forms of theology that will be rightly spurned and discarded by individual Thelemites, and more importantly, by our Church. These forms are superstitious faith on the one hand and systematic theology on the other.

As adherents in a Thelemic religious body, we are sometimes confronted with the difficulty that U.S.-American civic discourse has adopted "faith" as a synonym for "religion." This equation is a natural outcome of the rational Enlightenment background of political discourse in this country, asserting *freedom of religion* as identical with *liberty of conscience*. It is also consistent with the Deistic contempt for "revealed religion" asserted by many of the founders of American national polity.[*]

Our church cannot accurately be described as "faith-based." In our effort to implement scientific religion, we do not demand uniformity of belief, and certainly not on the basis of ancient superstitions. As a theological operation, superstitious faith places supreme metaphysical authority in the hands of religious professionals, or—perhaps just as frequently—in the unexamined, inherited prejudices of the individual "believer." As Nietzsche says, "Faith means not *wanting* to know the truth."[†] This fact is confirmed even by the ancient Christian proponents of faith, such as Irenaeus and Tertullian.[‡]

But our Past Patriarch remarked,

---

[*] See *The Faiths of the Founding Fathers* by D.L. Holmes.

[†] Nietzsche, *The Anti-Christ,* aphorism 51.

[‡] See K. Rudolph, *Gnosis: The Nature and History of Gnosticism* (1987), p. 373.

15

> I slept with Faith, and found a corpse in my arms
>   on awaking;
>
> I drank and danced all night with Doubt, and
>   found her a virgin in the morning.[*]

Some theologians and commentators have contrasted faith with knowledge, often using the Greek terms *pistis* and *gnosis*. Consistent with our professed identity as "gnostics," we must favor the latter. We should assist adherents to come to know the sources of belief, rather than to believe that they have found the sources of knowledge. While our clergy may know things worth teaching, we should value and encourage skepticism rather than credulity among those who seek our knowledge. To quote Nietzsche once more:

> I wage war on this theologian instinct: I have found traces of it everywhere. Anyone with theologian blood in his veins will approach things with a warped and deceitful attitude. This gives rise to a pathos that calls itself *faith*: turning a blind eye to yourself for once and for all, so that you do not have to stomach the sight of incurable mendacity.[†]

The fact that our church uses a creed does not implicate us in this "theologian instinct." The Gnostic Mass creed's primary function is *liturgical*, and its extra-liturgical role for the individual adherent is to indicate those subjects which we find it spiritually profitable to think *about*, not to circumscribe that which we are allowed to think. We do not and should not catechize our laity with any "correct" way to understand the words of our Creed, which is a text both numinous and multiply mysterious.

The second theological project with which Thelemites should find ourselves at odds is "systematic theology."

---

[*] Crowley, *The Book of Lies,* ch. 45, "Chinese Music."
[†] Nietzsche, *The Anti-Christ,* aphorism 9.

16

Although this phrase can refer more specifically to certain theological schools and tools, I use it here as a designator for the general project of creating a coherent body of religious teaching derived by rational intellectual enterprise on the basis of a specified set of scriptures and religious traditions. In its more advanced forms, systematic theology claims to discriminate those elements of "true" religious belief that are axiomatic and indispensable from those others which are peripheral and derivative. Well-meaning E.G.C. clergy have indeed from time to time suggested that this sort of enterprise ought to be undertaken on behalf of the Gnostic Catholic Church, or even for Thelema as a whole, with a goal of creating clarity about our supposedly shared gods and the divine prescriptions for Thelemites. Indeed, Crowley's sanction for "an enthusiastic putting-together of a series of doctrines, no one of which must in any way clash with Science or Magick"* seems nearly to be an exhortation to such work.

And yet the Tunis Comment to *Liber Legis* demonstrates the barriers to systematic theology for Thelemites. Crowley declared that "Short Comment" to be "the really inspired message, cutting as it does all the difficulties with a single keen stroke."† *The Book of the Law* is indisputably the cornerstone of Thelema, and yet to cite that book for theological justification is to invite shunning and contempt, by virtue of its most clearly authorized comment.

Furthermore, there is ample room for doubt that the "Great Ones of *Liber Legis*" (as Crowley calls them) are even "gods" in any customarily theological sense. The names Hadit and Ra-hoor-khuit are not even voiced in the Gnostic Mass; Nuit is named in an address to the Queen of Space where the Priest beseeches, "let them speak not of thee at

---

* Crowley, *Magick Without Tears,* p. 219.
† Crowley, *The Equinox of the Gods,* p. 126 *n.*

all." And this silence is consistent with what the Prophet elsewhere cautions:

> There are to be no regular temples of Nuit and Hadit, for They are incommensurables and absolutes. Our religion therefore, for the People, is the Cult of the Sun, who is our particular star of the Body of Nuit, from whom in the strictest scientific sense, come this earth, a chilled spark of Him, and all our Light and Life.[*]

The incommensurability and absoluteness of Nuit and Hadit are shown in the operations of "Liber Had" and "Liber Nu,"[†] which are severely magical in character, far from any conventional procedure of the religious sort, and rigorously solitary. They are not at all consistent with the abilities and aspirations of *theologians,* those whom Ludwig Feuerbach categorically scorns as hypocrites, fantasts, and speculative theorizers.[‡] Feuerbach's writings are of special value to us, as he is concerned to demonstrate in every particular how man creates god in his own image while still affirming the value of that creation.[§] As we say, "There is no god but man." Feuerbach wrote, "In religion man does not satisfy *other beings;* he satisfies his own nature."[**]

Consider also the paper in which Crowley theorizes most explicitly regarding "that energized enthusiasm which is the lever that moves God." In "Energized Enthusiasm," it almost seems as if a theology is being presented through its triad of Greek deities. But Crowley is not concerned with divine personalities named Dionysus, Apollo, and Aphrodite, nor does he want to establish the canonical mandates of these gods, the "proper" ways to show them reverence, or

---

[*] Crowley, *The Law Is for All,* p. 163 (commentary to *CCXX* III:22).
[†] *The Equinox* I:7, pp. 11-20 & 83-91.
[‡] *Lectures on the Essence of Religion,* 8th Lecture, p. 62.
[§] See J. Kripal, *The Serpent's Gift,* ch. 2.
[**] Feuerbach, *Lectures on the Essence of Religion,* 9th lecture, p. 76.

the rewards of service to them. On the contrary, it is in this paper that he remarks, "Easier I find it … to extend my connotation of 'man' than to invent 'God.'"[*] Crowley has taken these three gods from Plato's dialogue *Phaedrus* (and its later mutations in esoteric tradition). In a characteristically modern and Thelemic way he reduces the gods to indices, convenient signifiers for the three chief methods of inducing ecstasy in order to power human creativity.[†] His use of the ancient Greek god-names is to give us a sense of both the depth of the occult traditions on which he draws and the sanctity of the human genius into which he inquires.

Sigmund Freud's most confrontationally critical work on religion is *The Future of an Illusion*. In one of his devil's-advocate passages there he remarks, "If you want to expel religion from our European civilization, you can only do it by means of another system of doctrines," which would itself engender a functional religion, with all of the concomitant drawbacks.[‡] In replying to his own objection, Freud emphasizes the desired differences in his post-religious system: it is to be non-delusive and more capable of being corrected. It will be science, not religion. But Freudian psycho-analysis, for all of its scientific trappings, is already at some remove from the positivist territory of the physical sciences. It is no closer to, say, biology, than the monotheism of Moses was to the Canaanite religions of antiquity. In effect, Freud's proposal is that the superstitious religion of traditions focused on God should be replaced with a scientific religion trained on the soul.

This agenda is a match for Feuerbach's intentions, when he writes:

---

[*] "Energized Enthusiasm," *Equinox* I(9), .
[†] M.D. Rogers, "The Frenzied Beast," in *Aleister Crowley and Western Esotericism.*
[‡] Freud, *The Future of an Illusion* (Norton 1989), pp. 55-6.

that man, who is always unconsciously governed and determined by his own essence alone, may in future take his own, human essence as the law and determining ground, the aim and measure, of his ethical and political life. And this will inevitably come to pass. Whereas hitherto, misunderstood religion, religious obscurantism, has been the supreme principle of politics and ethics, from now on, or at some future date, religion properly understood, religion seen in terms of man, will determine the destinies of mankind.*

Do what thou wilt shall be the whole of the Law.

Rather than the theological understanding of human souls as accessories of God, Feuerbach's philosophy, Freud's psychology, and Crowley's magick alike see gods as accessories of the soul. And for Thelemites, the most important of these accessories, the "god of one's personal universe," is the *augoeides*, the personal genius or Holy Guardian Angel. As tempting as it might be to have a theology setting out the nature and attributes of such a being for the benefit of any curious aspirant, it would be false and counter-productive. Such knowledge and conversation can come only through practice and attainment, not through speculation, and not through the hearsay of bookish authority. Crowley writes that he prefers the title "Holy Guardian Angel" to its synonyms because of its absurdity, its ability "to mortify the metaphysical man," and thus to impede the theological impulse.†

Note that in a key letter of *Magick Without Tears* Crowley adamantly refuses to theologize. After blasting his correspondent's sloppy use of the word "god," he remarks that when *he* uses the word, he relies "on context to crystallize

---

* Feuerbach, *Lectures on the Essence of Religion,* 3rd lecture, pp. 22-3.
† Crowley, in "The Temple of Solomon the King," *Equinox* I(1), p. 159.

this most fluid—or gaseous—of expressions."* That is to say, he uses his occasional god-talk *rhetorically and heuristically*, not metaphysically, not morally, and not theologically. And he rebukes what he calls "the game of sanctimonious magniloquence," in which rhetorical effusions create theological mirages.[†]

Thelema encompasses a world-view structured through *initiation,* and thus we recognize that any particular theological position can itself only be contingent, subject to overturning as the initiate advances in light, wisdom, and understanding. As we read in "Liber Porta Lucis":

> To the adept, seeing all these things from above,
> there seems nothing to choose between Buddha
> and Mohammed, between Atheism and Theism.[‡]

Ultimately, the metaphysical consequences of Thelema include demonstrations of the non-exclusivity of idolatry and iconoclasm, monotheism and polytheism, theism and atheism, tradition and innovation. Initiation itself can be considered as a motion among these poles, tending toward the ultimate transcendence of them. In the words of the fourteenth-century Sufi poet Mahmud Shabestari Eleggua:

> If the moslem understood Islam he would become
> an idol-worshipper.[§]

Systematic theology is not only inadequate to the esoteric ambitions of initiation; it is also counterproductive with respect to the exoteric agenda of a mass movement. Theological training of clergy has time and again worked against the aims of propagating a religious message. Rodney Stark and other sociologists of religion have demonstrated

---

* *Magick Without Tears*, p. 206.

† *Ibid.,* p. 208.

‡ "Liber Porta Lucis," v. 19 (in *The Holy Books of Thelema,* pp. 40-1).

§ Quoted by Peter Lamborn Wilson in *T.A.Z.: The Temporary Autonomous Zone, Ontological Anarchy, Poetic Terrorism,* p. 10.

that the scholarly professionalization developed through seminaries creates destructive rifts between clerical and lay communities.* People come to a church for experience of the sacred and for social engagement, not for secondhand theological 'schooling.' Theological sophistication of seminarians and clergy is a primary cause for the decline of "mainstream" Protestantism as contrasted with its Evangelical and Fundamentalist competitors.

At the acknowledged risk of offending some readers, I would like to call out a certain form of speculative theology that is, in my opinion, commonly and counterproductively employed among contemporary Thelemites. The dependence of Thelemic writers and teachers on theories from so-called "depth psychology" is a bit dismaying to me. While I will happily admit the overlap in subject matter between that discipline and magick, I believe it is the proper role of initiates to explain profane theories in terms of esoteric principles, not the other way around. Too often in my experience we can see magicians emphasizing Jungian explanations of occult phenomena and doctrines. For all that Jung styled his work as "psychological" and insisted that he avoided theological claims—he certainly had no doctrinal authority in any traditional religious context—nevertheless his writings very commonly occupy a theological discursive register.

Jung's concerns do intersect with ours to a significant extent, and a case can easily be made that he was a crypto-occultist, albeit perhaps one in denial about the essential character of his work. In any case, Jungian psychology is certainly not a positive empirical science. "Archetypes of the collective unconscious" *may or may not exist* just like sephiroth, paths, spirits, conjurations, gods, spheres, planes, and

---

* See, for example, Stark & Finke, *The Churching of America 1776-1990: Winners and Losers in Our Religious Economy.*

so forth. I *earnestly warn you against attributing objective reality or philosophical validity to any of them.*[*]

Now, our central ceremony is professedly for the purpose of "the satisfaction of the religious instinct … by ceremonial means … through which people might enter into ecstasy."[†] We therefore exclude any sermonizing from the Gnostic Mass itself. This exclusion is a signal of the remoteness of theology from our chief objectives. Our mission as clergy is to organize sacramental ceremony for our communities and to provide just such teachings as will facilitate the ecstatic experience, while remaining consistent with the "series of doctrines" that emanate from the Sanctuary of the Gnosis and its sacred science.

Our Past Patriarch Baphomet was very explicit in his teaching that the mystical experience is not dependent on theology. He wrote:

> The mystic attainment may be defined as the Union of the Soul with God, or as the realization of itself, or – there are fifty phrases for the same experience. The same, for whether you are a Christian or a Buddhist, a Theist or (as I am myself, thank God!) an Atheist, the attainment of this one state is as open to you as is nightmare, or madness, or intoxication.[‡]

Intellectual positions in the metaphysical sphere, particularly when weighted with notions of theological *rectitude*, serve to create social division and to constrain mental freedom. Efforts to officially define and delimit the objects of popular devotion have served as engines of authority for superstitious religions, but they are not consistent with a ministry of Light, Life, Love and Liberty. To the extent that

---

[*] Liber O, I.2.
[†] Crowley, *Confessions*, p. 714.
[‡] *Crowley on Christ,* p. 116.

Gnostic Catholic clergy have any input to the theological views of the laity, our best contributions will help to keep such views *unsystematic, unsettled,* and *diverse*. "Convictions cause convicts."*

Consider the theological doctrine that is perhaps the most central to traditional Christianity and the source of the greatest theological contentions in Christian history: the Trinity. The relevant surviving documents—the Didache and the writings of the so-called New Testament—seem to indicate that the Trinity was not a teaching of the earliest Christianity. Yet Christians for many long centuries have persecuted one another in the public sphere regarding whether and how this concept was to be accepted. Crowley wrote that "Considerations of the Christian Trinity are of a nature suited only to initiates of the IX° of O.T.O., as they enclose the final secret of all practical Magick."† So such theological ideas which have been sources of dispute and discord should be reserved, *quarantined* among those who have sufficient knowledge, will, and courage to use them silently as intellectual instruments of Magick.

We must be on our guard against the suppositions of the profane that would demand a theological basis for our scientific religion! The troglodytes of Abrahamic cults insist that their worships were designed by the historically discrete will of the God of the ancient Hebrews: graven on tablets for Moses, enacted in the person of Jesus, or delivered angelically to Muhammad. These then become the grounds for theological explanations of religious origins. Aleister Crowley, on the other hand, boasted his restoration of "solar-phallic worship," citing such authorities as "General Forlong, Sir Richard Burton, Sir R. Payne Knight, Mssrs. Hargrave Jennings, Godfrey Higgins, [and] Gerald Massey."‡

---

* *Principia Discordia.*
† Crowley, *Magick: Book Four*, p. 138 *n.*
‡ *Crowley on Christ*, p. 189.

24

All of these seminal theorists of solar-phallic religion rejected the customary forms of theology, instead identifying the root of religion in the human capacity for communal ecstasy, awe, and reverence toward "the eternal miracle of abounding life, ever self-restored, triumphant over death, the return of the Sun and the resurrection of the Seed."*

And so I call upon you to join me in rejecting the superstition of individual faith along with the tyranny of exoteric theology. Love is the law, love under will.

---

* Op.cit.

Idol Idylls

One of the most fundamental dichotomies in the history of religions is the one between idolatry and iconoclasm. Egyptologist Jan Assmann coined the *Mosaic distinction* as a label for a concept that lies at the root of the broad tradition comprehending Judaism, Christianity, and Islam. This distinction severs monotheism not from "polytheism" (a late modern back-construction), but from *idolatry*.* The reality of יהוה is supposedly confirmed by the refusal to depict him, while the inert and perishable materiality of idols shows the impotence of the gods they represent and their remove from the true divinity. As with so many of the founding distinctions of Western religion, Thelema reverses this one. "Set up my image in the East: ... The other images group around me to support me: let all be worshipped, for they shall cluster to exalt me."† Little children understand representation! They understand projective participation with dolls. The refusal to understand and countenance the ways in which external images assist the spiritual imagination and the ways in which acts of worship ensoul material works, this refusal is a product of minds diseased with theology.

To return to Crowley's commentary on *CCXX* III:21-22, it continues:

> Our religion therefore, for the People, is the Cult of the Sun, who is our particular star of the Body of Nuit, from whom, in the strictest scientific sense, come this Earth, a chilled spark of Him, and all our Light and Life. His vice-regent and representative in the animal kingdom is His

---

* Assmann, *Moses the Egyptian,* p. 7 ff.
† *CCXX* III:21-22.

26

cognate symbol the Phallus, representing Love
and Liberty.*

Ra-Hoor-Khuit as the Sun and Phallus is thus set as a
henotheistic chief deity, after the manner of the New Solar
Theology of ancient Egypt. Unlike the Atenist error which
attempted to abolish earlier Egyptian cults, the Thelemic
priesthood is not to ban the worship of other gods and
goddesses, for they all "cluster to exalt" the one glittering
Image whose white and golden light streams forth to give
them their own potency as images.

In the classical Hermetic text *Aesclepius*, we find a hoary
and powerful advocacy of the magical power of idols:

> *Trism.* Mankind is ever mindful of its own par-
> entage and the source whence it has sprung,
> and steadfastly persists in following God's
> example: and consequently, just as the Father
> and Master made the gods of heaven eternal,
> that they might resemble him who made them,
> even so do men fashion their gods in the
> likeness of their own aspect.

> *Ascl.* Do you mean statues, Trismegistus?

> *Trism.* Yes, Asclepius. See how even you give way
> to doubt! I mean statues, but statues living and
> conscious, filled with the breath of life, and
> doing many mighty works; statues which have
> foreknowledge, and predict future events by
> the drawing of lots, and by prophetic in-
> spiration, and by dreams, and in many other
> ways; statues which inflict diseases and heal

---

* Crowley, *The Law Is for All,* p. 163.

27

them, dispensing sorrow and joy according to
men's desserts.*

The *Crater Hermetis*, a text of the Italian Rennaisance,
assigns procreative characteristics to this picture of spiritual
power. The author Ludovico Lazarelli uses a song to adumbrate the *arcanum arcanorum* of his Hermetic and cabalistic
gnosis:

> This is certainly the newest novelty of novelties
> and a greater miracle than all others
> that man has discovered the nature of God
> and knows how to make it.
>
> For just as the Lord or God the begetter *(genitor)*
> generates the celestials and procreates the angels
> who are the forms of things, the heads
> and first examples of all,
>
> just so the true man creates divine souls
> which the ancient host used to call gods of the earth,
> who are glad to live close to human beings
> and rejoice at the welfare of man.†

Crowley avers in *The Book of Lies,* "**That which causes
us to create is our true father and mother; we create in
our own image, which is theirs.**" Spiritual parentage is the
source of creative inspiration. Thus, "The Brothers of the
A∴A∴ are one with the Mother of the Child. … *They cause all
men to worship it.*"‡ Compare Mark III:31-35 (parallel in
Matthew XII:46-50):

---

* *Aesclepius* III, 23b-24a.
† Trans. Wouter J. Hanegraff, "Sympathy or the Devil: Renaissance
Magic and the Ambivalence of Idols," *Esoterica* 2 (2000).
‡ Crowley, *The Book of Lies,* pp. 52, 16-7.

There came then his brethren and his mother, and, standing without, sent unto him, calling him. And the multitude sat about him, and they said unto him, Behold, thy mother and thy brethren without seek for thee. And he answered them, saying, Who is my mother, or my brethren? And he looked round about on them which sat about him, and said, Behold my mother and my brethren! For whosoever shall do the will of God, the same is my brother, and my sister, and mother.

In Crowley's commentary to his chapter of *Lies* "The Blind Webster," he equates the title to "the Phallus in manifestation."[*] A webster is a *weaver*, and the phallus weaves new humans from threads of DNA, blindly and without fear. In "Liber Samekh," Crowley instructs that "The Holy Guardian Angel is the Unconscious Creature Self—the Spiritual Phallus."[†]

Hatred of idols is a value at the root of the Abrahamic traditions, embracing Judaism, Christianity and Islam. But the purest iconoclasm is ultimately untenable even in the orthodoxies of those religions, where man is created "in the image" of God, and thus any respect paid to man verges on idolatry. The ancient Hebrew scriptures sanction a number of sacred images, from the brazen serpent to the cherubim upon the Ark to the mysterious teraphim. As Peter Lamborn Wilson observes, "Even Islam has its popular icons—moon, minaret, rose, Kaaba and Buraq—which gain in intensity by their endless and musical repetition."[‡]

The Pauline episode of the "Unknown God" of the Athenians (Acts XVII) is precisely the text to which "The

---

[*] *Op. cit.,* p. 53.
[†] Crowley, *Magick,* p. 523.
[‡] Peter Lamborn Wilson, *Scandal: Essays in Islamic Heresy*, p. 158.

Blind Webster" is a rebuttal. Here I weave together the iconoclastic sermon of Paul with Perdurabo's opposed reply.

> *Paul.* That they should seek the Lord, if haply they might feel after him, and find him, though he be not far from every one of us:

> *Perdurabo.* It is not necessary to understand; it is enough to adore.

> *Paul.* For in him we live, and move, and have our being; as certain also of your own poets have said, for we are also his offspring.

> *Perdurabo.* We ignore what created us; we adore what we create. That which causes us to create is our true father and mother; we create in our own image, which is theirs.

> *Paul.* Forasmuch then as we are the offspring of God, we ought not to think that the Godhead is like unto gold, or silver, or stone, graven by art and man's device.

> *Perdurabo.* The god may be of clay: adore him; he becomes GOD. Let us create nothing but GOD!

> *Paul.* And the times of this ignorance God winked at; but now commandeth all men every where to repent:

> *Perdurabo.* Let us create therefore without fear; for we can create nothing that is not GOD.

Man has the right to to draw, paint, carve, etch, mould, build as he will. [*]

Again, a "webster" is a *weaver*. Weaving was a trade favored by the medieval Cathars,[†] and weavers were thereafter associated with heresy and insurrection. The Magick of Ra-hoor-khuit involves a vengeful revolt against iconoclasm.

Howard Eilberg-Schwartz's thoughtful and provocative book *God's Phallus, and Other Problems for Men and Monotheism* considers the peculiar ways in which divine maleness creates dilemmas for human masculinity, in the context of hetero-normative monotheism. He discusses the features of ancient Hebrew theophanies, as well as the aniconic dimensions of the tradition. He musters a persuasive case that it was the *maleness* of God that was problematic for Hebrews at the time of the composition of the Torah, rather than mere corporeality or even anthropomorphism. In an especially fascinating series of arguments, he links the disgrace of uncovering the nakedness of the father (as with Noah and his sons) to the Mosaic prohibition on images, citing especially Deuteronomy XXVII:15-16. This passage, like Acts XVII, is aggressively and succinctly contradicted by "The Blind Webster." Here is the resulting *textus*:

> *Moses.* Cursed be the man that maketh any graven or molten image, an abomination unto the LORD, the work of the hands of the craftsman, and putteth it in a secret place. (And all the people shall answer and say, Amen.)

---

[*] Liber LXXVII.

[†] Founding Patriarch Jules Doinel considered the Cathars or Albigensians to be the spiritual forebears of the Église Gnostique from which E.G.C. descends.

Perdurabo. The god may be of clay: adore him; he becomes GOD. Let us create nothing but GOD!

Moses. Cursed be he that setteth light by his father or his mother. (And all the people shall say, Amen.)

Perdurabo. We ignore what created us; we adore what we create. That which causes us to create is our true father and mother; we create in our own image, which is theirs.

The remainder of the passage from Deuteronomy (the "Twelve Curses") is concerned with further prohibitions on deceitful and malicious behavior, and on incest and bestiality. But of particular note is the curse (XXVII:18) against one who "maketh the blind to wander out of the way." Chapter 21 of *The Book of Lies* identifies "the phallus in manifestation" as blind, and Perdurabo is insistent that "the way" *not* be prescribed to this blind force: "Let this go free, even as It will. Thou art not its master, but the vehicle of It."* Love is the law, love under will.

---

* Crowley, *The Book of Lies,* p. 46.

2. Priesthood Is Service, and Nothing Else

The hierarchical structure of the E.G.C. clergy is not intended to exert a force of command over the laity. Clergy serve their congregations, the larger Church, and the public, not vice versa. A measure of respect and devotion offered to the priesthood makes them more effective in their service, and one of the ways that clergy serve their congregations is by *earning* that respect through service.

In addition, E.G.C. clergy in the United States are exhorted by our hierarchy to participate in public service activities on our own recognizance. This work we are to undertake as individual Thelemites, not as representatives of the Church. The benefits of such undertakings are several: clergy are brought into regular contact with the larger society beyond the self-selected membership of our congregations; the work itself develops the fundamental attitude of service within clergy; the experience of situations of need and crisis that may be encountered in various forms of community service fosters skills that clergy may also use in ministering to our brothers and sisters in the church.

There are certain cardinal examples of such service that might be considered. Volunteer work for the support and welfare of children is a signal activity for ministers of the Crowned and Conquering Child. Programs to promote literacy for adults and/or children are often in need of volunteers, and one can hardly understate the value of literacy in Thelemic culture. Hospices and other forms of end-of-life care may rely on volunteers in their efforts to provide services to the dying and to the bereaved. All of these sorts of work are closely tied to the sorts of integral initiation that clergy may expect to encounter and hope to support among members of their Church communities.

To reiterate and clarify: we should not present ourselves as "Thelemic chaplains," offering overtly religious or esoteric services to secular community institutions. For these sorts of community service there is no need to claim any credential other than that of *volunteer* (i.e. one who *wills* to act). Our task should be to see if we can supply the work these programs require to support their missions. We may then take satisfaction and learn from the experience of doing so.

In addition to public service, Thelemic clergy must be fortified by the experience of certain sorts of private, even *secret* service detailed in the following sections: we must serve our angels, and we must serve hell. Our service to the Church is grounded in the structure of our hierarchy and the sacraments of holy orders, directed toward the benefit of the larger Church. And finally, each priestess and priest, like the Church as a whole, must develop so as to be ready to serve the designs of the Secret Chiefs.

Priesthood and the Personal Genius

> [T]he Attainment of the Knowledge and Conversation of the Holy Guardian Angel ... is the essential work of every man; none other ranks with it either for personal progress or for power to help one's fellows. This unachieved, man is no more than the unhappiest and blindest of animals. He is conscious of his own incomprehensible calamity, and clumsily incapable of repairing it. Achieved, he is no less than the co-heir of gods, a Lord of Light. He is conscious of his own consecrated course, and confidently ready to run it.[*]

The matter of this accomplishment is a theme running throughout Crowley's writings, from the opening allegory of "The Wake World" in *Konx Om Pax* (1903 EV) to the "Epistola Ultima" of *Magick Without Tears* (mid-1940s). In the latter, he affirms, "It should never be forgotten for a moment that the central and essential work of the Magicians is the attainment of the Knowledge and Conversation of the Holy Guardian Angel."[†]

Nor should we presume that this attainment is peculiar to the system of A∴A∴, or even to Thelema. In the early journals of 666, he emphasizes the identity of various occult and religious traditions in this key feature, including Theosophy, the Golden Dawn, the Rosicrucian fiction of Bulwer-Lytton, Buddhism, the *Bhagavad-Gita*, the *I Ching*, the Hebrew Kabbalah, and ancient Zoroastrianism, each having each their own terminology to indicate the Holy Guardian Angel. Thelema may be exceptional merely in its injunction to *all* aspirants that this particular attainment can and should be pursued. In his diary of February 9, 1905 EV, the Priest and Apostle of Infinite Space had come to the realization

---

[*] "One Star in Sight," in *Magick: Book 4,* p. 494.
[†] *Magick Without Tears*, p. 502.

that his central mission would be to teach "THE KNOW-LEDGE AND CONVERSATION OF THE HOLY GUARDIAN ANGEL."[*] The post-theological character of our practice in this regard is evident not only from Crowley's radically syncretistic approach, but from his preference for the "patently absurd" label Holy Guardian Angel "so as to mortify the metaphysical man."[†]

Given that E.G.C. is the public, congregational rite of the holy Order to which this same teacher entrusted the global promulgation of his message, it may therefore come as something of a surprise to discover that nowhere in the official rituals or canonical regulations of our Church can we find the phrase "Holy Guardian Angel" *per se*. Still, since our Church is founded in a pre-existing tradition, it would not be surprising to find the Holy Guardian Angel instead appearing or alluded to under one of its many other names or titles, such as: Adonai, Yechidah, Adi-Buddha, Vishnu, augoeides, daimon, logos, Great Person, Imam-of-one's-own-being, true self, perfect nature, Silent Watcher, or personal genius.

That last term, the *genius*, is the one that Crowley ascribed to common usage in the Hermetic Order of the Golden Dawn, but it is also significant in being a recurrent term for the concept among Western philosophers from antiquity through the Enlightenment. Early literary examples occur in the works of Plautus in the third century BCE, where we find striking correlations between the concepts of *hospitality* and *geniality*—understood as rapport with one's genius. To exercise one's vitality and fulfill one's life is to *indulge* one's genius; while to submit to repression and failure is to *defraud* the genius.[‡]

---

[*] Quoted in *The Temple of Solomon the King,* in *The Equinox* I(8), p. 13.
[†] *The Temple of Solomon the King,* in *The Equinox* I(1), pp. 159-160.
[‡] Jane Chance Nitzsche, *The Genius Figure in Antiquity and the Middle Ages,* pp. 10-12.

During the European Renaissance, the Platonist Franciscan Francesco Giorgi wrote in *De Harmonia Mundi Totius* (1525 EV) about the essential congruity between one's astrological nativity and the guidance of one's genius.* In the eighteenth century EV, Giacomo Casanova wrote about encountering his genius in a garden, where it took the form of a serpent, just as it typically had for the ancients. Writing of his first hardships as a prisoner, Casanova reflected, "My Genius diverted himself in this fashion in order to give me the pleasure of making comparisons."[†]

In an early manifesto for Crowley's cultural and magical agenda, he allied himself with the Neo-platonism of pagan antiquity in an overt attempt to champion a deep European tradition in opposition to what he saw as the degeneracy of modern Christianity.[‡] And perhaps the greatest surviving exposition of the doctrine of the genius from such sources is *De Deo Socratis* by Apuleius, where we read:

> ... the dæmon who presides over you inquisitively participates of all that concerns you, sees all things, understands all things, and *in the place of conscience dwells in the most profound recesses of the mind.* For he of whom I speak is a perfect guardian, a singular prefect, a domestic speculator, a proper curator, an intimate inspector, an assiduous observer, an inseparable arbiter, a reprobater of what is evil, an approver of what is good, and if he is legitimately attended to, sedulously known and religiously worshipped, in the way in which he was reverenced by Socrates with justice and innocence,

---

* D.P. Walker, *Spiritual and Demonic Magic: from Ficino to Campanella,* pp. 112-15.
† Giacomo Casanova (Chevalier de Seingalt), *History of My Life* (trans. Willard R. Trask), vol. I, pp. 276-77 & vol. II, p. 36. See also vol. I, pp. 76 & 288; vol. II, pp. 86, 220, 225; vol. III, p. 30; etc.
‡ "Eleusis," in *The Collected Works of Aleister Crowley,* vol. pp. 225.

will be a predictor in things uncertain, a pre-monitor in things dubious, a defender in things dangerous, and an assistant in want. He will also manifestly, when the occasion demands it, to avert from you evil, increase your good, raise your depressed, support your falling, illuminate your obscure, govern your prosperous, and correct your adverse circumstances.[*]

How, the reader may ask, is the genius to be "religiously worshipped" after the manner of the ancients? In the Roman world of the beginning of the vulgar era, a living man would celebrate and propitiate his individual genius (or her *juno*, if a woman) on the anniversary of that individual's birth. The rites were performed in a white robe at a domestic altar, fires were lit and incense burned, and the sacrifice to the genius consisted of honey cakes and wine. And it is not at all unlikely that this "feast for life" contributed to the origin or at least eventual popularity of the Christian Eucharist. This ancient custom survived to Apuleius' time and beyond. In 392 EV, the Christianized law of Rome forbade sacrificing wine to one's genius—under penalty of death.[†]

Now consider our Gnostic Mass. As in a Christian Eucharist, the priest speaks words of institution: *This is my body,* and *This is my blood.* But who is the *me* of this *mine?* In the Christian context, the elements are embedded in a narrative that clearly identifies them as the body and blood of Jesus. Do *we* eat the body and blood of Jesus? Do we eat the sacrificial flesh of Aleister Crowley? Hardly. After the priest has consecrated the elements by identifying them as flesh and blood, he addresses the office of the anthem to "Thou who art I, beyond all I am": his personal genius or

---

[*] Apuleius, *The God of Socrates* (Heptangle Books ed.), pp. 39-40.

[†] Nitzsche, *op. cit.,* pp. 16-18. A modern Thelemite might consider a birthday regimen of the "Short Eucharist" at noon and "Daimonic Vespers" at sunset; for these rituals, see my book *Raise the Spell.*

Holy Guardian Angel.* And each congregant gets her own cake and his own goblet of wine. They are not communicating with the priest's genius, but with their own. And indeed, a reading of the gnostic Gospel of Phillip provides a Valentinian theory of the Eucharist, according to which "[t]he Eucharist anticipates the union of the gnostic with his 'angel image'; it effects a realization of the original oneness of the Pleroma."†

Liber XV instructs: *The PEOPLE communicate as did the PRIEST, uttering the same words in an attitude of Resurrection: There is no part of me that is not of the Gods.*

There is, in my experience, exactly zero variation in practice regarding the interpretation of the "attitude of Resurrection": it consists of crossing the arms over the breast in the X of the LVX signs, known in that context as the "Sign of Osiris Risen." There is no text of Liber XV prepared by Crowley where this gesture is made explicit, however. Is our practice entirely a matter of transmission through a series of witnesses? I don't think so.

The sign is significantly paired with the declaration "There is no part of me that is not of the Gods." This sentence ultimately derives from the Papyrus of Ani by way of the Adeptus Minor ceremony of the Hermetic Order of the Golden Dawn. The "attitude of Resurrection" is the "saluting Sign" of the Adeptus Minor grade in the old G.D. ritual.

The Gnostic Mass was written in part for public performance, with the knowledge that participating congregants would not necessarily be initiates of any particular rite or grade, and certainly not all G.D. Minor

---

* But see the essay "Reflections on 'Thou Who Art'" in this volume, for other possible interpretations of the Anthem.
† Kurt Rudolph, *Gnosis: The Nature and History of Gnosticism* (1987), pp. 230 & 241.

Adepts. By incorporating this coupled gesture and declaration at the climax of the ceremony, the Master Therion appears to have intended that each communicant, witting or no, would put him or herself in sympathetic resonance with the 5°=6□ grade of the Golden Dawn, in which the central obligation was to

> promise and swear that with the Divine permission I will, from this day forward, apply myself to the Great Work, which is, to purify and exalt my Spiritual Nature so that with the Divine Aid I may at length attain to be more than human, and thus gradually **raise and unite myself to my higher and Divine Genius**, and that in this event I will not abuse the great power entrusted to me.

Likewise, in Crowley's reform of the G.D. system, all that remains of the original obligation in that grade is "To prosecute the Great Work: which is, to **attain to the knowledge and conversation of the Holy Guardian Angel**."

Thus, by means of this artful device, the Gnostic Mass communicant benefits from a sort of *morphological field* generated by the work of the Vault of the Adepts, and reinforcing the basic Eucharistic process by which the magician

> becomes filled with God, fed upon God, intoxicated with God. ... matter is replaced by Spirit, the human by the divine; ultimately the change will be complete; God manifest in flesh will be his name.

> This is the most important of all magical secrets that ever were or are or can be. To a Magician thus renewed the attainment of the Knowledge and Conversation of the Holy Guardian Angel becomes an inevitable task; every force of his nature, unhindered, tends to that aim and goal of

whose nature neither man nor god may speak, for that it is infinitely beyond speech or thought or ecstasy or silence.*

In our ceremony of baptism, the candidate may declare, "I will rejoice in the will of my god," with that "god" understood as the Holy Guardian Angel. But this emphasis seems to fade at confirmation, with its focus on Ra-Hoor-Khuit the Lord of the Æon. And yet, these are not so far apart as they might at first seem. In his commentaries on *The Book of the Law,* Crowley remarks that the "Crowned and Conquering Child" refers both to Ra-Hoor-Khuit as cosmocrator, and to the true conqueror hidden in ourselves, the Silent Watcher or Guardian Angel who is "our own personal God." †

Moreover, we find in the ancient theories regarding the genius the idea that our common humanity is reflected in a "lord of dæmons; who from the first defined to every one his peculiar dæmon, according to his own proper will." And who should such a "lord of dæmons" be but the governor of the Æon and lord of initiation? Iamblichus makes this point, going on to aver that "when the peculiar dæmon is present with each of us, he then unfolds the worship which is proper to be paid to him and his name, and likewise delivers the proper mode of invoking him."‡

Hopefully, the present discussion clarifies ways in which the Thelemic concept of the Holy Guardian Angel underlies the magick of our Mass, and even how it informs our ceremonies of affiliation in baptism and confirmation. But these ecclesiastic practices were not the ones to which the Prophet addressed himself when prescribing a "proper mode of invoking" Knowledge and Conversation of the Angel.

---

* *Magick*, p. 269.
† *The Law Is for All,* commentary to *CCXX* III:22, p. 163.
‡ Iamblichus (trans. Thomas Taylor), *On the Mysteries,* ch. IX, p. 325.

Indeed, another of his reasons for preferring this term for it, is to refer to the method of *The Book of the Sacred Magic of Abramelin the Mage,* which Crowley calls "so simple and effective."[*]

With reference to this method, the most explicit and detailed instruction for Thelemites is that of "Liber Samekh": a revised and explicated version of the ritual that the Beast himself used in uniting himself to his genius. This ritual was grounded in a text that Crowley referenced as "The Preliminary Invocation of the Goëtia," although it was in fact a magical incantation from antiquity, only circumstantially associated with the *Goëtia* through the editorial activity of Golden Dawn chief MacGregor Mathers. Of the dozens of "barbarous names of evocation" comprehended by that ritual, Crowley singles out one for special treatment in Liber Samekh, one that "in its most secret and mighty sense declareth the Formula of the Magick of THE BEAST whereby He wrought many wonders":

> Let I and O face all; yet ward their A from attack. The Hermit to himself, the Fool to foes, The Devil to friends, Nine by nature, Naught by attainment, Fifteen by function. In speech swift, subtle and secret; in thought creative, unbiased, unbounded; in act free, firm, aspiring, ecstatic.
>
> Hermes to hear, Dionysus to touch, Pan to behold.
>
> A Virgin, a Babe, and a Beast!
>
> A Liar, an Idiot, and a Master of Men!
>
> A kiss, a guffaw, and a bellow; he that hath ears to hear, let him hear![†]

---

[*] *The Equinox* I(1), p. 159.
[†] *Magick,* pp. 533-4, corrected at Crowley's suggestion to replace correspondences of the 16th path with those of the 26th.

This formula IAO, which is the mainspring of "Liber Samekh," is none other than the name most crucially invoked in the Gnostic Mass. The Deacon calls on it to open the temple. The Priest calls on it to part the veil. And the consecrated elements are exhibited together as the Priest cries out: "Holy, holy, holy IAO!" And that Dionysus at the core of the formula, the Fool A, is himself a figure of the Holy Guardian Angel, in an allegory elaborated at length in Crowley's "Notes for an Astral Atlas": "Bacchus, twy-formed, man-woman, Bacchus, whose innocence tames the Tiger, while yet thy horns drip blood upon thy mouth, and sharpen the merriment of wine to the madness of murder!"[*]

Crowley was not the only occultist of his period to make this identification. The Theosophist James Morgan Pryse proposed that the figure of Dionysos was "the spiritual Mind, the true Self, represented as the Sun-God."[†]

According to the ritual of "Liber Samekh," the Angel is also identified with the devils BESZ and APOPHRASZ, whose "combined action ... is to allow the God upon whom they prey to enter into enjoyment of existence through the Sacrament of dividual 'Life' (Bread—the flesh of BESZ) and 'Love' (Wine—the blood or venom of APOPHRASZ)."[‡] In other words, the elements of the Eucharist can be construed as the faculties (Chiah and Neschemah) by which the Ruach is extruded from the Yechidah.[§] Their demiurgic power corresponds to the ancient belief that the genius was responsible for uniting the soul to the body.

---

[*] *Magick,* p. 511.
[†] James Morgan Pryse, *The Adorers of Dionysos (Bakchai)*, p. 33. Pryse emphasizes Dionysos as the image of the *genius* or *daimon* throughout his treatment of the text.
[‡] *Magick,* p. 524, brought to my attention in this context by Br. Robert Crow.
[§] See "Man" in *Little Essays Toward Truth,* pp. 9-17.

Long before the final composition of "Liber Samekh" in Cefalu, the Prophet had received and codified a Thelemic revision of the general method of Abramelin. That text, canonized for A∴A∴ as "Liber VIII," was originally formulated within his exploration of the Eighth Aethyr ZID of the Enochian system as documented in *The Vision & the Voice*. Within this episode in the North African desert, an angel declares to the seer, "And thus shall he do who will attain unto the mystery of the knowledge and conversation of his Holy Guardian Angel."[*] What follows reduces the hundreds of pages of Abramelin directions to just four or five pages, complete with new references to the symbol-system of *The Book of the Law*. After this instruction, the speaking angel, whom Crowley understood to be his own Holy Guardian Angel, identified himself as Aiwass, the dictating intelligence of *Liber Legis*. And then Aiwass corrected Crowley as follows:

> Thus hast thou erred indeed, perceiving me in the path that leadeth from the Crown unto the Beauty. For that path bridgeth the abyss, and I am of the supernals. Nor I, nor Thou, nor He can bridge the abyss. It is the Priestess of the Silver Star, and the Prophet of the Gods, and the Lord of the Hosts of the Mighty. For they are the servants of Babalon, and of the Beast, and of those others of whom it is not yet spoken. And, being servants, they have no name, but we are of the blood royal, and serve not, and therefore are we less than they.[†]

Crowley had previously assigned the Holy Guardian Angel to the qabalistic path of *gimel* between Kether and Tiphareth. But Aiwass insists that the personal genius is a

---

[*] *The Vision & the Voice,* p. 178.
[†] *The Vision & the Voice,* p. 183; corrected to conform to the original MS.

44

native of the supernals. No single identity can bridge the division of the Veil of the Abyss. But there are three *roles* that do, joining the Angel's awareness with the Magician's experience of Knowledge and Conversation in Tiphareth, and these three are indicated as those paths leading upwards from the center of the Tree of Life. They are figured by a set of tarot trumps which correspond to the principal officers of the Gnostic Mass: *gimel* is the Priestess of the Silver Star; *zain* is the Prophet of the Gods, the Lovers card showing the deacon Mercury; and *heh* is the Lord of the Hosts of the Mighty, the Emperor card with its red-robed priest.

In late medieval literature, the genius is typically figured as a priest, who marries the soul to the body, and who excommunicates the practitioners of unnatural vice.* But the passage from ZID suggests that—depending on the situation or disposition of the aspirant—any of the three principal officers of the Gnostic Mass can adumbrate the powers of the Holy Guardian Angel. "For they are the servants of Babalon, and of the Beast, and of those others of whom it is not yet spoken. And, being servants, they have no name...."

So when the clergy of our Church perform the genuine magick of sacramental service, we do so in a *nameless*, transpersonal fashion. The work is not a matter of expressing our individuality or achieving personal distinction; it is instead an offering of ourselves as instruments by which Babalon and the Beast can call others forth toward Knowledge and Conversation. And it is this work that makes us into ministers of the Law of Thelema, and which assists each aspirant toward his or her own True Will, the *summum bonum,* true wisdom and perfect happiness.

---

* Nitzsche, *op. cit.,* pp. 88-107, 116-19.

Priesthood from Hell: The Caste Pontifical

There is a very old teaching story identified with the Bektashi Dervish order. It concerns a young man whose father tended a famous shrine, where people would come from all the surrounding lands to pay their respects to the holy person who was interred there. In the normal course of events, the son could have anticipated gradually taking over the management of the shrine and deriving a comfortable and honored life from its maintenance.

However, as he came to maturity, this fellow was taken with an irrepressible thirst for knowledge and wisdom, and he set off in quest thereof. He saddled a donkey and took few possessions on his journey. The years of his travels saw him sojourn through Egypt, Arabia, Persia, and India. Having entered the formidable mountains beyond India, his long-suffering mount fell ill and died. This donkey had been the man's only companion during long stretches of his wanderings, and he was devastated by the loss. He buried the noble animal there in the mountain wilderness, and remained, wordless and disconsolate, at the crude grave.

Other travelers on the mountain trail could not fail to notice the mysterious mourner, and supposed that he must have been the disciple of a sainted teacher to whose grave he was now attached. Word traveled, and soon visitors began to arrive expressly to visit this nameless saint's resting place. A wealthy visitor even exercised his benevolence by having a shrine raised on the site.

It came to pass that this mountain shrine became so famous that its reputation carried all the way back to the father of the mourner. This man, craving some adventure in his declining years, made the long trip to the east and discovered his son at the site. "My son! You must tell me of what has passed! How did you come to set down here?" The son told the story, and the father replied in amazement, "I can now tell you that the shrine where you were brought up as a boy was founded through a similar circumstance, when my own donkey died many years ago."

There is so much sublime meaning in this story that I could scarcely unpack it for you. If it is not yet apparent to you, hopefully the remarks I will offer here may illuminate it.

In order to intimate what constitutes a "calling" to priestly service in the New Æon, I'll begin by considering how vocation may have differed in prior ages. And to this end, I want to reference the development of human values proposed by Saint ✠Friedrich Nietzsche in section 32 of *Beyond Good and Evil.* According to Nietzsche, the first and longest period of human existence was, as he put it, pre-moral. The value of any action was determined by its direct consequence. There was nothing like what we now understand as a sense of guilt or innocence related to malicious or benevolent intentions. The proof of the pudding was in the eating, or as someone once said, "By their fruits you shall know them."[*] Nietzsche refers to traditional societies where the character of children determines the honor of their parents.

The first priesthoods were hereditary, just as guilt and sin were hereditary in the earliest portions of the Hebrew Bible. It is interesting to note that just as Crowley was the son of a preacher, so too Nietzsche was a pastor's son, and Carl Jung also had a clergyman father.

Only over the last ten thousand years or so, in Nietzsche's estimation, have societies reoriented their valuations away from the results of human activity and toward the activity's supposed source in individual conscious purpose. In this properly "moral" phase, as he says, we arrived at "The intention as the whole origin and history of an action—almost to the present day this prejudice

---

[*] Matthew VII:16, 20.

dominated praise, blame, judgment and philosophy." It was the first turning-inward of the moral age when the conscious intention was set at odds with the Hell or "secret place" of the unconscious. Yet in the pre-moral age it had been by concession to Hell "that a few Men could be spared from Toil to cultivate Wisdom, and this was first provided by the Selection of a caste Pontifical," according to Crowley, who writes further: "By this Device came the Alliance of King and Priest, Strength and Cunning fortifying each the other through the Division of Labour."*

With the advancement of the moral system of values, especially exemplified in Christianity and Buddhism, the priesthoods no longer followed lines of genealogical descent. They became—*in principle*—the result of individual conscious choice and aspiration; even when—*in practice*—that choice was made for them by their families. The ideals of the priesthood were set against Hell, and directed toward a stale purity bounded by conscious purpose. Religion boasted that its chief value was as a moral resource.

But now, in Nietzsche's third phase, our New Æon, we see a return of the second to the first, but after another manner. Nietzsche foresees an "extra-moral" age, when, he writes, "The value of an action lies precisely in what is <u>unintentional</u> in it, while everything about it that is intentional, everything about it that can be seen, known, 'conscious,' still belongs to the surface and skin—which like every skin betrays something but conceals even more."

Nietzsche knows that the individual will is not something obvious, a mirror-gleam of waking awareness that can be seen as docile or rebellious by turns, but rather something deep and inexorable that reveals itself in dreams, in oracles, and ancestral traces. To use our Prophet's language, the True Will reposes in Hell.

---

* Crowley, *Liber Aleph,* p. 124.

In *Liber Aleph* Crowley writes:

> Now then thou seest that this Hell, or concealed place within thee, is no more a fear or hindrance to men of a free race, but the treasure house of the assimilated wisdom of the ages, and the knowledge of the True Way. Thus are we just and wise to discover this secret in ourselves, to conform the conscious mind therewith.[*]

Our priestesses and priests are called by the crackling sound of hellfire audible in the stellar core of every man and every woman. The priesthood knows the value of that fire, wills to embrace it, and dares to exhibit it, but refrains from explaining or justifying it.

Our priesthood is—*in principle*—summoned by unconscious forces; even when—*in practice*—we rely on a conscious estimation of those.

As Crowley wrote in *Liber Reguli*:

> Man is indeed not wholly freed, even now. He is still trampled under the hoofs of the stampeding mules that nightmare bore to his wild ass, his creative forces that he had not mastered, the sterile ghosts that he called gods. Their mystery cows men still; they fear, they flinch, they dare not face the phantoms. Still, too, the fallen fetich seems awful; it is frightful to them that there is no longer an idol to adore with anthems, and to appease with the flesh of their firstborn. Each scrambles in the bloody mire of the floor to snatch some scrap for a relic, that he may bow down to it and serve it.[†]

---

[*] Crowley, *Liber Aleph,* p. 128.
[†] Crowley, *Magick,* p. 580.

Is it our work to rehabilitate such spectres? Perish the thought. To quote Feuerbach once more, "In religion man does not satisfy other beings; he satisfies his own nature."* These "fallen fetiches" are the powers that still preside over the misery that Crowley calls "the hell of the slaves."†

The truly called priests and priestesses of the New Æon are those with the peculiar spiritual constitutions to stand bare and rejoicing, to worship with fire and blood, to work the work of wickedness with pure will unassuaged of purpose, so that others might come to understand the warmth and riches of Hell.

Nietzsche writes:

> The self-overcoming of morality—let this be the name for that long secret work which has been saved up for the finest and most honest, also the most malicious, consciences of today, as living touchstones of the soul.

There is no law beyond Do what thou wilt.

---

* Feuerbach, *Lectures on the Essence of Religion,* 9th lecture, p. 76.
† Crowley, *Liber Aleph,* p. 139.

Studying toward Sacerdotal Expertise

As organized in the United States, *Ecclesia Gnostica Catholica* includes a novitiate for members to undertake the practice and performance of the Gnostic Mass while working toward ordination. Any novice is under the supervision of a bishop, and can serve as a principal officer in a public Gnostic Mass as long as at least one of the other two officers (including the deacon) is an ordained member of the priesthood. But ceremonial practice should be only a part of the training involved in aspiration to the priesthood. There are various practical resources and forms of study that are pre-requisite to the realization of sacerdotal power. Experience of these should precede the sacerdotal authority transmitted through holy orders. Nor does ordination absolve clergy from the ongoing task of study and development.

Different bishops place various expectations and re-quirements on the novices they supervise: there is little uniformity throughout the Church on this score. I suspect that my own agenda for the training of clergy is among the more rigorous of those currently in place, and it has in fact become more demanding over time. (I was at first quite cautious of asking too much of ordinands, being aware that my own training had been more intensive than most, and aware that what suited me might not be fitting for others.) I will summarize that agenda here in the hope that even readers who are not *required* to fulfill this course of formation will be encouraged to do so.

One straightforward requirement of the Church is that those ordained to the priesthood must have received the *Mysteria Mystica Maxima* initiation entitled "Knight of East and West." This rank, a bridge between the first and second series of M∴M∴M∴ initiations, is the first *invitational* degree ceremony and stands outside of the system of triads that patterns the O.T.O. degrees. As our Patriarch notes, "Initiates of K.E.W. should be aware of ... special qualities they possess, by virtue of their initiation, that subtly prepare them for work as Priest or Priestess."[*]

In order to be eligible for K.E.W. invitation, an aspirant must have advanced through all the degrees of the Third Triad, *i.e.* the numbered degrees through IV° and the Council of Princes of Jerusalem which follows them. It is my custom to meet with a novice after his or her initiation to the III° for the purpose of tailoring an individual set of tasks and formative goals to prepare for both sacerdotal ordination and invitation to K.E.W. To generate one of those tasks, we discuss the obligations that the novice has already taken in M∴M∴M∴, identify which among them are the most personally challenging, and use that challenge as the basis for the task to be performed.

Crowley remarked, "Memory is of the very stuff of consciousness itself."[†] And in the words of a later magician and scholar, "The bond between eroticism, mnemonics, and magic is indissoluble to such at extent that it is impossible to understand the third without first having studied the principles and mechanisms of the first two."[‡] I assert that memory is both a necessary ingredient of our humanity, and a feature of our divine nature. In the grand chorus from Swinburne's *Atalanta in Calydon*, "memory fallen from heaven" is the complementary opposite of "madness risen from hell."

Properly prepared ordinands to the priesthood of E.G.C. should have fully memorized Liber XV, the Canon of the Gnostic Mass. The ability to reproduce the entire document from memory, rubrics and all, may be excessive; but a member of the priesthood should know by heart the structure of the Mass and its component ceremonies, all

---

[*] Hymenaeus Beta, "New E.G.C.-O.T.O. Policy," in *The Magical Link* V:3 (Fall 1991), 1.
[†] Crowley, *Little Essays Toward Truth*, p. 18.
[‡] Ioan Couliano, *Magic and Eros in the Renaissance*, p. xviii.

gestural cues and sequences, and all speeches and invocations of *all offices*. A priestess must still learn the speeches of a priest. A priest must still know the invocations of a deacon, *including the eleven Collects*.

Certainly, any and all members of E.G.C., lay or clerical, will benefit from persistent study and memorization of *Liber AL vel Legis*, the Revelation of the New Æon, upon which our mysteries are founded. In addition, however, I recommend particular courses of memorization for those working in or towards our clerical orders. They consist of chapters from oracular writings in our tradition, as itemized in the table on the following page.

This task is reminiscent of Crowley's requirements for memorization of the Holy Books of Thelema in the outer grades of A∴A∴. Functionally, these A∴A∴ tasks took the place of the old Golden Dawn "knowledge lectures," such as memorization of the Hebrew alphabet. In another way, Holy Book memorization became a substitute for the actual temple ceremonies in the elemental grades of that order. I can attest from personal experience that to memorize a chapter of one of the principal Holy Books of Thelema is to undergo a kind of initiation. The act of memorization demands an internal experience and integration of the contents of the text that can be achieved in no other way, and that will be unique for each aspirant. As it is written:

> [T]hey that sealed up the book in their blood were the chosen of Adonai, and the Thought of Adonai was a Word and a Deed; and they abode in the Land that the far-off travellers call Naught.*

---

* Liber LXV, V:59.

Text	Deacon	Priestess	Priest	Bishop
Liber Legis	Ch. III	Ch. I	Ch. II	Entire text, comment
Liber Cordis Cincti Serpente, sub figura LXV	Ch. II (Air, *ruach*)	Ch. III (Water, *neschemah*)	Ch. IV (Fire, *chiah*)	Ch. V (Spirit, *yechidah*)
Liber Liberi vel Lapidis Lazuli, sub figura VII	Ch. V (Mercury)	Ch. VI (Luna)	Ch. IV (Sol)	Ch. III (Jupiter, for male bishops) Chapter II (Saturn, for female bishops)
The Book of the Mysteries of God (Anna Kingsford)[*]	Ch. XII Z: "Proem," "Hymn to Hermes," & "An Exhortation of Hermes"	Ch. XIV θ: "The Hymn of Aphrodite," & "A Discourse of the Communion of Soules"	Ch. XIII H: "Hymn to the Planet God"	Ch. XI E: "Proem," & "Hymn to Phoebus"

[*] Published in *Clothed with the Sun*.

In his most concentrated and fundamental paper on ceremonial magic, *Liber O vel manus et sagittæ,* Crowley's first practical instruction is that the basic correspondences from *Liber 777* be "committed to memory." In fact, three of the six sections of that essential paper begin with instructions to exercise the memory. After their initiation to the III° and prior to their sacerdotal ordination, I examine novices in memorization of these correspondences *and their application in analyzing and developing magical formulae.*

I expect ordinands to have a familiarity with ecclesiastical theory and the relevant body of literature. In particular, I require substantial study of books drawn from the U.S. Primate Sabazius' "Book List for E.G.C. Priests and Priestesses."[*] For those who have exhausted that resource, there are of course further bibliographies to exploit, such as those included at the end of this book. In order to assure the institutional expertise of ordinands, I provide a written examination in E.G.C. policy and O.T.O. governance, as well as an oral examination in E.G.C. history.

There are a variety of tasks that can confirm a novice in his or her *subtle awareness of the Gnostic Mass temple.* Options include writing essays on the symbolism of various weapons and furniture, composing instrumental sacraments to bless them (my own are given later in this book), describing or even drafting a 'fantasy ideal' Gnostic Mass facility in great detail, or other creative work intended to explore and develop the understanding of the novice in this dimension.

An ordinand should have some orientation to pastoral work. Primarily this orientation will consist of an awareness of the sort of requests for and expectations of counsel with which members of the priesthood may be confronted, and an understanding of their own relevant abilities and

---

[*] Sabazius X°, *Mystery of Mystery,* pp. 326-8.

limitations, as well as a knowledge of how to perform appropriate referrals. The United States Grand Lodge of O.T.O. offers a recurring "Pastoral Counseling Workshop," which is a weekend seminar expressly tailored to provide this orientation. In the absence of (or in addition to) such a seminar, novices may undertake a course of text study, or receive training in a profane venue.

Novices should develop a personal *daily* practice of magick and/or yoga, and be able to relate that practice to their aspiration to the priesthood. They should have a working familiarity with at least one system of divination. They should have genuine experience with the method from Liber O called *Viator in Regnis Arboris.*[*]

When Crowley noted in Liber XV, "Certain secret formulæ of this Mass are taught to the PRIEST in his Ordination," he was patently engaging in purposeful mystification. Nevertheless, the statement has since caused enough anxiety that a certain amount of clarification may now be excused.

Eligible ordinands should be in possession of "the sublime and terrible knowledge that all real secrets are incommunicable."[†] The most important formulæ of the Mass can be grasped only through practice. I expect that an ordinand will have served in the appropriate ritual office many times as a novice, and ordination may include a celebration of the Mass in which the ordinand serves in that office. (Diaconal ordinations are *always* conducted thus.)

In addition, important formulae are communicated in the *Mysteria Mystica Maxima* degrees, when those are viewed as *gradual sacraments* preparing novices for ordination. This process is not even complete at the degree of Knight of East and West, which is the current prerequisite degree for

---

[*] Crowley, *Magick,* pp. 624-625.
[†] *Ibid.,* p. 189.

sacerdotal orders in E.G.C. Indeed, in one of the few instances where Crowley related an O.T.O. degree to a sacerdotal function, he indicates in the preamble to Liber CVI that a priestess administering last rites will do so in her capacity as a VI° initiate.

Finally, it should be noted that many important formulæ, "secret" in the sense that they are implicit rather than explicit in the text of Liber XV itself, have been discussed in the published writings of living bishops of the Church, including (but not limited to) those of the Patriarch, the U.S. Primate, and my own. Certain of these may indeed be emphasized in private instruction from a bishop to an ordinand. Even with the benefit of such instruction however, it remains vital to be open to other readings and alternate formulæ. Only thus can we further the establishment of Scientific Religion through our Gnostic and Catholic Church of Light, Life, Love and Liberty, the word of whose Law is Thelema.

The Nature of the E.G.C. Hierarchy

Ecclesia Gnostica Catholica has a sacerdotal (i.e. priestly) clerical class who act as official representatives of the Church in organizing and administering sacramental rites. However, we do not have any sacerdotalist doctrine which would require any of the Church sacraments under priestly auspices for the spiritual fulfillment or "redemption" of an individual, whether or not the individual is a member of the Church or an adherent to our doctrines.

It would be incorrect to conclude that we hold to a Protestant-style "priesthood of all believers" in which sacramental efficacy is considered to be divorced from training, proficiency, and ordination within the structures of the Church. Although each individual is inherently (and exclusively) qualified to seek and obtain her own access to the divine and to exhibit attainment *as an individual*, only the priesthood is authorized and empowered to demonstrate that divine access through the rites of the Church. Such demonstrations are intended to fortify and encourage the individual members who partake of our ecclesiastical sacraments.

The power informing E.G.C. priesthood is significantly different than that found in traditional Christianity. In Orthodox and Catholic Christian rites, priestly power and church hierarchies are founded on the basis of a concept of *apostolic succession*. According to their legends, there is an unbroken catena of spiritual transmission, effected through the imposition of hands, through all proper bishops, back to the "Twelve Apostles" and thence to the allegedly historical "Jesus." But as our contemporary E.G.C. is at pains to point out, **the traditional doctrines, theology, canon law, and insignia of the Roman Catholic, Orthodox, and Jacobite Churches do not operate within E.G.C.**

We can usefully contrast the "catholic and apostolic church" of the Nicene Creed with the "Gnostic and Catholic Church" of our own, in which the *apostolic* qualification is displaced by the *gnostic*. In popular discourse today, the word "gnostic" is often used to suggest a radical egalitarianism in mystical religion, as opposed to the hierarchism of traditional Christianity. Such was not typically the case among the heterodox sects labeled "so-called Gnostics" by the heresiologists of early Christianity, however. *Gnosis* was not something freely available to pious individuals; it was a secret knowledge transmitted through initiatory processes to chosen aspirants and realized through their own ineffable experience.[*] That sense is the one in which the word pertains to the Sanctuary of the Gnosis of O.T.O., wherein the Perfect Illuminati participate in the Supreme Secret to which they have been initiated.

The Sanctuary of the Gnosis is the root source of E.G.C. sacerdotal authority. Besides elevating the Law of Thelema to the principal religious code of O.T.O., Baphomet's reforms of both the E.G.C. and M∴M∴M∴ rites were intended to relate all ceremonial operations to the gradual adumbration of the Supreme Secret. And these two aspects are not very distinct from one another. In reference to the latter, 666 writes, "This Mass of the Holy Ghost is then the true Formula of the Magick of the Æon, even of the Æon of Horus, blessed be He in His Name Ra-Hoor-Khuit!"[†]

Today's universal Patriarch and national primates are heads within the Sovereign Sanctuary who act as the custodians and agents of those reforms. In an apostolic

---

[*] As Sabazius observes, "The elitism of most Gnostic systems led to their ultimate extinction in favor of the more popular and militant 'orthodox' systems of Christianity, Islam and Zoroastrianism." *Mystery of Mystery,* p. 30.
[†] Crowley, *Liber Aleph,* 85.

church, the sacramental contagion of cheirotonia is employed to transmit power and authority from some point of origin in history—or pseudo-history, like Jesus' commissioning of his disciples to ministry. In our Gnostic church, the same mechanism of contagion is used, but it communicates authority from the *continuous, capable,* and *contemporary* Sovereign Sanctuary, on the basis of the Supreme Secret, to the extent that the recipient has the individually-cultivated magick power to manifest that authority once received.

> I am ordained priest and consecrated Bishop and
> Arch bishop by the laying on of hands. Nothing
> else is valid.*

It is also the case that E.G.C. carries a legacy of apostolic transmissions, from the *Église Gnostique* of Jules Doinel, the Johannite Church of Bernard-Raymond Fabré-Palaprat, the Eliate Church of Eugene Vintras, and the Jacobite *episcopi vagantes* succession relayed by Joseph René Vilatte. Each of these has its own charms to add to the glamour of our ecclesiastical institution, but none of them are the essential basis of our work. The last of them is the one most closely associated with traditional Christian apostolic successions. Even in that case, its value to us has nothing to do with any putative link to the fiction of the pale Galilean, but rather to the Roman imperial church's incorporation of the earlier mysteries and state cults of paganism in antiquity.

Unfortunately, the ornamental nature of these apostolic histories was not always fully clear to the organizers of E.G.C. For some years during the 1980s, an episcopate was cultivated within E.G.C. that operated as if it were empowered by apostolic succession both to administer Thelemic sacraments and to further transmit the succession

---

* Crowley, letter to to C.S. Jones, March 13, 1919 (CSJ Papers), cited by Martin Starr in *The Unknown God: W.T. Smith & the Thelemites,* p. 72.

itself. At the end of that decade, aware of doctrinal inconsistencies and the possibility of practical abuses associated with this mode of development, Patriarch Hymenæus Beta suspended all further episcopal consecrations within E.G.C.* When he recommenced consecrations the following year, it was in combination with reforms that tied eligibility for E.G.C. holy orders to prior initiation in various degrees of M∴M∴M∴, identifying that of bishop with the VII°. As a direct consequence, the power to consecrate bishops in E.G.C. is now held only by a) the Patriarch, b) his appointed national Primates (holders of the X°), and c) any other members of the Sovereign Sanctuary of the IX° to whom he expressly delegates it. The relationship of the episcopate—and by extension, the clergy in total—to the Sanctuary of the Gnosis has thus been made more patent and efficient.

Compared to the proliferation of major and minor orders in the history of traditional Christianity, the hierarchy of E.G.C. is quite simple, with only five orders. Throughout the system, as in O.T.O. generally, authority is tied to service. Advancement in holy orders results in greater authority to administer and explicate the sacraments, but also greater responsibility to serve the lower ranks of the hierarchy.

The uppermost two orders are the headships invested in the Patriarch and his national primates respectively. These members of the Sanctuary of the Gnosis govern the rite, maintaining the authorized forms of rituals for the cardinal sacraments, and they superintend the bishops. In particular, the Patriarch (or Holy Father of the Church) determines the legitimate forms of the Gnostic Mass. Willful alterations of that ritual without his explicit permission are forbidden.

The bishops primarily serve the other orders of clergy, training them and providing them with authorization by

---

* Hymenaeus Beta, "On the Gnostic Catholic Church," in *The Magical Link* III:4 (Winter, 1990 EV), pp.25-30.

supervising their work. (Etymologically, the word bishop means 'supervisor.') Bishops admit members of the laity to the novitiate by agreeing to provide them with oversight. They also admit novices to the diaconal and sacerdotal orders through sacramental ceremonies of ordination. Short of the performance of episcopal consecrations, bishops hold a full measure of ministerial authority in E.G.C., with both the right and responsibility to administer all other sacraments of the church, and the license and obligation to expound those doctrines of the church which are not formally secret.

As mentioned earlier, only the regular inductees of the M∴M∴M∴ VII° are now eligible to be consecrated bishops. As part of that reform, a "grandfathered" class of *auxiliary bishops* was created, not yet initiated to the VII° but encouraged to aspire to that initiation. Yet another category, the *bishops in amity,* consists of bishops from other Gnostic churches who affiliate with E.G.C. in an advisory capacity, but they do not exercise episcopal functions within our hierarchy unless they have been consecrated also in E.G.C.

The priesthood serve local congregations and individual members of the laity through the teaching and sacramental functions discussed throughout this book. In particular, they have the authority and responsibility to preside over celebrations of the Gnostic Mass. They may also have the authority delegated to them by a bishop to perform baptisms and confirmations. In certain cases they may be authorized to perform weddings and last rites in the name of the Church. Priests and priestesses are equally vested with sacerdotal authority, even though their ceremonial offices in the Gnostic Mass are distinct.

Since the reforms of Anno III xxi, only initiates of the K.E.W. degree in M∴M∴M∴ have been ordained to the priesthood. Although the Patriarch extended an offer to grandfather priests and priestesses ordained under the prior circumstances, few applied, and there are currently no active members of the priesthood who do not hold the K.E.W. degree. Liber XV remarks that the Priestess is to be "Virgo Intacta, or specially dedicated to the Great Order." While the initials V.I. have been interpreted by some to mean that a Priestess should hold the VI° of O.T.O., ordination or supervised novice status are considered to be sufficient to make one "specially dedicated" to the Order of Oriental Templars, and sexual inexperience confers no effective qualification. Furthermore, while the original note from Baphomet indicated the communication of certain secret formulæ as a part of the ordination of a priest, the current Holy Father has revised this direction to apply to priestesses equally.

The diaconate is made up of clergy who have the authority and responsibility to assist the priesthood in sacramental tasks. A deacon also serves as the ceremonial leader of the congregation during the Gnostic Mass. Although English usage provides the feminine 'deaconess,' women are ordained 'deacons' in E.G.C. interchangeably with men, and there is no distinction between the duties of male and female deacons. Diaconal ordinands are currently required to hold the M∴M∴M∴ II°.

Novice clergy ('novices') are clergy members of E.G.C. who serve in ritual offices while aspiring and studying toward ordination. In addition to prior baptism and confirmation to establish E.G.C. membership, Minerval initiation in *Mysteria Mystica Maxima* and supervision by a bishop are essential elements of novice status.

There are thus six subclasses of clergy. (If we add the two further classes of laity and catechumens, the calculation yields eight levels to the entire hierarchy of E.G.C.) For purposes of public representation, the Patriarch, primates, bishops, priests and priestesses are all considered to be official representatives of E.G.C. Novices are not official representatives of E.G.C., and only some deacons (depending on their national situation and M∴M∴M∴ degree) have representative standing. The principal duties of E.G.C. clergy concern the Church's rituals and doctrines. While some (but by no means all) clergy have been trained in pastoral counseling and may be valuable resources in this regard, it is no part of their role to police the consciences of individual members of the Church, nor do they have any authority *as clergy* over the conduct of members *outside of the preparation and production of formal Church events.*

One of the curious allusions qualifying the sacerdotal power in E.G.C. is the statement in Liber XV that "The PRIESTESS and other officers never partake of the Sacrament, they being as it were part of the PRIEST himself."

The five Mass officers together illustrate the theophanic mechanism of a single individual, and thus no one of them is complete without the others. In qabalistic terms, the Priest is the *chiah*, the Priestess is the *neschemah*, the Deacon is the *ruach*, and the Children are the *nephesch*. (The duality of the *nephesch* relates to its dynamic of attraction/repulsion.) During the Ceremony of the Consecration of the Elements, the eucharistic elements are transformed from the *g'uph* into the *yechidah* (Kether in Malkuth and Malkuth in Kether), and thus, when the Priest communicates, all of the officers do so together: when the Priest says "no part of me," the *mezla* spills down the lightning flash from Eucharist to Priest to Priestess to Deacon to Children.

The Mass also prepares the people to communicate in their own persons, so that each popular communicant is an entire *chiah-neschemah-ruach-nephesch* composite who proclaims the continuity of *yechidah* ("the gods") and *g'uph* (the densest and least animate "part of me") within him or herself. When "There is no part of me that is not of the gods," *me* does not stop at my skin, it extends into my sensorium that includes everyone in the temple; it extends into my reason that includes everyone with whom I have interacted; it extends

64

into my intuition that includes humanity; it extends into my vital essence that includes the cosmos. All are parts of me in the exact reverse of the path by which we are parts of that Mystery of Mystery which is the One Father of Life.

The "part of the PRIEST himself" remark also should not be read as a suggestion that the Priestess (or any of the other officers) somehow *belongs to* the particular Priest as distinct from the larger body of the Church. In some places, limited resources, social inertia, or precedents regarding "Mass teams" has led aspiring clergy to believe that a priest or priestess should have a particular, ongoing partner as a regular co-celebrant in the Gnostic Mass. I think that making hardened dyads out of priest-priestess couples is not very helpful. If some ritualists want to work under such a restriction, so be it, but its general application poses serious problems for creating real communities of sacerdotal practice in which officers have an opportunity to learn and teach by working with a variety of other ritualists under orders.

As a bishop involved with training and supervision of clergy, I encourage novices to form and participate in such communities. In fact, I would go so far as to assert that a novice priestess who has only worked with one priest (or a novice priest, *mutatis mutandis*) is not optimally prepared for ordination.

Also, the convention of a Mass 'couple' has a tendency to radically subordinate the priestess to the priest in a way that is unsuited to the indications regarding her qualifications for office. Since the priestess is to be "Virgo Intacta or specially dedicated to the service of the Great Order" (this latter being glossed as "a sworn whore" in the Crowley marginalia preserved by Kenneth Grant), she should be a *free agent* with respect to the choice of priest, neither *married to* nor *pimped by* a particular priest, when it comes to her service to the Church.

At every level of the hierarchy, service is from the higher to the lower. The Patriarch and the Primates serve the bishops by maintaining the global and national institution of the Church, defining the powers of the various orders, and regulating the cardinal sacraments. The bishops serve the other clergy with instruction, ordination, and supervision. The priesthood serves local congregations by organizing and conducting the Gnostic Mass and other celebrations. The deacons serve the laity by leading them in the rites. The laity serve catechumens as examples and by pointing them to sources of knowledge about the Church.

Secret Chiefs and the Interior Church

Reading *The Confessions of Aleister Crowley* it is a recurring and unavoidable fact that he takes as given the reality of the Secret Chiefs and their involvement in his life. Although Crowley declared himself an atheist on any number of occasions, his memoirs show the Secret Chiefs to be the "higher power" to which he attributed his accomplishments and difficulties. In *Magick Without Tears*, a chapter that recounts anecdotes regarding the influence of the Secret Chiefs mentions that they might equally be called "The Masters" or "The Gods."*

> Now the Masters, the Secret Chiefs of the Order to which he owed his first initiation, are the directors of the spiritual destinies of this planet.†

But Crowley's accounts of his dealings with them are all a matter of synchronistic developments which he interpreted as their manipulation; or of communications received by him and his collaborators in visionary states of profoundly altered consciousness from such entities as Aiwass, Abul-Diz, Amalantrah, and Hermes Eimi.

It is perhaps little matter to someone living a century later that "They proved beyond all possibility of doubt to" Crowley, by his own lights "a firm sceptic accustomed to mathematical and scientific methods of criticism, their own existence, and their possession of power and knowledge far exceeding anything hereto conceived as human."‡ He later wrote:

---

* Aleister Crowley, *Magick Without Tears* (Tempe, AZ: New Falcon Publications, 1997), p. 320.
† Aleister Crowley, "The Master Therion—A Biographical Note," *The Equinox* III(10) (New York: 93 Publishing, 1986), p. 14.
‡ Aleister Crowley, "The Master Therion," p. 15.

> Since They are "invisible" and "inaccessible," may
> They not merely be figments invented by a self-
> styled "Master," not quite sure of himself, to prop
> his tottering Authority?[*]

Indeed they might. But Crowley never admits to having had such doubts during his work under the direction of Mathers in the Hermetic Order of the Golden Dawn. Moreover, their existence was necessary to Crowley's self-image as an honorable man. He wrote:

> Mathers and Westcott claimed to be working under
> one or more secret chiefs of the grade of 8°=3□. …
> It was then to those chiefs that I and other
> members of the Order were pledged.[†]

So that when Crowley split first with the other adepts of the Rosicrucian order within the Golden Dawn, and then later from Mathers himself, he could persist in what he saw as his original loyalty. Note that the Neophyte obligation that Crowley published in *The Equinox* refers simply and only to "the chiefs of the Order,"[‡] and that even this reference is absent in the original cipher manuscript, which simply mentions "a hostile current of will." (It does, in folio 59, give S.D.A. or Fraeulein Sprengel as "a chief among the members of the *Goldene Daemmerung*.")[§]

And yet the notion of **Secret** Chiefs or hidden masters seems to have been part of the culture of the Golden Dawn as fostered by Wescott and Mathers. Where did the Golden Dawn get this idea? Much of the founding membership of the Golden Dawn, including Wescott and Mathers, had been

---

[*] Crowley, *Magick Without Tears*, p. 93.
[†] [Aleister Crowley], Editorial, *The Equinox* 1910 I(4), p. 4.
[‡] [J.F.C. Fuller], "The Temple of Solomon the King," *The Equinox* 1909 I(3), p. 255.
[§] Darcy Kuntz (ed.), *The Golden Dawn Cipher Manuscripts* (Edmonds, WA: Holmes Publishing Group, 2001).

active in the Hermetic Society of Anna Kingsford, an organization first incubated in the London Lodge of the Theosophical Society under Kingsford's presidency. The creation of the separate Hermetic Society reflected a division between those members increasingly focused on "Esoteric Buddhism" who remained among the Theosophists, and the so-called "Hermetic" wing more interested in Western Mysteries, Rosicrucianism, esoteric Christianity, and so forth.[*]

From the inception of the Theosophical Society its organizers claimed to be working under instruction from hidden adepts even at that earliest phase when Theosophy had barely detached itself from the milieu of American Spiritualism. Theosophist leader Helena Petrovna Blavatsky had a spirit control named "John King"—what later occultists might call a "channeled entity." John King was first presented to Theosophical co-founder Colonel Olcott as a "Master," but was later demoted to a messenger of the Masters.[†] At this preliminary stage, the Orientalism of the Theosophists was directed to Egypt. Later, when it was transferred to Asia, these Masters became *Mahatmas* or "Great Souls." Key Theosophical Mahatmas included Koot Hoomi and Morya, but there were many others. Blavatsky described the Mahatmas in her correspondence to London Theosophist A.P. Sinnett with a quotation from Tennyson's poem "Wakeful Dreamer":

---

[*] Edward Maitland, *Anna Kingsford: Her Life, Letters, Diary, and Work*, 3rd ed. (London: Watkins, 1913), vol. II, pp. 153-54: Kingsford writes of creating two "sections" within the London Lodge of the T.S., one to owe allegiance to the Mahatmas through A.P. Sinnett, the other to pursue Hellenic and Christian mysticism under Kingsford. For the distinct Hermetic Society, *op. cit.,* pp. 186-87.

[†] Henry Steele Olcott, *Inside the Occult: The True Story of Madame Blavatsky* (Philadelphia, PA: Running Press, 1975).

How could ye know him? Ye were yet within
The narrower circle; he had well nigh reached
The last, which, with a region of white flame,
Pure without heat, into a larger air
Up-burning, and an ether of black blue
Invests and ingirds all other lives.*

In 1884, the Society for Psychical Research (S.P.R.), an English academy founded largely by Theosophists and on which Crowley later heaped much scorn in *The Equinox,* mounted an investigation of Blavatsky's claims of contact with the Masters, focusing on charges of conjuring tricks used by Blavatsky to produce magical phenomena and "apported" or mysteriously materialized correspondence at the Adyar Headquarters of the society in India.† Their conclusions were damning, and ever since then, those with opinions about the Mahatmas seem to be divided between the credulous believers for whom the Mahatmas are nearly ineffable realities, and scornful skeptics, who take them to have been purely fictions.

A very useful exception can be found in the research of K. Paul Johnson, who takes a middle route of considering that these were perhaps real men and women advancing intellectual, social, and political reforms, whose identities have been willfully obscured by conjuring antics and fabulous reputations alike.‡ Johnson notes for instance Joseph Maximillian Bimstein, a Polish kabbalist and magician who worked with Blavatsky in Cairo, and who later served in London as the Grand Master of the Exterior Circle for the

---

* H.P. Blavatsky, *The Letters of H.P. Blavatsky to A.P. Sinnett* (Pasadena: Theosophical University Press, 1997).
† A useful abridgement of Richard Hodgson's report to the S.P.R. is included in Tim Maroney, *The Book of Dzyan* (Hayward, CA: Chaosium, 2000).
‡ K. Paul Johnson, *The Masters Revealed: Madam Blavatsky and the Myth of the Great White Lodge* (Albany: SUNY Press, 1994).

Hermetic Brotherhood of Luxor, linking its governing initiates with an Interior Circle of hidden adepts, eventually understood to include both incarnate and disincarnate agents.*

As we read in a Theosophical text from 1889:

> The S.P.R. [Society for Psychical Research] now denies completely the existence of the Mahatmas. They say that from beginning to end they were a romance which Madame Blavatsky has woven from her own brain. Well, she might have done many things less clever than this. At any rate, we have not the slightest objection to this theory. As she always says now, she almost prefers that people should not believe in the Masters. She declares openly that she would rather people should seriously think that the only Mahatmaland is the grey matter of her brain, and that, in short, she has evolved them out of the depths of her own inner consciousness, than that their names and grand ideal should be so infamously desecrated as they are at present. At first she used to protest indignantly against any doubts as to their existence. Now she never goes out of her way to prove or disprove it. Let people think what they like.†

Another possible taproot of the Golden Dawn's teaching about Secret Chiefs is in the traditions of German Rosicrucianism. The *Goldene Daemmerung* of the cipher manuscripts seems to have been a cousin or portion of the

---

* Joscelyn Godwin, Christian Chenel, and John Patrick Deveney, *The Hermetic Brotherhood of Luxor: Initiatic and Historical Documents of an Order of Practical Occultism* (York Beach, ME: Samuel Weiser, 1995).
† H.P. Blavatsky, *The Key to Theosophy* (Pasadena: Theosophical University Press, 1946), pp. 297-8.

Gold und Rosenkreuzer: the lodge-based Rosicrucianism of eighteenth-century Germany that used a system of grades based on the qabalistic sephiroth, and focused their "practical" attentions on the work of alchemical magic and mysticism. Both Rosicrucian and alchemical traditions emphasize the possibility and desirability of aspirants being contacted by mysterious Adepts with knowledge otherwise unavailable.

Another eighteenth-century order with teachings comparable to and competing with those of the *Gold und Rosenkreuz* was the *Ritter des Lichts,* the Knights of Light, later known as the Asiatic Brethren, and as the Brotherhood of Light, whom we claim among the sources of traditional knowledge in the sanctuaries of O.T.O.*

Also in eighteenth-century Germany, the *Strikt Observanz* order of Baron von Hund popularized neo-Templar Freemasonry. Von Hund alleged to receive his authority from "Unknown Superiors," and he eventually had to compete with other organizers who claimed to be instructed by them as well as or better than he was.† Still, this notion so successfully fostered by Von Hund was perpetuated in many of the more esoteric strains of high-degree Freemasonry, including the Rectified Scottish Rite, which is yet another tributary of the O.T.O. initiatory stream.

The Rectified Scottish Rite was also, however, a manifestation of the Martinist tradition. And in nineteenth-century Martinism we see appeals to the *Supérieurs Inconnus*, or "Unknown Superiors," invoked as the means of

---

* L. Bathurst IX°, "Book 52—The Manifesto of the O.T.O.," *The Equinox* III(10) (New York: 93 Publishing, 1986), p. 153. On the *Ritter des Lichts,* see Antoine Faivre, *Dictionary of Gnosis & Western Esotericism,* s.v. "Asiatic Brethren," ed. Wouter J. Hanegraaff (Leiden: Brill, 2006), pp. 107-9.
† Pierre Mollier, *Dictionary of Gnosis & Western Esotericism*, s.v. "Neo-Templar Traditions," pp. 851-2.

transmission of the secret doctrines and methods of Martinism, from Louis Claude de Saint-Martin (himself called the "Unknown Philosopher") to the much later founders of the Martinist Order, among whom was Gérard Encausse, who became Supreme and Holy King of O.T.O. in France, and eventually a Saint of our Gnostic Catholic Church. When creating the lodge-based system of Martinism, Encausse made *Supérieur Inconnu* the title of the highest degree in that system.[*] Crowley and Mathers, conferring in Paris, appear to have been influenced by the initiatory techniques of Martinism when they planned for reforms of the Golden Dawn temples to add the custom of masking.[†]

All of this history aside, Crowley was prepared in advance for the idea of the Secret Chiefs by his first direct informant regarding the course to chart in occultism. Fresh from a reading of *The Book of Black Magic and Pacts,* Crowley had written to its author Arthur Edward Waite requesting from this expert what he should best study and how to receive initiated instruction. Waite directed Crowley to a little book titled *The Cloud Upon the Sanctuary* by Karl von Eckartshausen.[‡] And when Crowley wished to give what he called "An Account of A∴A∴" to aspirants, that is to say, an account of the Collegium Summum, the Third and Highest Order in his scheme of initiatory spiritual development, he simply edited the second letter or chapter of Eckartshausen's book.[§] For the phrase "a clear idea of the interior Church" Crowley substituted "a clear idea of the interior Order."

---

[*] Jean-Pierre Laurant, *Dictionary of Gnosis & Western Esotericism,* s.v. "Papus," pp. 913-915.
[†] Aleister Crowley, *The Confessions of Aleister Crowley*, ed. John Symonds and Kenneth Grant (New York: Arcana, 1989), 195-6.
[‡] Crowley, *Confessions,* p. 127.
[§] [Karl] von Eckartshausen, "An Account of A∴A∴," *The Equinox* 1907 I(1), pp. 5-13.

Eckartshausen wrote:

> [A]ll exterior societies subsist through this interior one giving them its spirit. As soon as external societies wish to be independent of the interior one, and to transform a temple of wisdom into a political edifice, the interior society retires and leaves only the letter without the spirit. It is thus that secret external societies of wisdom [are] nothing but hieroglyphic screens, the truth remaining inviolable in the sanctuary so that she might never be profaned.*

Note that this Councillor Eckartshausen was himself a product of the eighteenth-century esoteric milieu. He was trained for the Jesuit Order in Ingolstadt, studying under no less a teacher than Adam Weishaupt, founder of the Illuminati Order and a saint of our Church. But Eckartshausen was a monarchist and a theocrat, and after he discovered the supposed political ambitions of the Illuminati he quit them. He subsequently refused all secret initiations, even those of the Rosenkreuzer and Asiatic Brethren with whom he would have been in closer philosophical accord.†

And despite Crowley's attempt to fashion outer and inner orders for A∴A∴ that would call few and choose many to lead to the ultimate mystical brotherhood, both the original and the edited text admonish that the true Interior Church "knows none of the formalities which belong to the outer rings, the work of man."‡

Although Crowley said he had been "received among" the Secret Chiefs in a visionary episode in Japan in April of

---

* Karl von Eckartshausen, *The Cloud Upon the Sanctuary* (Edmonds, WA: Sure Fire Press, 1991), p. 47.
† Jacques Fabry, *Dictionary of Gnosis & Western Esotericism,* s.v. "Eckartshausen, Karl von," p. 236-8.
‡ Eckartshausen, "An Account of A∴A∴," p. 12.

1906 EV* and then "formally invited … to take [his] place officially" as a Secret Chief that December,† it was not until 1909, after certain experiences documented in *The Vision & the Voice*, that he accepted the grade. And those experiences presented the community of the Third Order to him not as a Church, but as a City: The City of the Pyramids, where those who have attained to mastery dwell in the Night of Pan.‡

In contemplating this topic, one angle that had occurred to me, would be to address the question: "How do you become a Secret Chief?" But of course, the answer to that is simple. You complete the Ordeal of the Abyss, so that <u>nobody</u> arrives in the City of the Pyramids. The Master of the Temple must have annihilated his or her prior personality, and therefore those who accomplish that attainment are *Nemo*, or "no one" at all. And "there is no path" to that station.

The mystic Ivan Vladimirovich Lopukhin was a Russian contemporary of Eckartshausen's. In his book on this topic, Lopukhin identifies the annihilation of the ego with the entry into the Interior Church.§ Likewise he points to the "pure disinterested love" which it is a task of the Master of the Temple to manifest.** Still, in keeping with the Gethsemane cry "not my will, but thine,"†† Lopukhin treats the human

---

* Crowley, *Confessions,* p. 526.
† Through the agency of George Cecil Jones, per Crowley, *Confessions,* p. 533.
‡ Aleister Crowley, Victor B. Neuburg, and Mary Desti, *The Vision & the Voice: With Commentary and Other Papers,* ed. Hymenaeus Beta (York Beach, ME: Samuel Weiser, 1988), pp. 137-142, 148-153.
§ I.V. Lopukhin, *Some Characteristics of the Interior Church,* trans. D.H.S. Nicholson, intr. A.E. Waite (Scriptoria Books, 2009).
** Aleister Crowley, "One Star in Sight," appendix II in Aleister Crowley, Mary Desti, and Leila Waddell, *Magick: Liber ABA, Book 4, Parts I-IV*, ed. Hymenaeus Beta, 2nd rev. ed. (York Beach, ME: Samuel Weiser 1997), p. 492.
†† Luke 22:42.

will as irreconcilable with the divine will, attaching only to the ego, rather than to that true Self which the ego's personality limits and oppresses. Perhaps such a teaching was suited to aspirants in the Old Æon.

Lopukhin's Interior Church does not, however, differ from the City of the Pyramids in our doctrines when it comes to the detachment needed in aspiring to it. "It is not enough to refrain from searching for this condition," he writes, "but the entrance to it must even be feared."[*] As declared by the Voice of the Fourteenth Æthyr:

> Bowed are their backs, whereon resteth the universe. Veiled are their faces, that have beheld the glory Ineffable. Herein no forms appear, and the vision of God face to face, that is transmuted in the Athanor called dissolution, or hammered into one forge of meditation, is in this place but a blasphemy and a mockery.[†]

Let us return to the matter of visions and synchronicities which Crowley interpreted as manipulation by the Secret Chiefs. In the chapter on "How to Recognize Masters" in *Magick Without Tears,* Crowley draws several anecdotes on these lines from his *Confessions*. In particular, he describes the clairvoyant guidance from the Wizard Abul-diz that enabled him and Mary Desti to find the Villa Caldarazzo outside of Rome as a refuge where work could begin on *Book Four*. He also relates an episode from 1920 in which he demanded a sign from the Secret Chiefs, feeling in despair about his work at that time. After an apt *I Ching* divination, he was presented by Jane Cheron—in an unrelated visit to her—with a large silk reproduction of the Stele of Revealing.[‡] It was episodes like these that caused Crowley to

---

[*] Lopukhin, *Some Characteristics of the Interior Church,* p. 94.
[†] Crowley, *The Vision & the Voice*, pp. 140-1.
[‡] Crowley, *Magick Without Tears,* pp. 323-333.

declare: "I am walking, not by faith but by sight, in my relations with the Secret Chiefs."[*]

But the chief illustration that Crowley used for the methods of the Secret Chiefs in arranging his affairs was the rediscovery of the manuscript of *The Book of the Law* in the attic of Boleskine House on June 28, 1909. Crowley insisted that the Secret Chiefs had arranged for him to have a house-guest with a love of skiing, so that Crowley would be led to discover some Enochian papers beneath his old skis, and below those, the manuscript.[†] Nor, if we are to believe the accounts of those still living, have the Secret Chiefs lost interest in the disposition of the original manuscript of *The Book of the Law*.

The article "Raiders of the Lost Basement" by Tom Whitmore recounts the author's discovery of a hoard of Crowley papers in the basement of a house he had just purchased. Whitmore wasn't entirely sure what he had, but he knew an O.T.O. member. In short order he found himself talking to O.T.O. Grand Secretary General Bill Heidrick, and then to Crowley's pupil Israel Regardie. Ultimately, for very little personal reward, Whitmore returned to the O.T.O. a considerable number of pieces of original correspondence and Crowley manuscripts, including the authorizations to Grady McMurtry known as "the Caliphate letters," an O.T.O. charter from the 1920s, and the original MS of *The Book of the Law*. Some of these to be sure, though perhaps not all, had been stolen in a house robbery from Karl Germer's widow. But their delivery to the basement is still a mystery. Whitmore writes, "The one lead we had as to how the papers got into the basement turned out to be false; we may never know."[‡]

---

[*] Crowley, *Confessions*, 601.
[†] Crowley, *Magick Without Tears*, 321-3.
[‡] Tom Whitmore, "Raiders of the Lost Basement," *Baphomet Breeze* vol. VII, no. 3, Autumnal Equinox 1992 EV.

From Whitmore's perspective, these events were a little windfall, and "a story to dine out on." But from the perspective of the organizers of O.T.O. the recovery of the manuscript of *Liber Legis* affirmed the continuity of the Order and the currency of our mission through a very tangible approbation from the Secret Chiefs. More recently, with the sixty-five pages of the manuscript duly secreted in a safe repository by and for the Order, the Prophet's own handwriting appeared again from an unexpected quarter to affect our custodianship of the text of the Law.

There is a complicated editorial history of the verse paraphrase of the Stele of Revealing which is inserted in the text according to the instructions of Aiwass. The verses themselves do not appear in the holograph manuscript. They were to be interpolated from another notebook where Crowley had already written them prior to the April reception. But that notebook has never been recovered. As mentioned earlier, Crowley himself lost the manuscript for some years prior to 1909.

There are a variety of parallel and supplementary texts that problematize the line of verse beginning with "Aum!" Virtually all twentieth-century editions of *The Book of the Law* III:37 give the line as: "Aum! Let it fill me," But the separate publication of the verses from the Stele in *The Equinox* I:VII and in earlier proofs for Crowley's *Collected Works,* and in later volumes under Crowley's editorship, all have instead: "Aum! Let it <u>kill</u> me." There are a variety of interesting considerations and arguments that have been made concerning this inconsistency. The upshot of them is that the original holograph manuscript gives no guidance, since the "fill" that appears there is a pencil marking by Crowley after the reception of the book but prior to its publication and prior to the other publications of the Stele verses.[*] Our

---

[*] Hymenaeus Beta, "On the kill me/fill me correction to *Liber Legis*," online at http://oto-usa.org/static/legis/legis1.pdf;

Frater Superior was laboring in 2013 on the still-forthcoming new edition of *The Holy Books of Thelema*, and he was not at liberty to passively contemplate this dilemma. As an editor he *had* to make a decision. The more he had learned about the editorial history of the text, the less obvious that decision had become.

It was at that very point that the O.T.O. again recovered some of the Order's important historical properties. James Thomas Windram, had been Crowley's O.T.O. Viceroy for South Africa. His surviving son very generously returned some papers, books, and regalia to the O.T.O. archives. Among these was the copy of *Thelema* (i.e. the 1909 Holy Books volume) that had served as Crowley's own desk copy between 1909 and 1913. It includes a variety of penciled corrections, most of them already adopted in later editions of the Holy Books. But it also clearly corrects fill to kill.* The receipt of this information—again, from an entirely unlooked-for quarter—is not only another case of synchronistic providence concerning the Law, where Secret Chiefs might have arranged for the restoration of the text at a time when it could finally be corrected with sufficient transparency and promulgated at sufficient speed. It is the written instruction of one who was a Secret Chief himself: Aleister Crowley after 1909.

I once gave a shorter, simpler version of this chapter as a talk at a synaxis for E.G.C. clergy. Afterwards, I was approached by several attendees. They wanted to know what

"Further on the kill/fill correction" online at http://oto-usa.org/static/legis/legis2.pdf; "On the kill/fill correction (3)," online at http://oto-usa.org/static/legis/legis3/legis3.pdf (all consulted 2017.02.12).

* Hymenaeus Beta, "News from International Headquarters," April 10, 2013 EV, online at http://oto.org/news0413.html (consulted 2017.02.12).

I *really* thought about the Secret Chiefs. It was a fair question then, and it is a fair question now.

Doctor Marco Pasi is a scholar of modern occult movements. He observes that the Secret Chiefs, and their various counterparts and homologues—the Interior Circle, the Mahatmas, the Unknown Superiors, the Hidden Adepts, and so on—all function in the manner of conspiracy theories. But rather than indicating a menacing influence that orchestrates the chaos of the world and makes us into victims, the Secret Chiefs are supposed to be benevolent, developing humanity's latent potentials, and rescuing the world from the wrong turns of society. Dr. Pasi seems to think that the Secret Chiefs are a great consolation: a style of eunoia in esoteric rhetoric, to balance or counteract the paranoia so often fostered in the modern world.[*] But that doesn't mean they are *real*.

Crowley, sure of their reality, insisted, "They may be incarnate or disincarnate: it is a matter of their convenience." Also, he remarked that the system of the outer G.D. and inner R.C. Orders that he organized for attainment "is only one of many" superintended by the Secret Chiefs.[†]

As for me, I live in a world where it seems that the heavens stretch away just as far as the hells. Considering any person I have met who has seemed to me to be the most contemptible, the most delusional, powerless, self-absorbed, worthless bag of crap, I imagine that there must be one who exceeds my integrity, my insight and my capabilities, and my concern for humanity by at least as much as mine exceed that of the miserable wretch. I suppose that that higher one must have peers, and that these, the Secret Chiefs of the Third Order, recognize one another just as Eckartshausen and Crowley wrote.

---

[*] Marco Pasi, *Aleister Crowley and the Temptation of Politics* (Bristol, CT: Acumen, 2014), pp. 118-119.
[†] Crowley, *Magick Without Tears*, p. 93.

If I already knew better than anyone else how the world should be and how to make it that way, if I had nothing to learn about the basis of reality and the destiny of humanity, then, if I were an adept in fact, I would be a Black Brother, accursed, one who seals up the Pylon with blood, who shuts himself off from the company of the saints, who keeps himself from compassion and from understanding.

And so I seek to make myself a fit instrument for the designs of the Secret Chiefs, and to make myself sensitive to their direction. It is my fervent wish and benediction that you will as well.

3. Magisterial Priestcraft: Promulgating the Law

> I'm sick of your teaching—teaching—teaching—as if you were God Almighty and I were a poor bloody shit in the street!
>
> —George Montagu Bennet,
> 7th Earl of Tankerville,
> addressing Aleister Crowley
> 7 July, 1907 EV*

Tankerville's revulsion may have had as much to do with his own character as with Crowley's social tactics. But it does interestingly highlight a challenge faced by Thelemic clergy. As official representatives of the Gnostic Catholic Church, priests and priestesses participate in the Church's magisterium, and thus possess both the authority and the responsibility to provide teaching about the Law, the Church, and the mysteries of our rite. *Deus est homo,*† and we do therefore indeed preach and teach as *God Almighty,* but the knowledge of our vocation as servants among other almighty gods should preserve us from treating our auditors as *poor bloody shits in the street*—even if we are standing on the curb to address them.

> Do not therefore 'select suitable persons' in thy worldly wisdom; preach openly the Law to all men. ... The open preaching of this Law, and the practice of these precepts, will arouse discussion and animosity, and thus place thee upon a rostrum whence thou mayst speak unto the people.‡

---

* Quoted in Martin Booth, *A Magick Life,* p. 249.
† "There is no god but man," in the words of Liber LXXVII.
‡ Liber CCC, "Khabs Am Pekht."

At the same time, despite even the Prophet's direction in this regard, considerations of the short "Comment" ("Those who discuss the contents of this book...") impel our clergy to avoid a traditional Christian homiletic approach, in which selected passages from scripture are expounded and illustrated with anecdotes for the moral improvement of listeners. This limitation is perhaps the one which 666 had in mind when he wrote, "We are not to add to this gift by preaching and the like." Still, he insists in the same document:

> Note, pray thee, in verse 42 of this chapter [III of *CCXX*] the injunction: "Success is thy proof: argue not; convert not; talk not overmuch." This is not any bar to an explanation of the Law. We may aid men to strike off their own fetters; but those who prefer slavery must be allowed to do so.*

One route out of this impasse is provided by the review and explanation of Crowley's Extenuation† and other commentaries on *Liber Legis*. Readings and recitations of the Holy Books are among the purest forms of promulgation, but even those need to be supplemented with enough context to give listeners a chance to appreciate their significance.

While promulgation of the Law must always be an ingredient in any priestly teaching stemming from the E.G.C. magisterium, it does not have to be the only or dominant focus in a particular sermon or discourse. Thelemic preaching may consist of straightforward exhortation to the Great Work, encouragement to each listener to seek and execute the one true purpose of his or her individual manifestation on this plane, renouncing all goals and values that interfere with its accomplishment. Similarly, it is fitting for a member of the priesthood to issue denunciations and

---

* *Op. cit.*
† Abridged with added materials as *The Law Is for All.*

84

anathemas against the forces of tyranny and oppression. One may attempt assessments of secular conditions vis-à-vis the Law of Thelema.

Focusing within our rite, as is likely when addressing fellow members of the Church, there are many possibilities for exercising the instructional role of the priesthood. A talk may furnish an account of the life of one of the Saints and his work, or similarly address an inductee of the Order of the Lion or the Order of the Eagle. Sermons may offer explication of various articles of the Creed, or discussion of the power and significance of certain sacraments. Clergy may reflect on the condition of the local sanctuary or the universal Church.

We can address our magisterial efforts to the outer world of the profane, the intermediate world of our fellow initiates, and also to the inner world of the spirit. In Sura LXXII of the Qur'an, ✠Mohammed engages in *preaching to the djinn*, sharing the divine message with these rational non-human beings. Alluding to the very same context, the instruction of 666 on "The Astral Journey: How to Do It" counsels magicians to ascertain of an encounter in the spirit-vision "if he is 'one of the believing Jinn'" by demanding from him the Word of the Law.* Rather than interrogating a visionary entity with arcane words and signs, one can simply consider its reaction to the plain statement: "Do what thou wilt shall be the whole of the Law."

While many spirits have doubtless already resolved themselves to champion the New Law or to slave for the Old, there will often—and especially in the experience of magicians whose own initiation is as yet preliminary—be those who are undecided and who will therefore profit from contact with the priestly will-to-promulgation. Even if we accept the argument of "The Initiated Interpretation of

---

* Crowley, *Magick without Tears,* p. 147.

Ceremonial Magick" that evoked spirits are all subsidiary mental entities of the magician's own consciousness,* the process of preaching to the djinn consolidates that consciousness in the light of the Æon and liberates it for the performance of the Great Work. As ✠Friedrich Nietzsche put it, "In this way the person exercising volition adds the feelings of delight of his successful executive instruments, the useful 'under-wills' or under-souls—indeed our body is but a social structure composed of many souls—to his feelings of delight as commander."†

And so we promulgate to the profane, teach our brothers and sisters, and test the spirits, all as functions of an active priesthood. When considering these three realms of magisterial activity, a priestess or priest will in all likelihood find one of them especially attractive. "But since one is naturally attracted to the Angel, another to the Demon, let the first strengthen the lower link, the last attach more firmly to the higher."‡ It is vital to recall the *principle of equilibrium* which is the "basis of the work."§ Clergy should not at first follow their natural attraction, but rather its reverse. Crowley offers this approach as a course of political training in his story "Thien Tao"—political in the sense of Plato's *Republic*, which instructs that an enlightened and initiated aristocracy is required for sound government.** But the best models of social government ultimately apply also to the discipline of the individual: "For, in True Things, all are but images one of another; man is but a map of the universe, and Society is but the same on a larger scale."††

---

* Crowley, *The Goetia* (1st ed. & facsimiles) pp. 1-5, (illus. 2nd ed.) pp. 15-19.
† Nietzsche, *Beyond Good and Evil,* §19. Kaufmann trans. quoted.
‡ Liber Tzaddi sub figura XC, v. 41.
§ Liber Librae sub figura XXX, v. 0.
** Crowley, *Konx Om Pax,* pp. 53-67.
†† Liber CXCIV, pt. 1.

By challenging ourselves to magisterial operation in the realms we find most daunting, we avoid the trap of valuing that activity for its pleasurable byproducts, and we keep it in perspective as work by which we realize the will to sacerdotal power according to the Law of Thelema.

Ritual Settings
for the Thelemic Magisterium

While the Gnostic Mass is indeed the "broad base of public association" in E.G.C. and O.T.O.,* and may yet become so for Thelema as a whole, it is not *in itself* conducive to the teaching function of the priesthood. Since the *cultivation of ecstasy* among congregants was Baphomet's express intention in designing the ceremony of our Mass, there seems to be a basic conflict with the sort of articulate conscious engagement that would be optimal for an instructional event. This observation is not to deride the important fact that the Gnostic Mass always provides instruction on a certain plane, in that it constantly adumbrates the Supreme Secret of O.T.O. Still, the ritual of Liber XV provides no opportunity within the Mass for teaching by means of expositions, sermons, or instructional readings. Even to attach such a feature to the beginning or the end of an unmodified Gnostic Mass would require some ritual engineering. Current episcopal consensus, along with the advice of the U.S. Primate, discourages full-on sermonizing by the deacon prior to admitting the people, suggesting that a deacon's preamble be kept to a minimum of procedural information for the benefit of new attendees.

A certain measure of preaching is comprehended by Crowley's diary notes regarding E.G.C. baptism (and realized in the current ritual authored by U.S. Primate Sabazius), in the form of an 'exhortation' to the new catechumens at the end of the ceremony. This function is consistent with the nature of the sacrament as an admission to the cate-chumenate: those baptized are inaugurating a course of learning about the Church. Some explicit instruction is fitting as part of that event. But with that sole exception, the magisterial function seems to be largely segregated from the

---

* Aleister Crowley to Karl Germer, 12-14 March, 1942.

sacramental function, at least with respect to the cardinal sacraments that carry the authorization of the full hierarchy. This situation should not be interpreted as discouraging magisterial work among the priesthood, but rather as offering an opportunity to teach creatively, without being constrained by sacramental circumstances.

At the same time, Thelemic priestesses and priests are necessarily *magicians* with an interest in ceremony, and we commonly have an appetite for ritual vehicles that will place our teachings in relief. We have some pointers from 666 in this regard, and I have also developed some original ritual for the purpose.

Liber Israfel

The ritual of Liber LXIV was called "Liber Anubis" in its original form, which was developed principally by Allan Bennett. Later, when issuing it as an official publication of A∴A∴ in class B, the Prophet renamed it "Liber Israfel," an allusion to the Islamic angel of the trumpet, the being who was supposed to announce the Final Judgment and turn of the age, corresponding to "the 20th Key, the Angel," which is to say the Tarot trump now known as The Æon. The original title *Anubis* refers to a psychopomp, a god-form concerned to lead and instruct the adherent, while the new name *Israfel* more specifically alludes to the communication of the Word of the New Æon and the promulgation of the Law, i.e. the Thelemic magisterium.

While often viewed simply an invocation of Tahuti (a god of the Word), Liber Israfel includes three further components after the initial invocation of the god:

- Points 1-14 invoke the deity.

- Points 15-17 prepare the hearers and the speaker for inspiration.

- Points 18-19 consist of a "Lection" (a reading, recitation or speech), prefaced by a version of the General Exordium of the Golden Dawn Neophyte Grade.

- Points 20-21 are a dismissal and closing.

These four sections correspond to the formula of Tetragrammaton, just as the first section alone embraces the entire formula.[*] Alternatively, they may be understood in terms of the gods Thoth, Asi and Hoor-Apep, with the final section corresponding to the magician/aspirant (identified with Asar).[†]

Liber Israfel continues to be a viable and engaging ceremonial context for Thelemic sermonizing, although it is rarely applied in this manner. It may be used in full to frame an exposition regarding the Law, either in a temple as noted in the text, or in a more public setting. An adaptation would have a speaker employ the first fourteen points alone to fortify him- or herself immediately prior to an event where he or she would offer public teaching on the Law.

The text of Liber Israfel follows, for ease of use and reference. Regardless of how it is put into further practice, memorization of this brief ritual is strongly recommended as training for the magisterial dimension of Thelemic priesthood.

---

[*] Points 1-5, 6-7, 8-11, 12-14; see *Magick in Theory & Practice* Chapter II, pp. 149-50.

[†] See the ritual of "Liber Pyramidos sub figura DCLXXI," in Crowley, *Commentaries on the Holy Books and Other Papers* (*The Equinox* IV:1).

LIBER ISRAFEL
sub figura XLIV

0. *The Temple being in darkness, and the Speaker ascended into his place, let him begin by a ritual of the Enterer, as followeth.*

1. Procul, O procul este profani.

2. Bahlasti! Ompehda!

3. In the name of the Mighty and Terrible One, I proclaim that I have banished the Shells unto their habitations.

4. I invoke Tahuti, the Lord of Wisdom and of Utterance, the God that cometh forth from the Veil.

5. O Thou! Majesty of Godhead! Wisdom-crowned Tahuti!
   Lord of the Gates of the Universe! Thee, Thee, I invoke.
   O Thou of the Ibis Head! Thee, Thee I invoke.
   Thou who wieldest the Wand of Double Power! Thee, Thee I invoke!
   Thou who bearest in Thy left hand the Rose and Cross of Light and Life: Thee, Thee, I invoke.
   Thou, whose head is as an emerald, and Thy nemmes as the night-sky blue! Thee, Thee I invoke.
   Thou whose skin is of flaming orange as though it burned in a furnace! Thee, Thee I invoke.

6. Behold! I am Yesterday, To-Day, and Brother of To-Morrow!
   I am born again and again.
   Mine is the Unseen Force, whereof the Gods are sprung! Which is as Life unto the Dwellers in the Watch-Towers of the Universe.
   I am the Charioteer of the East, Lord of the Past and of the Future.
   I see by mine own inward light: Lord of Resurrection;
   Who cometh forth from the Dusk, and my birth is from the House of Death.

7. O ye two Divine Hawks upon your Pinnacles!
   Who keep watch over the Universe!
   Ye who company the Bier to the House of Rest!
   Who pilot the Ship of Ra advancing onwards to the heights of heaven!
   Lord of the Shrine which standeth in the Centre of the Earth!

8. Behold, He is in me, and I in Him!
   Mine is the Radiance, wherein Ptah floateth over the firmament! I travel upon high!
   I tread upon the firmament of Nu!
   I raise a flashing flame, with the lightning of Mine Eye!
   Ever rushing on, in the splendour of the daily glorified Ra: giving my life to the Dwellers of Earth.

9. If I say "Come up upon the mountains!" the Celestial Waters shall flow at my Word.
   For I am Ra incarnate!
   Khephra created in the Flesh!
   I am the Eidolon of my father Tmu, Lord of the City of the Sun!

10. The God who commands is in my mouth!
    The God of Wisdom is in my Heart!
    My tongue is the Sanctuary of Truth!
    And a God sitteth upon my lips.

11. My Word is accomplished every day!
    And the desire of my heart realises itself, as that of Ptah when He createth his works!
    I am Eternal; therefore all things are as my designs; therefore do all things obey my Word.

12. Therefore do Thou come forth unto me from Thine abode in the Silence: Unutterable Wisdom! All-Light! All-Power!
    Thoth! Hermes! Mercury! Odin!

By whatever name I call Thee, Thou art still nameless to Eternity: Come Thou forth, I say, and aid and guard me in this work of Art.

13. Thou, Star of the East, that didst conduct the Magi!
Thou art The Same all-present in Heaven and in Hell!
Thou that vibratest between the Light and the Darkness!
Rising, descending! Changing ever, yet ever The Same!
The Sun is Thy Father!
Thy Mother the Moon!
The Wind hath borne Thee in its bosom; and Earth hath ever nourished the changeless Godhead of Thy Youth!

14. Come Thou forth, I say, come Thou forth!
And make all Spirits subject unto Me:
So that every Spirit of the Firmament
And of the Ether,
Upon the Earth,
And under the Earth,
On dry land
And in the Water,
Of whirling Air
And of rushing Fire,
And every Spell and Scourge of God the Vast One, may be obedient unto Me!

15. I invoke the Priestess of the Silver Star, Asi the Curved One, by the ritual of Silence.

16. I make open the gate of Bliss; I descend from the Palace of the Stars; I greet you, I embrace you, O children of earth, that are gathered together in the Hall of Darkness.

17. *(A pause.)*

18. The Speech in the Silence.
The Words against the Son of Night.
The Voice of Tahuti in the Universe in the Presence of the Eternal.
The Formulas of Knowledge.

The Wisdom of Breath.
The Root of Vibration.
The Shaking of the Invisible.
The Rolling Asunder of the Darkness.
The Becoming Visible of Matter.
The Piercing of the Scales of the Crocodile.
The Breaking Forth of the Light!

19. *(Follows the Lection.)*

20. There is an end of the speech; let the Silence of darkness be broken; let it return into the silence of light.

21. *The speaker silently departs; the listeners disperse unto their homes; yea, they disperse unto their homes.*

The Ritual Ordained for Public Service

Crowley later wrote another ceremony to support Thelemic preaching. The centerpiece of that operation was the Mass of the Phoenix, an A∴A∴ ritual consisting of a solo Eucharist. His own description of the ceremony was as follows:

> The Priest is seated before the altar in meditation. The Priestess is in the throne of the N.E. The Acolyte is in the throne of the S.E.
>
> The Acolyte rises, and knocks 1-3-7, bearing Bell, Book, and Candle to Priest.
>
> The Priestess rises, and plays *Abide with Me* or *Abendlied*.
>
> The Priest rises, and performs the Mass of the Phoenix.
>
> The Priestess plays what she will, while the Acolyte binds the Priest to the cross, which he unveils.
>
> The Priest preaches.
>
> The Priestess plays, while the Acolyte draws the veil.
>
> The Acolyte comes forward to the Altar, and knocks 7-3-1 saying, "Go: it is finished."
>
> The Priest is robed in white and gold, his breast bare.
>
> The Priestess wears a green robe.
>
> The Acolyte wears a red robe, and is girt with a sword. He may be masked.*

Crowley seems to have performed this ritual a few times circa 1912 EV, with Leila Waddell as his priestess. He discontinued its use after composing the Gnostic Mass, and it is officially regarded as **obsolete** in E.G.C. In fact, bodies within O.T.O. have been officially discouraged from sponsoring *public* presentations of the Mass of the Phoenix.

Nevertheless, the "Ritual Ordained for Public Service," as he called it, contains several features that may provide

---

* Crowley, *The Vision & the Voice (The Equinox* IV:2), p. 370 *n.*

worthy inspiration to today's Thelemic clergy. The precedent of combining a sermon with a brief demonstration of Eucharistic magick is not a negligible one.* The idea of pairing a preacher with an instrumental musician offers great possibilities for powerful presentations. Finally, delivering a discourse from a fixed ritual posture—crucifixion being but a single example—can be a way of adding drama and intensity to the event.

On the other hand, it should probably be noted that in the Gnostic Mass, Crowley deliberately declined to follow the Christian precedent of connecting preaching with the Eucharistic operation. For a free-standing ceremony to contextualize preaching, with a more ecclesiastical character than that of Liber Israfel, see "The Liturgy of the Word of the Law" in my book *Raise the Spell*.

---

* See, for an example of a Eucharist that could be enacted thus, the "Short Eucharist" published in *Raise the Spell*.

The Tracts Are for All

Addressing his "Son" Parzival X° regarding the cultivation of the Thelemic movement, the Master Therion wrote:

> The special tracts written by Us, or authorized by Us, should be distributed to all persons with whom those who have accepted the Law may be in contact.[*]

A little later, he expressed particular interest in having such literature consecrated through the efforts and understanding of the Magicians distributing it. He instructed his Australian organizer Progradior,

> <u>In haste.</u> I want every member of the Lodge to rewrite *The Law of Liberty* in such language as should appeal to his own friends and class. Present pamphlet is over the heads of many.[†]

Regardless of the effect it had in making Crowley's message intelligible to the *recipients* of such rewritten literature, that exercise would be valuable in promoting a more thorough comprehension of it by those who *distributed* them. Similar work can be pursued by today's E.G.C. clergy, for both reasons.

Paper tracts may seem a bit antiquated in a society where glowing screens are so effective at monopolizing attention. But they have many advantages. The format does not obsolesce. It does not require a host device or distribution platform other than the ones that ordinary people are

---

[*] Liber CCC Khabs Am Pekht. The whole of this short text is worth repeated study by clergy seeking to understand our magisterial responsibilities.
[†] Crowley to Frank Bennett, c. 1917 EV (*The Progradior Correspondence*, p. 59).

equipped with. It has a *talismanic materiality* that commends its use to the magician.

The most effective use of such a talisman is to give it singly, in person, to someone who is intended to read it. In this manner, the Thelemite's knowledge is courageously applied to the willed promulgation of the Law in a way that demonstrates its significance and allows the work to continue in the Thelemite's silent absence. It is a crucial complement to the "elevator pitch," when clergy are asked about their obscure religion or the symbols or insignia that they might display. Of course, it is also possible to leave a small stack of tracts on the counter of a friendly merchant (with her permission), to post one to a kiosk or notice board, to place one in a relevant book on the shelf of a school or public library, and to set copies in the entry area of a dedicated O.T.O. temple.

Modern technology allows print tracts to be produced rapidly and inexpensively. They can be in color or on color paper. Trifold brochures work well, as do postcards, or even small staple-bound chapbooks. Art can help to spark the interest of potential readers, but there needs to be enough text to supply actual instruction. It is important that there be an encouragement to action and that the document include some sort of contact address, phone number, Web URL, or other reference allowing the reader to pursue further information.

It may seem as if the work done by a print tract is more easily carried out online, leveraging existing networks on "social" internet platforms and dispensing with material encumbrances. Increasingly though, one of the foremost challenges of contemporary culture and organizing is to break out of the matrix of digital simulation and passive online engagement. As part of a stream of online content, your magisterial efforts to communicate a world-changing Law will be set on an equal footing with the latest political controversies, celebrity rumors, and pop culture nonsense, engineered to seize the attention and deaden the reflective capabilities of ubiquitous "users." It is important to make Thelema available and accessible online to those who are actively seeking sound resources regarding the Law and our Magick. But introducing these to people in a way that can re-orient their religious ambitions is still best achieved in "meatspace," and the humble tract is one of our best instruments for the purpose.

Eliciting the Exploration of the Law

At the outset of this section on magisterial priestcraft, I mentioned the importance of avoiding a traditional "homiletic approach" to religious instruction. It is customary for Christian ministers to explicate their scripture, focusing on a short passage and providing it with context, and often with illustrations from daily life intended to make the text relevant to its hearers. This method tends to attribute interpretive authority to the religious official, rather than emphasizing the actual responsibility of each adherent to apply individual reason and experience to the understanding of shared sacred texts. For the Holy Books of Thelema generally, and *The Book of the Law* in particular, a different strategy is required, one that allows for more initiative from, and makes more demands of, each Thelemite.

This work can and should be carried on by individuals for themselves, but at the social level where clergy may facilitate it, the small discussion group is perhaps the optimal format. Somewhere from three to eleven Thelemites may take up a text, ranging from a verse to a chapter of a holy book. Eleven continuous verses can make a digestible amount of material. If a consistent group can meet on a regular basis, that can be useful, but it may also be illuminating to have a regular influx of new participants.

A facilitator should avoid making positive statements of interpretation. Certainly, it is unhelpful to assert, "Where the text says X, it means Z." It is marginally better to say, "I have myself read X to mean Z." But it is best to simply ask, "What could X mean?" If multiple meanings are proposed, they can be set in dialogue with one another. If there is only one, it should be subjected to questioning. Proposed meanings can be exposed to apparent contradiction from elsewhere in the text or from premises that the participants are willing to aver.

An understanding of the text can be tested for its truthfulness: "Does this reading really reflect what we see in the world around us?" It can be tested for its usefulness: "How does this reading incline us to conduct ourselves?" It can be tested for its consequentiality: "What other ideas or actions does this reading lead to?"

Participants should not be encouraged to think that the discussion will produce a single correct interpretation.

A facilitator can ask participants to identify other texts (written by the Prophet or otherwise) to which the one under consideration has a relationship. Such comparisons may help to provide clarity and/or complication.

It may be especially helpful in the later stages of discussion for the facilitator to attempt to summarize conclusions or judgments made by the participants. Such summaries are best made in the form of further questions. "Do you then think that X means Z in this passage?"

This entire process bears a great deal of similarity to what has often been termed the "Socratic method," and there is a large body of relevant literature that may be useful to clergy who wish develop the skills to employ it effectively.

4. Sacramental Priestcraft: Sustaining and Celebrating the Law

The medieval Christian theologian Peter Lombard provided a definition of *sacramentum* that is still often cited by Catholics today: "an outward sign of inward grace." Since Thelemites accept neither grace nor guilt as the basis for interaction with the divine, it is evident that at a minimum this definition would need to be altered for our purposes to reflect a signification of "will" rather than "grace." But even then, the relationship between "outward" and "inward" is suspect on such grounds as *CCXX* I:8. Thomas Aquinas' definition of sacrament as "the sign of a sacred thing in so far as it sanctifies men," may perhaps be of use, as long as it is understood that the condition of sanctification in Thelemic Gnosis differs considerably from that found in the slave-religion Christianity.

Certainly, we do not make the sacramental status of a practice dependent on its institution by Aleister Crowley, any more than we do by Jesus of Nazareth. While Crowley's precedent may lead us to consider certain practices as sacraments (and to define the regular form of those practices), it is in no way a necessary ingredient for those sacraments which are demanded by the vital circumstances of the Church or its members.

I have been resistant to the wholesale adoption of the Orthodox and Catholic Christian system of seven sacraments for use in Thelemic Gnosticism. In former times, my proposed alternative was to reduce the system of sacraments to five, in keeping with the precedent of Bricaud's Gnostic church and my own set of corre-spondences. On further reflection, however, I am dissatisfied with any reduction of the number of sacraments, largely because it seems to me counter to a basic sensibility of magick: "every act must be a ritual, an act of worship, a Sacrament."[*] To simplify the sacramental system is to follow the degenerate course set by Protestantism. At the same time, I am mindful of the usefulness of those ecclesiastical traditions which assign importance to certain formal rituals as "sacraments of the Church." The enumeration of such sacraments serves to define and to concentrate the powers and purposes of the ecclesiastical body.

Before the development of the sevenfold system— which began near the end of the first Christian millennium and was not complete until the twelfth century—*sacramentum* was a term of much wider application, comprehending such diverse functions as benedictions of all sorts, public prayer services, foot washing, alms giving, reading of scripture, speaking in tongues, exorcisms, etc. etc. Many of these practices were later reclassified as "sacramental" but not "sacraments proper," when rubrics were consolidated and subjected to regulation by the hierarchy.

My current disposition is to open up the term *sacrament* to a more diverse significance within our Gnostic Catholic Church so that any ritual, any act of worship, any practice that draws on and perpetuates the Church's system of sacred signification can be accorded the status of sacrament. Rather than the simple seven sacraments of the Christian system, I now employ a system of seven *classifications*, which can among them accommodate countless particular sacraments. These classifications are:

- natural
- cardinal
- punctual
- instrumental
- remedial

---

[*] Crowley, "The Law of Liberty" (Liber DCCCXXXVII), in *The Equinox* III(10), p. 48.

- occasional
- practical

Each sacramental category is detailed in its own following section of this book.

These categories are not reliably exclusive. For example, the administration of the virtues to the sick in their homes* might be understood to combine features of cardinal (Eucharist of the Gnostic Mass), remedial (addressing the illness and/or isolation of the communicant), and practical genres—and all genuine sacraments necessarily include the natural sacraments within their effective operation. But the seven sorts do cover what I view as a comprehensive array of Thelemic sacraments within the rite of the Gnostic Catholic Church.

By combining the five cardinal sacraments with the two natural sacraments, we arrive at a very close approximation of the seven-fold "sacramental system" set forth for E.G.C. by the U.S. Primate of the Church.†

It is also noteworthy that the degree rituals of the Church's sister rite *Mysteria Mystica Maxima* (which are, among other things, prerequisites for clerical ordination in E.G.C.) are sacramental in character. They are not, however, part of the Church's repertoire of ritual *per se*. They may, if desired, be considered to constitute an eighth category: the **gradual** sacraments, from *gradus*, meaning "degree."

---

* An approved ritual for Administration of the Virtues to the Sick is in Sabazius, *Mystery of Mystery,* pp. 324-5.
† Sabazius, *Mystery of Mystery,* pp. 283-95.

Natural Sacraments

The **natural** sacraments are Love and Will. They are the fundamental principles upon which all possible manifestations and hidings of divinity are founded. E.G.C. holds no authority over the natural sacraments, these being the magical preconditions of the Church and of life and existence generally. The maximal fulfillment of these sacraments in the life of the individual is indicated by the final clause of the Oath of a Master of the Temple: "That I will interpret every phenomenon as a particular dealing of God with my Soul."

> It is love which is the centripetal power of the universe; it is by Love that all creation returns to the bosom of God. The force which projected all things is Will, and Will is the centrifugal power of the universe. Will alone could not overcome the evil which results from the limitations of Matter; but it shall be overcome in the end by Sympathy, which is the knowledge of God in others — the recognition of the omnipresent Self. This is Love. And it is with the children of the Spirit, the servants of Love, that the dragon of Matter makes war.[*]

> Oh, the dazzling, dazzling brightness! Hide me, hide me from it! I cannot, cannot bear it! It is agony supreme to look upon. O God! O God! Thou art slaying me with Thy light. It is the throne itself, the great white throne of God that I behold! Oh, what light! What light! It is like an emerald? A sapphire? No; a diamond. In its midst stands Deity erect, His right hand raised aloft, and from Him pours the light of light. Forth from His right hand streams the universe, projected by the omnipotent

---

[*] Anna Kingsford, *Clothed with the Sun,* p. 8.

repulsion of His will. Back to His left, which is depressed and set backwards, returns the universe, drawn by the attraction of His love. Repulsion and attraction, will and love, right and left, these are the forces, centrifugal and centripetal, male and female whereby God creates and redeems. Adonai! O Adonai! Lord God of life, made of the substance of light, how beautiful art Thou in Thine everlasting youth! With Thy glowing golden locks, how adorable! And I had thought of God as elderly and venerable! As if the Eternal could grow old! And now not as Man only do I behold Thee! For now Thou art to me as Woman. Lo, Thou art both. One, and Two also. And thereby dost Thou produce creation. O God, O God! Why didst Thou create this stupendous existence? Surely, surely, it had been better in love to have restrained Thy will. It was by will that Thou createdst, by will alone, not by love, was it not? – Was it not? I cannot see clearly. A cloud has come between.[*]

—Dame Anna Kingsford

---

[*] *Ibid.,* p. 181.

Cardinal Sacraments

Cardinal sacraments are those by which the Church distinguishes its members from the profane and distinguishes among its members. In the rituals and doctrines that Jean Bricaud outlined for *Église Catholique Gnostique*, the immediate institutional predecessor of the Gnostic Catholic Church of O.T.O., he advanced a system of five proprietary sacraments. We still exercise a corresponding set of five: Baptism, Confirmation, Ordination, Last Rites, and the Eucharist of the Gnostic Mass.

Cardinal sacraments are also the ones that might be viewed by the Church as requiring episcopal and/or sacerdotal participation to be valid. This stipulation makes obvious sense in the cases of both the Eucharist of the Gnostic Mass and the sacraments that affect affiliation and status in the Church. Last Rites is a trickier instance. Since we don't hold any doctrine that penalizes those who die without Last Rites, the responsibility and concern for their cardinality lies not with the adherent, but with the Church. While non-clergy might effectively administer to the spiritual needs of the dying, they could not absolve the Church of the responsibility for action from its clergy, if needed or desired by a member at death.

Sacrament	Magick Power	Element
Baptism	To Know	Water
Confirmation	To Will	Fire
Ordination	To Dare	Air
Unction	To Keep Silence	Earth
Mass	To Go	Spirit

As shown in the table above, our cardinal sacraments can be attributed to the various key emblems of the pentad: the pentagram, the square-based pyramid, and the Jerusalem cross. If we were a Christian church, I might suggest their attribution to the five wounds and to the letters of יהשוה. In the context of O.T.O., they may be seen as elements in the formula of ΑΙΘΗΡ (invoked during the Consecration of the Elements of the Gnostic Mass),* and they may be attributed to the clauses of the Priestess' injunction from *CCXX* I:63.

Sing the rapturous love-song unto me!	Baptism
Burn to me perfumes!	Confirmation
Wear to me jewels!	Ordination
Drink to me,	Gnostic Mass
for I love you! I love you!	Unction

The natural and cardinal sacraments together form a set of seven parallel and analogous to the seven sacraments of Orthodox Christianity, where Love and Will can be read as Marriage and Penance, respectively. 'Marriage' is here understood in the sense of the Collect from the Gnostic Mass regarding "**all** who unite with love under will," regardless of the institutional status of their union. (For purposes of the sacramental types, a wedding ritual or benediction of marriage is classed among the punctual sacraments.) 'Penance' must be *inverted* to discover its role as the sacramental reflection of individual will.

Gnostic Mass

The cardinal sacraments are all clearly concerned with the Church's institutional participation in the life of the individual. Yet the Eucharistic Mystery stands out as the first among equals, the spiritual operation that empowers and motivates the others. It was also the first of the cardinal

---

* See Crowley, *The Book of Lies*, cap. 86, for the full analysis of this formula.

sacraments to be given a regular form in E.G.C., and that by the hand of the Prophet of the Law himself. Accordingly, the other four each receive individual treatment in this section, while an entire further section "Features and Formulæ of the Gnostic Mass" provides an assortment of materials pertaining to the Mass.

As noted in the introduction to this book, I have chosen not to include the full ritual of the Gnostic Mass in a volume intended primarily for those who will doubtless have routine access to an approved copy of Liber XV already. (See the bibliography for a list of approved editions as of this writing.) For casual reference or preliminary study, a variety of editions are conveniently available, including many on the Internet.

Baptism

Although baptisms are commonly administered by members of the priesthood, the authority to do so is not conferred *carte blanche* with sacerdotal initiation. A priestess or priest must have their bishop's express authorization in order to baptize into E.G.C. Members of the priesthood should make sure that the form of ritual they are using meets the bishop's requirements. Novices may assist at baptisms, but the presiding ritualist must always be a bishop or a member of the priesthood acting with license from a bishop.

My own ritual for baptism varies slightly from the one originally authorized by Sabazius and published in his book *Mystery of Mystery*. The chief difference consists in the names invoked during the affusion of the candidate. Most baptizing clergy, whether they use Sabazius' ritual or another form developed by a bishop with the approval of the Primate and Patriarch, baptize in the names of the three Great Ones of *Liber Legis,* according to a precedent set by Past Patriarch Hymenæus Alpha. Christian tradition places great emphasis on the use of a Trinitarian formula in the ceremony of

110

baptism, and it does indeed make sense to use the trinity of Nuit, Hadit, and Ra-hoor-khuit for a ceremony understood as a reception of an aspirant into Thelemic society.

However, there are other trinities that might be as apposite for this purpose. During the ceremony of the Mystic Marriage in the Mass, the priest invokes (in Greek) the "masculine trinity" of the Father, Son, and Holy Spirit, which is perverted in exoteric Christian doctrine. I prefer yet a third option, based on the fact that although Christian baptism was originally the seal of membership concluding a catechumenal period, with us it is instead a reception into the catechumenate. This feature is emphasized in the obligations of our baptismal sponsors to guide the catechumens in their study of the Creed. The Creed is presented as the principal synthesis of our mysteries to be addressed in study by those who have been baptized. Accordingly, my practice is to baptize in the names of the three persons identified in the first three articles of the Creed: CHAOS, BABALON, and BAPHOMET.

Sabazius' ritual for baptism includes an instruction for the baptizing clergy to exhort the new catechumens regarding their role in the Church. This practice is very valuable. It can serve not only to instruct those just baptized, but also the variety of members and guests who may be in attendance. In keeping with the nature of the catechumenate, this exhortation is actually one of the points in which the magisterial function of the priesthood surfaces most conspicuously among the cardinal sacraments. While the ability to deliver a rousing exhortation *ex tempore* is invaluable,[*] I have found that repeated preparation has improved my own. Here is one sample that I wrote many years ago:

---

[*] "The really great Magus speaks and acts impromptu and extempore." (Crowley, *Magick,* p. 190 *n.*)

In the Creed of our Church, we profess belief in "one Baptism of Wisdom." This ceremony has not been that baptism. You partook of the true baptism when you were actually born to the flesh, but this baptism symbolizes that one, in the form of a wet entry into a new world.

Among other religions, the rite of baptism is often accorded the power of saving the candidate from sin. We do not expect or encourage you to condemn or disavow your life before your reception among us, any more than a child should condemn or disavow her mother's womb. We do expect and encourage you to explore and question the Church, just as a child must explore and question the world of matter in which she finds herself.

We also trust that this process of exploring our mysteries will provide you with opportunities better to learn and to know your own will, and to develop a greater intimacy with the divine as you come to understand it.

Through baptism, you have become a cate-chumen of our Church. You have been formally received among us, and we have undertaken obligations to defend your freedom, and to guide you in your study of our mysteries. You have undertaken obligations only to yourself and to your god, and it is through fulfilling those obligations that you may come to decide whether you will seek confirmation to full membership in our Church.

Here is another baptismal exhortation, this one inspired by the ancient *procatechesis* of the fourth-century Cyril of Jerusalem:

> There is a savor of blessedness upon you, even as you take your first steps in quest of our Sacred Gnosis. There is a light in your eyes to be answered by the light from our altars. The fragrance of our Mother, Mystery of Mystery, is upon you. You are now in the outer court of the palace of our Church's knowledge; may Wisdom herself invite you to penetrate further. We know you by name and we applaud your aspiration.
>
> Soon you will join in the great feast of our Mass. May it nourish and intoxicate your spirit. If you are true to our mysteries, our sacraments will answer to the hungers and thirsts of your deepest being, and you will gradually attain to what our ceremonies shadow forth.
>
> But perhaps your motives in joining us are not so direct. Perhaps you have taken this step to impress someone else among us, or someone not among us, or merely to challenge or entertain yourself. We do not worry about your past intentions, if only you will *now* live up to the words you have spoken: to know your will and to do it.
>
> You are now a catechumen: one who hears with ears that have been blessed for the reception of what it is that our Church has to say. And yet it is your own god in whom you must rejoice. As you participate in our rites, words that you have heard before will come to have new meanings for you. When you discover that your god is indeed the Crowned and Conquering Child who is the Lord of the Æon, or one of those others who cluster to

exalt him, then you may pursue confirmation to full membership among us.

> Leave behind you whatever fear, guilt, and shame you may once have carried. Study the matters of which we speak in the Church. Reflect on the conduct of those you find here. Be the star that beams within you. For indeed, there is no law beyond Do what thou wilt.

The baptismal Mass follows the ceremony of baptism, to demonstrate the hospitality to catechumens that the baptismal ceremony declares and to place a sacramental seal upon the act. (In primitive Christianity, new catechumens were provided with a sacramental taste of bread and salt.) Although I prefer the clergy who preside over baptism also to preside over the Mass, it is certainly possible to make other arrangements. A baptismal Mass, like the baptism itself, must be a *public* ceremony, open to interested non-members.

Communion in a baptismal Mass is given only to the priest and the newly-baptised catechumens. There are many good reasons for this constraint, which is explicit in Liber XV, and which applies similarly for confirmation Masses.

The exclusive communion of baptisands and confirmands integrates these Masses with the ceremonies of baptism and confirmation. They are not simply two different Church ceremonies happening on the same occasion. The Eucharist in these cases empowers the act of baptism or confirmation, as the case may be, and emphasizes the integration of new catechumens and members into the sacramental system of the Church.

Removing the expectation of popular communion makes baptism and confirmation Masses ideal for first-time guests, who may not (yet) be actively interested in Thelema or our Order. Baptisands and confirmands can and should be encouraged to bring family and friends as witnesses to these ceremonies, where there will be no pressure or even opportunity for them to actually partake of our sacrament.

Scheduling and time-economy are served by balancing the addition of our relatively brief baptism or confirmation ceremonies against the removal of the full popular communion, which takes a comparable period of time

Anyone who has been baptized in E.G.C. is eligible to serve as a Child in public enactments of the Gnostic Mass. Doing so provides catechumens with an important supplementary perspective in their appreciation of the Church. However tempting or convenient it may be, new catechumens should *not* serve as a Children in their own baptismal Mass. It is essential that they *take communion* in that Mass. As Children they would not be able to do so.

Confirmation

Like baptism, confirmation is a sacrament dispensed by members of the priesthood only with specific license from their bishops. The term "confirmation" is familiar to many people from the Christian liturgical tradition. Our custom does in fact resemble Christian confirmation, to the extent that it is a ceremonial initiation subsequent to baptism. However, the respective weights of these two sacraments are rather different in E.G.C., where baptism is merely preparatory for the membership status established through confirmation. (In many Christian traditions, confirmation merely reaffirms the status established through baptism.) It was fitting that in the Piscean Age, a watery sacrament was the one that conferred membership; the force and fire of the Lord of the New Æon are better communicated through our ceremony of confirmation.

Before a Confirmation Mass, clergy should meet privately with each confirmand to be sure he or she is both materially and mentally prepared. Candidates must know the Creed by heart. If they cannot recite it in private, they should not be put to the public humiliation that would eventuate in the public ceremony. The candidate should possess a white robe for Church use and wear it when confirmed.

As contrasted with baptism, confirmation should *follow* the public Gnostic Mass at which only confirmands communicate. In this manner, the Eucharist serves to fortify and encourage a candidate approaching the ceremony. The confirmand also demonstrates that he or she is a participant in our mysteries, prior to making the commitment of confirmation.

The white robe of the confirmand is comparable to the one worn in the ancient mysteries, from which we ultimately derive the term *candidate* ("white-clothed"). It also forms the basis of the regalia worn by officers in the Gnostic Mass. It is thus the generic uniform of the Church. The stipulation that it open in front, while it will later be helpful for the procedure in diaconal ordination, is unnecessary in the ceremony of confirmation. So while it may assist members to economize and to invest continuing sentiment in a single robe, it does not need to be insisted upon.

The confirmation ceremony by Sabazius published in *Mystery of Mystery* can be analyzed qabalistically as a descent through the ten sephiroth, understood as the process of emanation by which True Will (*Kether*) manifests in the events of the aspirant's life (*Malkuth*). Here is an outline, which not only has interpretive value, but should also serve as an aid to memorization:

CROWN—The presiding clergy exchanges the Summary of the Law with the confirmand.

WISDOM—The confirmand's name is elicited and asserted.

UNDERSTANDING—The confirmand formulates his or her aspiration as a will to membership in the Church.

MERCY—The confirmand identifies a comrade (already a confirmed member), to stand with him.

POWER—The confirmand recites the Creed from memory.

BEAUTY—The presiding clergy performs cheirotonia, anoints the confirmand, and speaks the words of confirmation, in the name of Ra-hoor-khuit, the Lord of the Æon.

VICTORY—The presiding clergy recites the doxology from Liber XXXVI.

SPLENDOUR—An officer rings a bell and the Nepios is recited.

FOUNDATION—The presiding clergy addresses a charge, quoting from the third chapter of *Liber Legis,* to the confirmand(s).

KINGDOM—The presiding clergy delivers an admonitory cuff, with appropriate explanation, to each confirmand.

The ceremony of confirmation includes at its central point the procedure of cheirotonia, known colloquially as "laying on of hands." This physical and subtle contact communicates to the confirmand participation in the egregore of the Church: he or she is now *incorporated as a member of the body,* a soldier of the army, a worshiper in the true metabolism of the congregational being.

Ordination

The sacrament of ordination comprehends three specific ceremonies of the Church, corresponding to three orders of clergy: diaconal ordination admits to the diaconate, sacerdotal ordination admits to the priesthood (also called the presbyterate), and episcopal consecration admits to the episcopate. All ordinations involve the mechanism of cheirotonia in order to refine the immediate and physical connection to the living gnosis of the E.G.C. rite. Each ordination involves an increasing conscious apprehension of the *egregore* to which the cheirotonia of confirmation connects all members of the Church.

As mentioned in the earlier discussion of the E.G.C. hierarchy, the authority to consecrate bishops reposes within the Sanctuary of the Gnosis, while the bishops in turn ordain the other orders of clergy.

Accordingly, the rituals for sacerdotal ordination are only circulated among the episcopate, but an authorized ceremony for diaconal ordination has been published by Sabazius in *Mystery of Mystery,* as the work of such ordinations formerly might be delegated to members of the priesthood. Sabazius' diaconal ordination ritual has a structure that suggests a descent of power through the planetary spheres. Here is an analysis:

Saturn—The ordinand commits him or herself to the path of service in E.G.C.

Jupiter—The ordinand acknowledges the authority of the hierarchy as expressed through Church policies and instruction from the bishops, with the ultimate intention of serving the congregation.

Mars—The ordinand identifies his or her will with a vocation as E.G.C. clergy.

Sol—The ordinand receives cheirotonia, anointing with Holy Oil, and the officiant's words of ordination.

Venus—The officiant vests the ordinand with a yellow stole or mantle, and recites the doxology from Liber XXXVI.

Mercury—The officiant presents the ordinand with a copy of *Liber Legis*.

Luna—The officiant proclaims the new deacon to the congregation.

E.G.C. ordination has key prerequisites including specific M∴M∴M∴ degrees, as established by the Patriarch. Bishops must hold the VII°, which completes the entire M∴M∴M∴ system. Priests and priestesses prior to their ordinations are required to have advanced to the degree of Knight of East and West (K.E.W.), which is the first of the invitational degrees (immediately preceding V°). A diaconal ordinand may have M∴M∴M∴ initiation as modest as the II°, but in order to serve as public representatives of the Church, deacons also must progress to the K.E.W.

Bishops vary in their programs of training and their specific expectations of novices regarding accomplishments prior to ordination. For my own, please see the earlier section of this book, "Studying toward Sacerdotal Expertise."

Even after ordination, clergy remain under supervision, and it is important for all deacons, priests, and priestesses to remain in regular, open communication with a bishop who is responsible for their continuing development and ongoing fidelity to the Church.

Extreme Unction

It should be obvious that no deathbed "absolution of sins" is part of our sacramental agenda. Sabazius has described the sacramental function of our ritual for the dying as being "to assist in the alleviation of fear [and] concern ... so that those who approach death may set their sights squarely on the ultimate accomplishment of their True Wills."[*]

The ceremony of last rites in E.G.C. is founded in Past Patriarch Baphomet's Liber CVI "On Death." Sabazius has supplemented that address at the deathbed with a procedure for final administration of the Eucharist in his ritual, published in *Mystery of Mystery*. In that procedure he provides for a simple unction with oil applied to the forehead. I suggest the following fuller method, based on Liber DCLXXI *vel Pyramidos*, the object of which is to support the communicant in composing his or her subtle body to the Adventure which awaits.

> *The* PRIESTESS *(preferably, but* PRIEST *if necessary) has administered the Eucharist to the extent feasible and has read Liber DCLXXI through the stanzas from the reverse of the Stele of Revealing. (S)he administers the unction by tracing a* ✠ *with consecrated Holy Oil at each point named:*

---

[*] Sabazius, *Mystery of Mystery*, p. 310.

I gild thy left foot with ✠ the light

I gild thy Phallus with ✠ the light[*]

I gild thy right knee with ✠ the light

I gild thy right foot with ✠ the light

I gild thy left knee with ✠ the light

I gild thy Phallus with ✠ the light[*]

I gild thine elbows with ✠ the light

I gild thy navel with ✠ the light

I gild thy heart wedge with ✠ the light

I gild thy black throat with ✠ the light

I gild thy forehead with ✠ the light

I gild thy Phallus with ✠ the light[*]

The Threefold Star Cross-crowned, Thou art

Mighty shouldst thou now depart!

> The PRIEST(ESS) *places open palm upon the forehead of the Communicant, saying:*

The Benediction of the All-Begetter, All-Devourer be upon thee.

> The PRIEST(ESS) *recites the Doxology of Liber XXXVI ("Gloria Patri") and the Nepios ("Now I begin to pray"), and then converses with, reads to, or simply sits quietly with communicant. Before departing (s)he says:*

Love is the law, love under will.

---

[*] Alternately: "I gild thy Vulva with the light." The holy oil would presumably be applied to covering clothing for these points, but with a gentle pressure that would be perceptible.

Punctual Sacraments

Punctual sacraments are the ceremonies celebrated within the community of the Church to mark critical events in the lives of individual members. The punctual sacraments "of will" are the Feasts for Water and Fire (passage to maturity). The punctual sacraments "of love" are the Feast for Life (infant benediction), Marriage (nuptial benediction), and Greater Feast for Death (funeral ceremony).

All of these sacraments have the highest sanction. They are referenced in the Collects of the Gnostic Mass. Except for Marriage, they are listed in *CCXX* II:41. (Marriage is mentioned in the text of Liber XV.) Unlike the cardinal sacraments however, these only provide festivity, solemnity and benediction to events that happen *with or without* the participation of the Church. No one is any less "married" for not having an E.G.C. wedding, than they are *less dead* for not having a Greater Feast ceremony.

The U.S. Primate Sabazius has circulated rituals composed by T Apiryon and Helena for each of the punctual sacraments of love. Those treatments of the Feast for Life and Greater Feast for Death are both fully sufficient for the use of E.G.C. clergy. While the wedding ceremony of their ritual is elegant (and I have myself administered it with the happiest of results), the additional complications likely to be involved in the benediction of marriage will call for some further remarks below.

Feasts for Fire and Water

These ceremonies are intended to celebrate a boy's puberty and a girl's menarche. I have prepared full ritual texts for use by E.G.C. members. They will not be published, because portions are confidential (i.e. they are performed in secret with the youth or maiden concerned).

As these are not cardinal sacraments, there is no requirement that the ritual officers be under orders or even serving as novices. However, my rubrics do indicate certain roles as Deacon, Priest and Priestess, in order to stress that these officers would be members of the local community who are recognized as responsible leaders. While the Deacon (or Deacon-substitute) may be of any gender, the Priest (or Priest-substitute) must self-identify as a man, and the Priestess (or Priestess-substitute) must self-identify as a woman. The Feast for Fire involves a Priest, and the Feast for Water calls for a Priestess. For young people who aspire to genders other than men or women, one may postulate Feasts for Air and/or Earth, conducted by officers who *actually hold and express* the genders which those young people are seeking to manifest. Such cases are (at present) sufficiently exceptional that they will require significant ingenuity on the part of ritual organizers, and standards or rules from the Church are likely to be inadequate to particular circumstances.

Prior to the Feast, the child who is to be honored must prepare two or three pieces, as demonstrations of competence to the community. The first piece is a demonstration of **intellectual proficiency**, and it will consist of the recitation of text, chosen in consultation with parents or guardian, followed by a talk interpreting the text and explaining its significance. The recitation must be from memory, but the talk may employ notes. The other piece(s) will demonstrate **aesthetic** and/or **athletic proficiency**, and they may consist of musical recital (instrumental or vocal), dance, dramatic monologue, gymnastics routine, martial arts demonstration, or other activities in this broad orbit. Each piece should be at least eleven minutes in length. Ideally, the child will spend several months in preparing these pieces.

The Feast begins with the child's demonstrations, and concludes with a banquet. The private ceremonies take place between these two community events. Ritual texts for the two public phases are given here.

RECITALS

> *Adult members of the community irrespective of gender are gathered in a convenient place where they may be seated to observe the Examination of the parents (or guardian) and the child. There is a small altar or podium at which a speaker may stand.*

> *The* DEACON *is at the altar in a plain white robe, and the child and parents are seated nearby.*

DEACON: Do what thou wilt shall be the whole of the Law. I proclaim the Law of Light, Life, Love and Liberty, in the name of BABALON.

ALL: Love is the law, love under will.

DEACON: We are gathered here today to celebrate a Feast for Fire/Water in honor of *Nn.*, who this day leaves childhood in a journey towards manhood/womanhood. Is it your will to witness his/her departure?

ALL: It is.

DEACON (*recites from Kingsford's Book of the Mysteries of God*):

(Feast for Fire)

Be thou master of the fire, and command it; let not the cloven tongue of the serpent beguile thee; neither barter thy liberty for the fruit of enchantment. For the fire shall be quenched by the water, and the water shall be resolved into spirit. But if the fire consume thy soul, it shall be scattered abroad as ashes, and return to the dust of the earth. For it is fire that tries every man's work, and purifies the substance of all souls. By fire is the initiate baptized, by fire the oblation is salted; and the flame shall devour the dross of the crucible. That which endureth unto the end, the same shall be saved.[*]

(Feast for Water)

All things are of the sea-salt, for without salt matter is not, whether of the outer or of the inner, whether of the small or of the great. Behold the manifold waves of the sea, which rise and sink, which break and are lost, and follow each other continually; even as these are the transmutations of the soul. For the soul is one substance, as is the water of the deep, whose waves thou canst not number, neither tell their shapes, for the form of them passeth away; even as these are the incarnations of the soul. And the secret of Thetis is the mystery of the Metamorphosis. Out of the sea the horse ariseth; strength and intelligence are begotten of the deep. She is the mother of Avatârs, and her cup is the chalice of bitterness: whoso drinketh thereof shall taste of power and knowledge, and of tears of salt.[†]

DEACON *turns to the* PARENTS, *who rise.*

DEACON: [*Names of* PARENTS], do you recognize that *Nn.* has stepped onto the path away from childhood?

PARENTS: We do.

> DEACON *yields altar to* PARENTS, *who introduce child as they will, and then retire to their seats.*
>
> *Child makes recitals.*
>
> *General applause. All rise.*

---

[*] Kingsford, *Clothed with the Sun,* p. 161.
[†] *Ibid.,* p. 162.

The DEACON *advances to the altar and blesses the child:*

DEACON *recites blessing:*

(Feast for Fire)

Our Lord whose flames burn within all living things, Holy Father CHAOS, inspire this youth with your energy and endurance, that he may attain to power and knowledge.

(Feast for Water)

Our Lady who sittest upon many waters, Holy Mother BABALON, pour out upon this worthy maiden your strength and your delicacies, that she may attain to power and knowledge.

ALL: So mote it be.

Parents congratulate the child; after which all begin to circulate and socialize.

(Two private ceremonies follow.)

BANQUET

A great banquet is held, with the youth or maiden in the place of honor. The PRIEST *or* PRIESTESS *leads Will over meat as follows:*

PRIEST(ESS): Do what thou wilt shall be the whole of the Law.

ALL (led by DEACON): What is thy will?

PRIEST(ESS): To eat and drink.

ALL: To what end?

PRIEST(ESS): That we may fortify our bodies thereby.

ALL: To what end?

PRIEST(ESS): That we may celebrate this Feast for Fire/Water in honor of N*n*.

ALL: To what end?

PRIEST(ESS): That we may live to see him/her accomplish his/her True Will, his/her Great Work, his/her Summum Bonum, True Wisdom, and Perfect Happiness.

ALL: Love is the law, love under will.

> *In this section of the ceremonies, and this section only, children who have not yet reached their own adolescence may attend.*

> *The youth or maiden receives gifts and adulation.*

Marriage Ceremonies

Marriage had existed in pagan Europe since time immemorial as the means by which families were united in support of a couple who aspired to have children. Such a social mechanism was unavoidable and naturally invested with a great deal of attention and importance. Parents, local leaders, gods and goddesses might be called as witnesses to the nuptial decision.

In the eleventh century of the Christian era, the Roman Catholic Church began to assert the desirability of marriage on parish premises along with a requirement for a priest to preside over the ritual. What had been a ceremonial elaboration of a civil contract began a shift into becoming a proprietary sacrament of the Church. Opposition to this trend characterized many medieval heretics, including the Cathars.

E.G.C. has its traditional origins in part from the Cathar revivalism of Jules Doinel, elaborated by Jean Bricaud. In Bricaud's Catechism, the following point appears:

Is marriage a sacrament?

No, but there has always existed in the Church a nuptial benediction, which is a simple religious ceremony.

When we have a wedding in E.G.C., it includes a nuptial benediction for the couple. But the **marriage** is not contingent on that benediction. Nor is it simply a civil contract. In our view, marriage is the fundamental sacred act in manifest existence. Marriage is any union resulting from love under will, and especially sexual union, whether procreative in its intention or not. In the Gnostic Mass, marriage is defined as the act of "all that ... unite with love under will." In an E.G.C. wedding ceremony, the couple graciously permits the congregation to appreciate their marriage, while the clergy offer a nuptial benediction and the church members offer communal approbation.

In the U.S.A., separation of the civil and religious authorities has led to the development of the civil "marriage license." Since no single church holds authority over the wedding process and since the contractual elements of patrimony and common property are of concern to the civil system of justice, there is an argument in favor of this piece of bureaucracy. The civil authorities cannot issue a "wedding license" without infringing on the prerogatives of the religious bodies that provide weddings. But Thelemites should understand that marriage is always a matter of liberty, not of license.

**Man has the right to love as he will:—
"take your fill and will of love as ye will,
when, where, and with whom ye will." ***

There's no dishonor in playing the game of bureaucratic wedding licensure. There are certain advantages to the legal recognition provided in that system. But there can be a hesitation involved, a basic philosophical dilemma: "If I accept this license, am I betraying my own liberty?" Marriage is a right, not a privilege. E.G.C. invites our members to formally proclaim that right within our ceremonial confines. But it is not, and never will be, for the church or the state to determine who is really married.

It is now usual for weddings, especially between Thelemites, to become an exercise in personal expression by the couple and to strive for uniqueness in liturgical form that will reflect the particularity of the event. Consequently, it is ordinary for wedding liturgies to be written for the occasion by the couple being married, or by the clergy presiding in consultation with the couple.

The following ceremony is intended to emphasize the liberty of the couple and the absolute nature of love under will. I have never presided at a wedding using this ritual: it was the text of the ceremony for my own marriage to Sister Sheba in 2004 EV. We held a "surprise wedding," in the form of a party where the guests did not realize they were being invited to our wedding. Br. Omega Baphomet was the officiant.

----

* Liber LXXVII, quoting *CCXX* I:51.

OFFICIANT: The Prophet writes, "[I]t was the marriage of the Beast which made possible the revelation of the New Law. This is **not** an apology for marriage. Hard cases make bad law."

OFFICIANT: Do what thou wilt shall be the whole of the Law.

ALL: Love is the law, love under will.

OFFICIANT: Marriage is union in love under will. [*Brother N.*] and [*Sister Nn.*] have you married each other already?

COUPLE: We have.

OFFICIANT: Are you marrying each other now?

COUPLE: We are.

OFFICIANT: Will you continue to marry each other henceforth?

COUPLE: We will.

OFFICIANT: Having confessed these facts, do you demand to have your marriage recognized by this community?

COUPLE: We do.

OFFICIANT: And is it your will to have your marriage recognized by the state?

COUPLE: It is.

OFFICIANT: Then your will be done! Witnesses, do your duty.

(They sign marriage document.)

OFFICIANT: Know ye all that [*Sister Nn.*] and [*Brother N.*] are united in love under will. There is no law beyond Do what thou wilt.

There are many different ritual components that can go to make up a given wedding ceremony. Here is a rough list of possibilities, arranged in a typical sequence. Of these, I consider only the *assent of the couple* to be indispensable.

- Introit of couple
- Opening Greeting
- Preliminary Invocation
- Readings and/or admonishments
- Vows regarding married conduct
- Consecration and Exchange of Tokens
- **Assent of Couple to Marriage**
- Proclamation
- Other petitionary prayers
- Benediction*
- Eucharist or other Magick

Many of these components can be so composed as to exhibit important sentiments of Thelemic Gnosticism, without unduly alienating members of a larger community whose presence may be desirable. For example, here is the text of a Preliminary Invocation, tacitly addressing Nuit:

> Perfect majesty of earth and heaven, we are made in your image in love and for love, and our hearts are restless until we respond in love to you through each other. Bless [N.] and [Nn.], who stand before us now. We are thankful for all of the joy which they bring to this occasion, as we are grateful for all those who have taught them how to love. There is no bond that can unite the

---

* *CCXX* I:18-19 is my preferred benediction to offer the couple.

divided but love. Let their thoughts, words, and deeds express that bond. So mote it be.

Here is a set of petitionary prayers directed to Ra-hoor-khuit:

> Supreme and uttermost god, look with favor upon this world, and especially upon this man and this woman who have joined together as partners in honor and celebration of life.

> Make open their paths to knowledge and understanding in the ordering of their common life, that each may be to the other a strength in need and a companion in joy.

> Grant them your light and make their life together a sign of love in the world, that unity may overcome estrangement, courage conquer fear, forgiveness heal guilt, and joy dissolve shame.

> Bestow upon them the gift and heritage of children, and the power and subtlety to bring them up with love and respect as their legacy to the earth.

> Give them such fulfillment of their mutual affection that they may reach out in love and concern for others.

> May all persons who have witnessed this rite find their lives strengthened and their loyalties confirmed.

> Grant that they may triumph over adversity, and that through your power they may increase in light, life, love and liberty all the days of their lives together.

Here is a blessing of the couple addressed to Hadit:

> Thou who art life and the giver of life, infuse the vigor of your blessing into the blood of this man and this woman. Defend them from every enemy. Lead them into all prosperity. Let their love for each other be a seal upon their hearts, a mantle about their shoulders, and a crown upon their foreheads. Bless them in their work and in their companionship; in their sleeping and in their waking; in their joys and in their sorrows; in their life and in their death. Finally, in your splendor and rapture, bring them to that table where your saints feast forever.

Different states have various expectations and requirements with respect to the ceremonial officers presiding at wedding ceremonies. Accordingly, E.G.C. reserves the function of performing weddings to the bishops, to be delegated to members of the priesthood on a case-by-case basis. In some states it is easy for anyone, regardless of religious or court credentials, to serve as an officiating witness to a legally effective ceremony. In others, restrictions make it impractical for E.G.C. clergy to conduct the legal component of the operation; even then, the couple can approach the church for a ceremonial benediction after transacting the legal business with a civil court official.

Instrumental Sacraments

Instrumental sacraments address the sanctification of environments and implements, and they fall into two classes. Instrumental sacraments "of the sanctuary" are those that address the materials used by officers and congregations of the Church as such. They also include practices and ceremonies intended to spiritually provision ritualists for ceremonial work, distinct from the permanent change of status involved in baptism, confirmation, or holy orders. Instrumental sacraments "of the home" are those directed to personal and routine objects and spaces. While some sacraments of the home will be undertaken by laity as a natural part of domestic routine, such as saying "Will" over the main meal of the day, others may usefully involve the assistance of ceremonially proficient clergy. Three instrumental sacraments of the home have been published in my book *Raise the Spell:* invocations at table, the blessing of a domicile, and the installation of a domestic relic. In addition to the instrumental sacraments of the sanctuary detailed below, T Apiryon's ritual for Consecration of the Oil* is of the greatest use to clergy.

Generally speaking, instrumental sacraments are at the option of the administering clergy, and their omission in any particular form (such as the ones detailed here) does not as such impair the work which they would otherwise bless and facilitate.

---

* Sabazius, *Mystery of Mystery*, pp. 322-3.

Blessing the Primitive Cake

The underlying mechanism and motive of this ceremony is to transform the bloodied cake from a personal object into a transpersonal one, using sacerdotal power to convert its association with the organism supplying the blood into an incontrovertible purpose for the sustenance of the ecclesiastical egregore. It is for performance on the cake that will be reduced to ash for admixture into the substance of further cakes to be used in E.G.C. ceremonies. This work is in some respect the converse of the process of the consecration and consummation of the elements in the Mass, where they begin as transpersonal properties of the Church and are changed into the substance of the individual divinity of the priest and people.

Stele 666 in the East (i.e. toward Boleskine).
Small altar, set with:

- *CCXX*
- candle
- paten bearing a cake of light smoothed down with blood
- a small folded linen that can be used to cover the paten

The Priest or Priestess is present alone, wearing white only.

Knocks 55555-1-55555 (or uses bell for knocks throughout).

Lights candle, invoking the Continuity of Light by his or her own ingenium.

Kisses Book.

Knocks 1-999999999-1.

Makes the Sign of Mystery, and recites from *The Ship*: "I am that I am, the flame ..." to "... And is daily born again."[*]

Takes the cake, touches it to the three points indicated by the penal signs, and declares, "Hoc est enim corpus meum."[†]

Says, "I devote this cake unto the nourishment of the spirit of the Church and those in Her fold."

Makes a cross with the cake on the paten, "By the Sign of Light, so mote it be."

Places the cake in the flame of the candle, saying: "Behold, there appeared a chariot of fire, and horses of fire, and he went up by a whirlwind into heaven."[‡]

Returns the burnt cake to the paten.

"The offerings of the LORD made by fire, and the bread of their God, they do offer: therefore they shall be holy."[§]

Covers the paten and cake with the linen.

Knocks 22-77777-22.

Raises the covered paten, saying:
"a ka dua tuf ur biu bi a'a khefu dudu nur af an nuteru."

Returns the paten to the altar and adores. Knocks 333-5555-333.

The cake is then retained on the covered paten until its immolation can be completed with an oven or other appropriate technology. (The candle flame is insufficient for the full treatment.)

---

[*] Full text on pages 156-7, below.
[†] "For this is my body," words of consecration in the Roman Mass.
[‡] 2 Kings II:11.
[§] Leviticus XXI:6.

Preparatory Regimen for Mass Officers

This five-fold regimen takes as its point of departure the שׁ of Spirit, and then traces the elements in the reverse order of Tetragrammaton, i.e. proceeding mystically from Earth up through Fire.

I. Daily Stations of the Sun - שׁ

Thelemites who observe the ritual of Liber Resh (or some suitable substitute) often have periods of increased or diminished rigor in that practice, even—or especially—when we engage in it over many years or decades.* But even when we are in a period of laxity, we should be especially punctual and punctilious with those adorations in the twenty-four hours prior to serving as an officer in the Gnostic Mass. We should not scruple to interrupt sleep or other activities for this purpose.

For those clergy who have not opted to include the daily stations of the sun among their routine disciplines, it is also useful to make it a special observance during the immediate period of preparation for serving in the Mass. (And may they come through this experience to realize its more general value!)

---

* The most authoritative presentation of Liber Resh is that of Aleister Crowley, *Magick,* pp. 655-6 and 786-7. A reproduction is included among the appendices to my book *Thelema for the People.* Useful introductions to the practice can also be found in Lon DuQuette's *The Magick of Aleister Crowley* and in Nancy Wasserman's *Yoga for Magick,* Appendix Two. An alternative ritual for solar adorations is supplied in my book *Raise the Spell.*

II. Fasting - ה

The observance of the Stations of the Sun can help to define the period of fasting prior to serving as a Mass officer.[*] To be specific, a minimal fast should have begun before the last of the four solar adorations observed before the Mass itself. I think of this as a "quarter-Resh fast." A "half-Resh fast" carried out through the span of two adorations, or "three-quarter Resh fast" through three, would be more a more rigorous alternative.

Also, we can be sensitive to the use of various sorts of fasting that do not go so far as full abstinence from food. Some of these are helpfully inventoried in the Eighteenth Illumination of Dame Anna Kingsford's *Clothed with the Sun*.[†] An incremented procedure constructed on this basis might go as follows:

- Beginning with the Sunset adoration: all foods permitted other than human flesh and horse meat (per Kingsford's mysteries of Bacchos)
- Beginning with the Midnight adoration: only fruit, vegetables and fish permitted (mysteries of Aphrodite)
- From the Dawn adoration: strictly vegetarian (mysteries of Hermes)
- From the Noon adoration: a complete fast (mysteries of Phoibos)
- Gnostic Mass at sunset

---

[*] For the Thelemic theory of fasting, see the later chapter of this book: "Conditions for Eucharistic Magick," as well as my discussion of *sawm* in "The Sharia of the Great Beast," in *Neither East nor West: Proceedings of the Ninth Biennial National O.T.O. Conference,* pp. 13-15.

[†] Anna (Bonus) Kingsford, *Clothed With the Sun,* pp. 48-52.

III. **Holy Meditation** - ו

In point 5 of Liber CC, the adorant is instructed to "compose Thyself to holy meditation." Many Thelemites working Liber Resh omit this part of the ritual in practice. If included, it is open to considerably varying interpretations. For the final Station of the Sun before serving as a Gnostic Mass officer, I would especially encourage reflection on a passage from the Holy Books of Thelema, after the manner of *lectio divina*. Read slowly, with both mind and voice engaged, open to associations at the personal and the general level. Be attentive to the promptings of your individual genius, and allow these to take intelligible form. Finally, permit the words of the book to be swallowed in the silence of your innermost being.

IV. **Bathing** - ה

Bishops Helena and Tau Apiryon observe: "Vestments of all officers should be donned ceremonially before the Mass, after ceremonial ablutions. All officers took a bath and meditated for a time before commencing the Gnostic Mass at Agapé Lodge." In the Mathers/Crowley edition of the *Goetia*, a Latin "conjuratioun" is prescribed for use "atte ye bathes of art":

> *Asperges me, domine, hyssopo, et mundabor;*
> *lavabis me, et super nivem dealbabor.*

The text is in fact Psalms 51:9 from the Vulgate Bible (which is 51:7 in the KJV and most English Bibles). Given that the "hocus-pocus" language of Liber XV is Greek rather than Latin, clergy preparing for Mass may prefer to use the Greek version from the Septuagint:

> ραντιεις με κυριε υσσωπω και καθαρισθησομαι
> πλυνεις με και υπερ χιονα λευκανθησομαι

The words *domine* and κυριε are actually not present in the biblical versions, being the added "Lord" of direct address for invocatory use. In the form given by Crowley in Chapter XIV of *Magick in Theory and Practice*, the word *Therion* is substituted for *domine*, and he remarks the connection of this conjuration with the mysteries of the VII° O.T.O. He also recommends replacing it wholesale with *CCXX* I:44:

> For pure will, unassuaged of purpose, delivered
> from the lust of result, is every way perfect.

V. **Prayer -** ʼ

Some sort of deliberate, practiced prayer (in addition to any spontaneous adorations and petitions) should be undertaken by a Mass officer after ceremonial ablutions and prior to the Mass proper. I have provided some of my own prayers for this purpose in the next section. But the best prayers will be carefully composed and refined by individual clergy for their own use.

I have found it useful in such invocations to punctuate them with magical gestures, particularly ones that I have learned through my initiation.

Sacristy Prayers

Here are a few prayers effective for recital and devotional meditation by priests and priestesses immediately prior to the work of the Gnostic Mass. Whether or not the architecture of the space in which the Mass is conducted has a dedicated sacristy, there must be a time and place for the final preparations of the clergy. As Priest, my "sacristy" has often been the tomb itself.

Anima Therion

This prayer is based on the *Anima Christi* of Roman Catholic tradition, which is documented as early as the fourteenth century—and which was not, therefore, written by Ignatius Loyola, who did however popularize it. It is equally suitable for use by priestesses and priests.

> Soul of the Beast, sanctify me.
> Body of the Beast, nourish me.
> Blood of the Beast, inebriate me.
> Thou shalt purge me with hyssop, O Therion,
> and I shall be clean;
> Thou shalt wash me, and I shall be whiter than snow.
> Inflame in us Therion the fire of your love
> and the flame of eternal devotion.
> To Mega Therion, hear me:
> Turn thine heads towards me;
> On thine horns exalt me;
> Grant the death forbidden unto me,
> And bid me shine forever.
> Blessing and worship to the prophet of the lovely star.
> AUMGN.

Song of the Sphinx

Our Lady declares of this incantation: "that which thou hearest is but the dropping of the dews from my limbs, for I dance in the night, naked upon the grass, in shadowy places, by running streams." It is drawn from the Second Aethyr of *The Vision & the Voice*, and it is well suited to the preparations of a priestess prior to Mass.

Silence! the moon ceaseth (her motion),
That also was sweet
In the air, in the air, in the air!
Who Will shall attain!
Who Will shall attain
By the Moon, and by Myself,
and by the Angel of the Lord!

Now Silence ceaseth
And the moon waxeth sweet;
(It is the hour of) Initiation, Initiation, Initiation.
The kiss of Isis is honeyed;
My own Will is ended,
For Will hath attained.

Behold the lion-child swimmeth (in the heaven)
And the moon reeleth: —
(It is) Thou! (It is) Thou! (It is) Thou!
Triumph; the Will stealeth away (like a thief),
The Strong Will that staggered
Before Ra Hoor Khuit! — Hadit! — Nuit!

To the God OAI
Be praise
In the end and the beginning!
And may none fall
Who Will attain
The Sword, the Balances, the Crown!

Ambrosial Prayer

The prayer of St. Ambrose is a text used by Roman Catholic priests preparing for Mass since the eleventh century. But its sentiments are largely inappropriate to our Church and her officers. Consequently, the following radical revision preserves much of its form, while inverting many of its contents. It is best suited to the use of a priest.

Thou highest and only One, in Thy Holy Name Mystery of Mystery: be mighty within me, a man among men: a magician whose art and craft are but glamour; strengthen the servant priest by whose hand and tongue the sacrifices are made: grant O Lord the manifestation of my will, which is Thine: vouchsafe the hiding of Thy love, which is mine, for the knowledge of me is the knowledge of death. May I be devoured by the light and eaten up with blindness: O Lord, the desires and energies of our flesh record Thy memory, reflect Thine understanding, and execute Thy will. Yea, though we perceive not the heaven through which we move, Thy Prophet has given us a Law by which our righteousness may be esteemed. O Holy Child, accept my adoration. O Thou whose will is Light, Life, Love, and Liberty: grant Majesty and Might unto us whom Thou hast established in the spirit, so that by virtue we may redeem the Earth as Thy perfect Kingdom throughout the Æon. AUMGN.

Miles Domini

"The soldier of the Lord" is an original prayer that I devised for my own use as an E.G.C. priest.

O Thou Lord of Energy and Endurance,
Mystery of Mystery,
Thou hast charged me
as an officer of Thy conquering army.
With the Light in my eyes,
the Law in my heart,
and the Lance in my hand,
I am ready and willing to fight
in the cause of Our Lady.
On Her fields
let my body be broken and my blood poured.
With Thy force
may I administer the virtues unto the brethren
in the fulfillment of my Will, which is Thine.
AUMGN.

Consecration of the Hallows

The four principal ritual implements (or "Hallows") of the Gnostic Mass are the Lance, Cup, Paten, and Sword. The fifth of these four is the Stele of Revealing, corresponding to the element of Spirit. They may be magically consecrated to their purpose by a bishop, priest or priestess using the following ritual. Note that in order to maintain the effect of the consecration, they must thereafter be touched by none other than ordained clergy, or charged ritual officers of the Church in the performance of their duties. They may of course be *re*-consecrated by means of the original procedure, and such re-consecration may in fact be a routine element of preparation for a Gnostic Mass. Note that the elemental references in the verses appear reversed; the idea is to temper each weapon with its opposing element, and thus to strengthen it.

Consecration takes place at the high altar, with the veil open. The candles are lit, and a vial of consecrated Holy Oil and The Book of the Law *are close at hand upon the altar top.*

The Hallow to be consecrated is placed upon the center of the altar. It must already be clean and in good material condition.

CONSECRATOR: "For pure will, unassuaged of purpose, delivered from the lust of result, is every way perfect."

CONSECRATOR *takes* The Book of the Law *in his or her right hand, touches it to the Hallow, and recites the appropriate stanza of consecration.*

Lance Be this consecrated lance
      A shaft of light. The Lord who grants
      His power to our work this day
      Ensure its strength. I duly pray
      That I may bear this sacred rod
      With all the fitness of a god.
      May waters rush to meet its thrust;
      May it inspire the force of lust.
      So may each heart and tongue fulfill
      The law, that is love under will.

Cup Be this consecrated graal
      The well of joy beyond the veil.
      As into it our woe has rained
      Let happiness therefrom be drained.
      The flower of its brimming cup
      Of nectar shall be offered up
      To light the fire upon the tongue
      Of God. Now let the song be sung:
      So may each heart and tongue fulfill
      The law, that is love under will.

Sword Be this consecrated sword
      The key of freedom. May the Lord
      Most Secret its chill steel imbue
      With perfect justice, sharp and true.
      This weapon wrought for mortal strife
      May cleave asunder human life
      From that more cosmic realm unknown:
      The World's hidden heart of stone.
      So may each heart and tongue fulfill
      The law, that is love under will.

Paten Be this consecrated plate
The solar disc: the eye of fate,
That turned to Earth gives life and death—
The life that stirs in every breath,
And in the searing southern ray
The fatal end to breathing. May
It come from darkness to the East
To bear for us the holy feast.
So may each heart and tongue fulfill
The law, that is love under will.

Stele Let this ancient prophecy
Crown our holy sorcery.
Set to witness from above
Our life and liberty and love;
Its light from beyond time and space
Illuminating every face,
With color that will never fade:
Abomination fitly made!
So may each heart and tongue fulfill
The law, that is love under will.

> *The* CONSECRATOR *sets down the Book, and places some oil on his right thumb. With the thumb he makes a* ✠ *upon the Hallow, with a brief invocation, according to the following pattern:*

CONSECRATOR *traces from center to top arm:* Ο ΠΑΤΗΡ
back to center: ΕΣΤΙΝ
to bottom arm: Ο ΥΙΟΣ
back to center: ΔΙΑ
to left arm: ΤΟ ΠΝΕΥΜΑ
back to center, to right arm: ΑΓΙΟΝ.
and return to center: ΑΥΜΓΝ.

Ante-Mass Ritual

This entirely unofficial ceremony designed to precede the Gnostic Mass has several possible applications. For example, it may be used to appoint a temple that has not been previously or continuously used for work with the Mass, or it may be used to formalize a new working relationship among Mass officers. In any case, it is designed to be performed with only three ritualists: the PRIEST, PRIESTESS and DEACON. The PEOPLE should not be present, and the CHILDREN are not required.

The temple is arranged as specified in Liber XV, with the following exceptions and additions:

- The Consecrated Stele, Book of the Law, Graal, and Lance are in the closed tomb.

- The Veil of the Shrine is closed.

- The PRIESTESS is standing within the Veil, in her full regalia.

-I-

The DEACON *admits the* PRIEST, *who is clad only in a white robe and carries a lit candle.*

The PRIEST *gives the candle to the* DEACON, *who places it on the Altar of Incense.*

The PRIEST *stands in the East (before the closed veil) while the* DEACON *recites the Nepios:*

DEACON: Now I begin to pray: Thou Child,
Holy Thy name and undefiled!
Thy reign is come; Thy will is done.
Here is the Bread; here is the Blood.
Bring me through midnight to the Sun!
Save me from Evil and from Good!

That Thy one crown of all the Ten
Even now and here be mine. AMEN.

> *From behind the veil, the* PRIESTESS *chants
> the Song of the Sphinx in Bathyllic:*

PRIESTESS: Mu pa telai,
   Tu wa melai
   a, a, a.
   Tu fu tulu!
   Tu fu tulu
   Pa, Sa, Ga.
      Qwi Mu telai
   Ya Pu melai;
   u, u, u.
   'Se gu malai;
   Pe fu telai,
   Fu tu lu.
      O chi balae
   Wa pa malae: —
   Ut! Ut! Ut!
   Ge; fu latrai,
   Le fu malai
   Kut! Hut! Nut!
      Al OAI
   Rel moai
   Ti — Ti — Ti!
   Wa la pelai
   Tu fu latai
   Wi, Ni, Bi.*

> *The* DEACON *opens the veil. (Left side, then
> right, crossing behind the* PRIEST.*)*

---

* From the 2nd Aethyr of *Liber 418;* see the English translation in
"Sacristy Prayers," above.

The PRIESTESS *is revealed, standing on the dais. She makes the Sign of Mystery*, *which the* PRIEST *answers with the Hailing Sign.*

PRIEST: Divine prophetess, I entreat you to admit me to the Nadir of Heaven.

> *The* PRIESTESS *descends and leads the* PRIEST *to the West.*

-II-

> *He kisses her hand once, and she opens the tomb.*

> *She reaches within and produces the Stele, which she shows to the* PRIEST.

PRIEST: "Above, the gemmed azure is
The naked splendour of Nuit;
She bends in ecstasy to kiss
The secret ardours of Hadit.
The winged globe, the starry blue,
Are mine, O Ankh-af-na-khonsu!"   (*CCXX* I:14)

PRIESTESS: ΤΟΥΤΟ ΕΣΤΙ ΤΟ ΚΕΦΑΛΗ ΜΟΥ.†

> *She gives him the Stele. He bears it widdershins to the East.*

> *He kisses it five times, once each on Nuit, Hadit, Ra-hoor-khuit, Ankh-f-n-khonsu, and the heiroglyphic text; he places it on the super-altar, and*

---

* A novice uninstructed in this sign may instead do as follows: a) place the fingertips of both hands at the throat, b) draw them simultaneously out to the tops of the shoulders, c) bring them together overhead, palm-to-palm, and d) lower the joined hands to the forehead.
† *Touto esti to kephale mou.* Gk. "For this is my head."

returns widdershins. (If the super-altar is too high to reach, the PRIEST *may leave the Stele at the Shrine with the* DEACON, *who then takes any needed measures to complete its placement.)*

She reaches within the tomb and produces the Book, which she shows to the PRIEST.

PRIEST: "There is great danger in me; for who doth not understand these runes shall make a great miss. He shall fall down into the pit called Because, and there he shall perish with the dogs of Reason." (*CCXX* II:27)

PRIESTESS: ΤΟΥΤΟ ΕΣΤΙ ΤΟ ΚΑΡΔΙΑ ΜΟΥ.*

She gives him the Book. He bears it widdershins to the altar of incense. He kisses it thrice, places it on the altar, and returns widdershins.

She reaches within the tomb and produces the Graal, which she shows to the PRIEST.

PRIEST: "But your holy place shall be untouched throughout the centuries: though with fire and sword it be burnt down & shattered, yet an invisible house there standeth, and shall stand until the fall of the Great Equinox; when Hrumachis shall arise and the double-wanded one assume my throne and place. Another prophet shall arise, and bring fresh fever from the skies; another woman shall awake the lust & worship of the Snake; another soul of God and beast shall mingle in the globed priest; another sacrifice shall stain the tomb; another king shall reign; and blessing no longer be poured To the Hawk-headed mystical Lord!"   (*CCXX* III:34)

PRIESTESS: ΤΟΥΤΟ ΕΣΤΙ ΤΟ ΚΟΛΠΟΣ ΜΟΥ.†

---

* *Touto esti to kardia mou.* Gk. "For this is my heart."
† *Touto esti to kolpos mou.* Gk. "For this is my vulva."

152

She gives him the Graal. He bears it widdershins to the font. He kisses it once, fills it with wine, and covers it. He gives it to the DEACON, *who takes it deosil to the Shrine. The* PRIEST *returns widdershins.*

He kisses the PRIESTESS *once on the mouth, and she closes him into the tomb.*

-III-

The PRIESTESS *meets the* DEACON *at the altar of incense. She unsheathes her sword.*

PRIESTESS: "Do what thou wilt shall be the whole of the
Law."   (*CCXX* I:40)

DEACON: "Love is the law, love under will."   (*CCXX* I:57)

The DEACON *drops to one knee, and the* PRIESTESS *rests the flat of the sword's blade on the* DEACON's *right shoulder, then left.*

PRIESTESS: Be thou bright and beautiful.

The DEACON *stands.*

PRIESTESS: Fail not. Sorrow not. Fear not.

With each "not" she traces a circle with the sword over the head of the DEACON.

DEACON: Thou hast spoken it.

The PRIESTESS *sheathes the sword.*

PRIESTESS: ΑΥΜΓΝ. ΑΥΜΓΝ. ΑΥΜΓΝ.

The PRIESTESS *exits to the sacristy.*
The DEACON *strikes the bell once.*
The DEACON *exits to the narthex.*
The ceremony is ended, and the Mass follows.

Candle Blessing

A prior blessing is highly desirable for all candles to be burned on altars.* This ceremony may be undertaken by any clergy. If multiple candles are on hand to be blessed, the prayers may be recited for all collectively except where indicated. This method is an option.

Candles to be blessed are placed on an antimension or another red cloth. Clergy performing the blessing recites:

Unknowable enigma of revelation, thou limit who art not, invisible Magician, whose illusions reveal the truth, devouring us and eating us up with blindness; mayst thou stream from perfection to perfection in the hidden life of all. AUMGN.

Caress each candle individually with its own recitation of the following formula.

ACCENDAT IN NOBIS THERION IGNEM SUI AMORIS ET FLAMMAM AETERNAE CARITATIS.

Recite once for all:

Station of the Light,
food of the flame,
burn with love in the Temple of Truth!

Conclude with a recitation of the doxology from Liber XXXVI (raising hands in blessing):

GLORIA PATRI ET MATRI ET FILIO ET FILIAE ET SPIRITUI SANCTO EXTERNO ET SPIRITUI SANCTO INTERNO, UT ERAT EST ERIT IN SAECULA SAECULORUM, SEX IN UNO PER NOMEN SEPTEM IN UNO, ARARITA.

---

* For background on the significance of the ritual, see Alexander Hislop, *The Two Babylons*, pp. 191-197.

Ordinary Hallowing of a Bell

The bell that rings in the Gnostic Mass is not described in any detail. Its location is unspecified, and there is not even any clear direction as to who should ring it. Many clergy have justifiably interpreted the chapter on "The Bell" in *Liber ABA* (Part II, Chapter XIV) to offer a description of the ideal material design of the bell itself, but such is only an educated inference.

The ritual which follows details the procedure for an instrumental sacrament performed by clergy to confer a durable consecration on a bell for use in Church ceremonies. Given the absence of such direction from past or present patriarchs, it is obviously not *required* of any bell in Church use. In the rubric for "ordinary hallowing" below, the HALLOWER may be any member of the clergy under orders, and the ASSISTANT may be any confirmed member of the Church. The ceremony may be conducted publicly if desired.

The ritual calls for the use of another, previously-hallowed bell. By this means, the bell being hallowed is brought into a vibratory communion with the larger Church. On the occasion of this ceremony, the owner (clergy or congregation) of the bell being hallowed should document both the name of the saint to whom the new bell is dedicated, and (to the extent known), the series of bells through which the call of the Church descends to it.

Necessarily, this feature raises the question of "extraordinary hallowing," in which no previously-hallowed bell is available. Such a ceremony can and should be conducted privately by a bishop.

A bell consecrated by this ritual is considered to hold its charge unless actively desecrated.

The bell to be hallowed hangs above a central double-cube altar. It is suspended by a thong or chain so that it hangs freely to resonate with the vibrations made by the voices of the HALLOWER and the others gathered. There is a lit candle, a copy of *Liber Legis*, a small bowl of salt water, a burning censer, a vial of holy oil, and for ordinary hallowing, another bell which has already been hallowed. These tools may be on the central altar or otherwise near to hand.

HALLOWER (*facing East with the appropriate gesture*):
Απο παντος κακοδαιμονος!

ASSISTANT (*in the East*): Do what thou wilt shall be the whole of the Law. (*CCXX* I:40)

ALL: Love is the law, love under will. (*CCXX* I:57)

ASSISTANT *recites the Nepios*:

Now I begin to pray: Thou Child,
Holy Thy name and undefiled!
Thy reign is come; Thy will is done.
Here is the Bread; here is the Blood.
Bring me through midnight to the Sun!
Save me from Evil and from Good!
That Thy one crown of all the Ten
Even now and here be mine. AMEN. (*XLIV*)

The HALLOWER *lights the incense.*

HALLOWER: I am that I am, the flame
Hidden in the sacred ark.
I am the unspoken name
I the unbegotten spark.

I am He that ever goeth,
Being in myself the Way;
Known, that yet no mortal knoweth,
Shewn, that yet no mortal sheweth,
I, the child of night and day.
I am never-dying youth.
I am Love, and I am Truth.

I am the creating Word,
I the author of the aeon;
None but I have ever heard
Echo in the empyrean
Plectron of the primal paean!
I am the eternal one
Winged and white, the flowering rod,
I the fountain of the sun,
Very God of very God!

I am he that lifteth up
Life, and flingeth it afar;
I have filled the crystal cup;
I have sealed the silver star.
I the wingless God that flieth
Through my firmamental fane,
I am he that daily dieth,
And is daily born again.   (from *Liber DCCC*)

> *The* HALLOWER *cleanses the bell with salt
> water.*

HALLOWER: Asperges me Therion hyssopo et mundabor,
lavabis me, et super nivem dealbabor.

> *The* HALLOWER *collects smoke from the
> censer in the mouth of the bell.*

HALLOWER: Accendat in nobis Therion ignem sui amoris,
et flammam aeternae caritatis.

> *The* HALLOWER *circumambulates the altar
> deosil thrice, reciting each time:*

HALLOWER: O Lion and O Serpent that destroy the
destroyer, be mighty among us.

> *The* HALLOWER *makes the Sign of the
> Enterer at the beginning of each recitation, while
> passing the East. He stops to the west of the altar,
> faces the bell, and raises his hands in prayer.*

HALLOWER: Oremus, dilectissimi nobis, pro ecclesia sancta gnostica: ut eam Dominus et Domina nostra fortificare, adunare et custodire dignetur toto orbe terrarum: subjiciens ei principatus et potestates: dentque nobis audentiam et liberam vitam degentibus, glorificare Legem verum. Oremus.

> *The* HALLOWER *recites the First Collect of the Gnostic Mass (The Sun).*

ALL: So mote it be.

> *The* HALLOWER *makes a* ✠ *with oil upon the outside of the Bell.*

> *The* HALLOWER *recites the Second Collect of the Gnostic Mass (The Lord).*

ALL: So mote it be.

> *The* HALLOWER *makes a* ✠ *with oil upon the outside of the Bell.*

> *The* HALLOWER *recites the Third Collect of the Gnostic Mass (The Moon).*

ALL: So mote it be.

> *The* HALLOWER *makes a* ✠ *with oil upon the outside of the Bell.*

> *The* HALLOWER *recites the Fourth Collect of the Gnostic Mass (The Lady).*

ALL: So mote it be.

> *The* HALLOWER *makes a* ✠ *with oil upon the outside of the Bell.*

> *The* HALLOWER *recites the Fifth Collect of the Gnostic Mass (The Saints), omitting the list of individual saints.*

ALL: So mote it be.

The HALLOWER *makes a* ✠ *with oil upon the outside of the Bell.*

The HALLOWER *recites the Sixth Collect of the Gnostic Mass (The Earth).*

ALL: So mote it be.

The HALLOWER *makes a* ✠ *with oil upon the outside of the Bell, completing the points of a hexagram.*

The HALLOWER *recites the Seventh Collect of the Gnostic Mass (The Principles).*

ALL: So mote it be.

The HALLOWER *makes a* ✠ *with oil upon the top point of the Bell.*

The HALLOWER *recites the Eighth Collect of the Gnostic Mass (Birth).*

ALL: So mote it be.

The HALLOWER *makes a* ✠ *with oil upon the inside of the Bell.*

The HALLOWER *recites the Ninth Collect of the Gnostic Mass (Marriage).*

ALL: So mote it be.

The HALLOWER *makes a* ✠ *with oil upon the inside of the Bell.*

All stand, head erect, eyes open.

The HALLOWER *recites the Tenth Collect of the Gnostic Mass (Death).*

ALL: So mote it be.

The HALLOWER *makes a* ✠ *with oil upon the inside of the Bell.*

159

The HALLOWER *recites the Eleventh Collect of the Gnostic Mass (The End).*

ALL: So mote it be.

The HALLOWER *makes a* ✠ *with oil upon the inside of the Bell, completing the corners of a square.*

HALLOWER: "I await Thee in sleeping, in waking. I invoke Thee no more; for Thou art in me, O Thou who hast made me a beautiful instrument tuned to Thy rapture." *(VII, VII:13)*

The ASSISTANT *rings the other, previously hallowed bell.*

HALLOWER (*makes each* ✠ *with bell*): May this bell be hallowed and consecrated. In the name of ✠ CHAOS and of ✠ BABALON and of ✠ BAPHOMET. In honour of the worthy Saint ... [*names a saint chosen from the canon of Liber XV*]. Might and majesty be thine. ΑΥΜΓΝ.

ALL: So mote it be.

HALLOWER: Do what thou wilt shall be the whole of the Law. *(CCXX I:40)*

ALL: Love is the law, love under will. *(CCXX I:57)*

HALLOWER: May all those who attend the sound of this bell always profess the Law of Liberty.

ALL: So mote it be.

The HALLOWER *rings the new bell. All depart.*

Remedial Sacraments

Remedial sacraments are those intended to relieve distress or resolve disharmony in an individual, a household or a congregation. Without any sort of doctrine of original sin or universal sorrow, Thelemic religion relegates the therapeutic and rehabilitative functions to a relatively minor corner of the sacramental universe.

The foremost of these remedial sacraments are those for the relief of the individual, typified by the **administration of the virtues to the sick**. In this operation, the clergy act on the cue provided in Liber XV: "The Sacrament may be reserved by the Priest, for administration to the sick in their homes." Priestesses are equally empowered to serve in this capacity. Bishops T Apiryon, Helena, and T Sir Hasrim have composed an effective ceremony for this purpose. In this ritual the administering clergy visits an indisposed member at home or another site of convalescence, and transacts an abbreviated form of the Gnostic Mass in which the member communicates.* It mixes formal ceremony and blessings with opportunities for counsel and consolation.

While the administration of the virtues to the sick exhibits a kinship to the cardinal sacrament of the Eucharist of the Gnostic Mass, there is another remedial sacrament that can be viewed as having a relationship to the initiatory operations of baptism, confirmation, and holy orders. This sacrament of **renouncing slave-religion** is one that was contemplated by the Prophet, but never received an authorized form from him. Similarly, no sanctioned ritual for the purpose has been issued by the Patriarch or our Primate. Nevertheless, the need for such a ceremony is not at all uncommon, even as we find ourselves more than a century into the New Æon. The ritual form that I have used for the purpose is published in *Raise the Spell*.

---

* Sabazius, *Mystery of Mystery,* pp. 324-5.

Exorcism

Exorcism is an obvious practice from ecclesiastical tradition to be considered as a candidate for a remedial sacrament. There are, however, certain complications involved and objections to be raised. At the outset, it is necessary to distinguish between the treatment of "possessed" persons and "haunted" spaces or artifacts.

The exorcism of persons has doubtless served legitimate therapeutic purposes at numerous points during its long history. In the setting of ecclesiastical institutions, however, it has had many terrible consequences. For a highly detailed case study from the seventeenth century, see Aldous Huxley's *The Devils of Loudun*. (The book is also of interest for its epilogue "in amplification of material in Chapter Three," which forms a parallel treatment of the central topics in Crowley's "Energized Enthusiasm.") Such exorcisms are apparently now gaining in popularity for Christians, both among Roman Catholics and Protestant Evangelicals, but they are not a part of Thelemic practice.

Above and beyond the coercive use of exorcism by religious authorities, recent decades have seen the emergence of secular forms of exorcistic practice by psychologists using such diagnoses as "multiple personality disorder" (MPD) and "dissociative identity disorder" (DID). There is a significant body of research literature reaching back into the twentieth century that discusses the iatrogenic basis for many of the symptoms and complexes involved in this nosology. Within the psychotherapeutic culture, there are strong connections (often simple identity) among MPD/DID specialists and proponents of "ritual abuse" who have been shown to promote confabulations of childhood trauma. Of course, the media-fueled accounts of "ritual abuse" have been inimical to propagation of Thelemic culture and the welfare of

Thelemites. These have repeatedly led to rumor-panics and moral crusades hostile to Thelema.*

Exorcism of persons by sincere religious agents can pose genuine hazards to the exorcist. In the first volume of Giacomo Casanova's memoirs he recounted the apparent demonic possession of thirteen-year-old Bettina. Casanova noticed that her demoniac condition gave her complete freedom from responsibility in her family, and that the demons preferred a handsome exorcist to an ugly one.† Even the innocently "possessed" may exercise alarming amounts of inducement and control over their would-be healers.

On the other hand, the exorcism of evidently baleful influences from places and objects is a largely blameless exercise, as long as it is not a mercenary operation.‡ For Thelemic clergy, the techniques will be the canonical banishings and cleansings of ceremonial magick, as detailed in Liber O and *Magick in Theory & Practice*. More "ecclesiastical" forms would be superfluous.

Magick (not just legerdemain) is sometimes a matter of misdirection. In the case of the widely-publicized 1967 exorcism of the Pentagon building in Washington, D.C., the genuine effect was on the larger population, as one of the magicians involved explained:

> The levitation of the Pentagon was a happening that demystified the authority of the military. …
> The Pentagon was symbolically levitated in people's minds in the sense that it lost its

---

* See Jeffrey S. Victor, *Satanic Panic: The Creation of a Contemporary Legend* (1993). For one "expert" (blinkered and/or dishonest) indictment of Thelema and O.T.O. as part of a "satanic" tapestry of crime and violence, see Carl A. Raschke's *Painted Black* (1990).
† Casanova, Giacomo (Chevalier de Seingalt), *History of My Life*, trans. Willard Trask (1966), Vol. I, pp. 70-87.
‡ See Crowley, *Magick: Book Four*, Pt. III, Ch. XXI, §I, pp. 275-6.

authority which had been unquestioned and unchallenged until then.[*]

While the promised 300-foot levitation of architecture failed to take place, that operation was a success in the terms of its designers' intentions. It helped to shift American attitudes about military imperialism for a full generation.

Dissolution of Marriage

The purpose of this ceremony is to assist in the social and emotional resolution of a consensual marital divorce between members of the Church. The officiant may be any member of the Church, although preferably a member of the priesthood who has provided counseling to the couple undergoing divorce. Obviously, the ceremony will not have the legal consequence of divorce. It should be understood as a benediction of the individuals; an opportunity for each to explicitly recognize the independence of the other; a recognition by the community of the inherent value of each, distinct from their marital history; and an expression of support during the difficult work of dissolving a partnership.

This sacramental function should **not** be performed in conjunction with a Gnostic Mass. It should instead follow directly on a banquet provided by the divorcing couple as a final act of joint hospitality.

My own ritual for dissolution of marriage is in draft form and not suited for publication, but the notes above should be sufficient guidelines for any clergy called upon to perform this function. In such a circumstance, clergy will draw on their own ingeniums, the wills of the couple divorcing, and the guidance of a bishop.

---

[*] Allen Ginsberg, quoted by Peter Manseau in "Fifty Years Ago, a Rag-Tag Group of Acid-Dropping Activists Tried to 'Exorcize' the Pentagon," *Smithsonian.com*, October 20, 2017.

Occasional Sacraments:
A Thelemic Liturgical Calendar

Occasional sacraments are communal observances oriented to annual or other periodic dates, including astronomical phenomena, anniversaries of historical events, and commemoration of saints and heroes. Some of these are specified in the Calendar of *Liber Legis* II:34-44, which is recited in every Gnostic Mass.

As a general rule, no clergy standing is needed in order to conduct ceremonies celebrating any occasional sacrament as such. On the other hand, to do such work can be an important expression of service by the clergy under orders, and it can serve as a valuable means by which novices can gain proficiency and express their aspiration.

The calendar which follows is neither official, nor exhaustive. Some dates are traditional and not historically verifiable. When possible, feast days attributed to individuals are set on the anniversaries of their deaths. Occasions noted [in brackets] pertain to the obsolete traditions of Valentinian Gnosticism, but may be of interest to clergy. A cross pattée (✠) before a name indicates a saint invoked as such in the Gnostic Mass. The chivalric titles Sir and Dame are used for inductees of the Orders of the Lion and the Eagle, and/or high-degree initiates of O.T.O.

Underlined occasions are the designated dates for suitable liturgies included my books *Mysteries of the Great Beast Aleister Crowley* and *Raise the Spell*.

SPRING

March

20 – <u>*Feast for the Supreme Ritual and the Equinox of the Gods*</u>,
   Feast of Sir John Yarker, <u>BEGIN HOLY DAYS</u>

22 – *Feast of ✠Wolfgang von Goethe*

24 – *Feast of ✠Priapus*

26 – *Feast of ✠Johannes Dee, Feast of Mansur al-Hallaj*

April

8 – *Feast for the First Day of the Writing of the Book of the Law*

9 – *Feasts for the Second Day of the Writing of the Book of the Law,
   and of ✠Rabelais, and ✠Francis Bacon Lord Verulam*

10 – *Feast for the Third Day of the Writing of the Book of the Law,
   and of ✠Swinburne,* <u>HOLY DAYS CONCLUDE</u>

12 – *Feast of Dame Mary d'Este Sturges*

25 – *Feast of ✠Manes*

27 – *Feast of Sir Wilfred T. Smith*

May

1 – <u>*Feast of Cattle*</u>

5 – *Feast of Sir James Branch Cabell*

8 – *Feast of ✠Paul Gaugin, Feast of Dame Helena P. Blavatsky*

11 – *Feast of Lady Frieda Harris*

18 – *Feast of ✠Elias Ashmole*

23 – *Feast of Sir Henry Klein, Apparition of the Daughter of
   Fortitude*

24 – *Feast of ✠Hermes*

26 – *Feast of ✠Siddartha*

30 – *Feast of Joan of Arc*

31 – *Feast of ✠Alphonse Louis Constant, and Dame Phyllis Seckler*

June

1 – *Feast of Marguerite Porete*

7 – *Feast of ✠Carl Kellner*

8 – *Feast of ✠Mohammed*

10 – *Feast of ✠Basilides*

13 – *Feast of ✠Ludovicus Rex Bavariae*

17 – *Feast of Sir Jack Parsons*

SUMMER

June
21/22 – *Summer Solstice*
27 – *Feast of ✠Andrea*
29 – *Feast of ✠Simon Magus*

July
11 – *Lesser Feast of ✠Bardesanes*
12 – *Feast of Sir Grady Louis McMurtry*
24 – *Feast of Marjorie Cameron*
28 – *Feast of ✠Tahuti*
29 – *Feast of Sir Paschal Beverly Randolph*

August
1 – *Feast of the Lion-Serpent*
7 – *Feast of Sir Franz Hartmann*
12 – *Feast for the First Night of the Beast and His Bride, and of*
      ✠Heracles, and of ✠William Blake
13 – *Feast of ✠Hippolytus*
15 – *[Feast of the Assumption of the Holy Sophia]*
18 – *Feast of ✠Roderic Borgia, Pope Alexander VI*
25 – *Feast of ✠Friedrich Nietzsche*
26 – *Feast of ✠Krishna, and of ✠Cagliostro*
29 – *Feast of ✠Ulrich von Hutten*

September
4 – *Feast of ✠Mosheh*
8 – *Feast of ✠Robertus de Fluctibus, [Descent of the Holy Sophia]*
13 – *Feast of ✠Dante Alighieri*
14 – *Feast of Dame Leila Waddell*

AUTUMN

September
21 – *Autumnal Equinox, Feast of* ✠*Virgilius*
24 – *Feast of* ✠*Paracelsus*
27 – *Feast of Cosmus & Damianus*

October
2 – *Feast of Dame Emma Hardinge Britten*
7 – *Feast of* ✠*Dionysus*
12 – *Crowleymas (Lesser Feast of the Prophet)*
16 – *Feast of Dame Ida Craddock*
20 – *Feast of* ✠*Sir Richard Francis Burton*
25 – *Feast of* ✠*Gérard Encausse, Feast of Sir Karl Johannes Germer*
28 – *Feast of* ✠*Theodor Reuss*
31 – *Feast of the Dragon*

November
13 – *Feast of* ✠*Osiris*
17 – *Feast of* ✠*Jacob Boehme*
18 – *Feast of the First Initiation of the Prophet, and of*
    ✠*Adam Weishaupt*
25 – *Feast of* ✠*Sir Edward Kelly*
27 – *Feast of Harry Smith*

December
1 – *Feast of* ✠*Sir Aleister Crowley*
3 – *Feast of the Annihilation of the Prophet*
13 – *Feast of* ✠*Frederick of Hohenstaufen*

WINTER

December
21/22 – *Winter Solstice*
29 – *Feast of* ✠*Molinos*

January
1 – *Feast of* ✠*Pan*
28 – *Feast of* ✠*Carolus Magnus*

February
2 – *Feast of the Stars*
11– *Feast of Dame Rose Edith Kelly*
13 – *Feast of* ✠*Richard Wagner*
14 – *Feast of* ✠*Valentinus*
17 – *Feast of* ✠*Giordano Bruno the Martyr*
22 – *Feast of Doctor Dame Anna Mary Bonus Kingsford, and of
        Dame Leah Hirsig*
24 – *Feast of Sir Charles Stansfeld Jones*

March
3 – *Feast of Saladin*
5 – *(Lesser) Feast of* ✠*Lao Tzu*
10 – *Feast of Sir Israel Regardie*
17 – *Feast of* ✠*Dionysus*
18 – *Feast of* ✠*Jacobus Burgundus Molensis the Martyr*

Practical Sacraments

Practical sacraments are routine rituals and disciplines used by individual Thelemic Gnostics for personal realization. The most succinct piece of instruction that we have on this score is *"De Cultu,"* the sixteenth chapter of *Liber Aleph vel CXI*:

> Now, o my Son, that thou mayst be well guarded against thy ghostly Enemies, do thou work constantly by the Means prescribed in our Holy Books.
>
> Neglect never the fourfold Adorations of the Sun in his four Stations, for thereby thou doest affirm thy Place in Nature and her Harmonies.
>
> Neglect not the Performance of the Ritual of the Pentagram, and of the Assumption of the Form of Hoor-pa-Kraat.
>
> Neglect not the daily Miracle of the Mass, either by the Rite of the Gnostic Catholic Church, or that of the Phoenix.
>
> Neglect not the Performance of the Mass of the Holy Ghost, as Nature herself prompteth thee.
>
> Travel also much in the Empyrean in the Body of Light, seeking ever Abodes more fiery and lucid.
>
> Finally, exercise constantly the Eight Limbs of Yoga. And so shalt thou come to the End.

There are some Crowlier-than-thou folks who seem to think that these instructions from 666 must be followed by every Thelemite. It is important to keep in mind, however, that *Liber Aleph* is an extended epistle to "777" (Crowley's "magical son" Charles Stansfeld Jones), who was both a Perfect Illuminatus of the Sovereign Sanctuary of the IX° and a Magister Templi of A∴A∴. The total level of discipline indicated is therefore rather in excess of what might be expected of a lay Thelemite. Still, it provides valuable direction for the priests and priestesses of the Holy One.

In the following sections, I offer some illustrations drawn from my own practice regarding the first two disciplines: adorations of the sun, and the ritual of the pentagram.

While the Gnostic Mass of E.G.C. is certainly a cardinal sacrament, it may also contribute to the practical sacrament of a *daily* Eucharistic observance for the individual Thelemite. For this practical concern, 666 expresses indifference whether that be drawn from the O.T.O. canon of Liber XV or the A∴A∴ ritual in Liber XLIV (i.e. the Mass of the Phoenix). One might well work up original ceremonies for one's own use in this important discipline. In my book *Raise the Spell*, I have published "A Short Eucharist" which I developed for the purpose. Among the following rituals in the present volume I include both my own translation of the Mass of the Phoenix into Enochian and a private Eucharist "of three elements" according to the program outlined in *Magick in Theory & Practice*.

The general principles of travel in the Body of Light are detailed in section V of Liber O, in Chapter XVIII of *Magick in Theory & Practice*, in "Notes for an Astral Atlas," in Letter 17 of *Magick Without Tears*, and in the original Golden Dawn Flying Rolls IV, IX & XXV.

The eight limbs of yoga are thoroughly discussed in Part I of *Magick: Book 4* and in Crowley's *Eight Lectures on Yoga*. A helpful contemporary approach to this material is Nancy Wasserman's book *Yoga for Magick*.

Ultimately, each practitioner must establish his or her own regimen of practical sacraments.

Solar Adorations

The injunction to observe the "fourfold Adorations of the Sun" refers to the practices described in "Liber Resh vel Helios." 666 remarked that advanced practitioners could use this ritual to draw on the spiritual power of the sun. In my experience, this ritual properly performed has the further effect of converting the power of the physical rotation of the earth—which produces the effect of the motion of the sun—into the practitioner's spiritual aspiration to (or communion with) his or her star, i.e. personal genius. It effectively induces a current through the continual observation of the circular motion of the outer world, propelling the ritualist on a linear path of interior initiation.

> O my darling, I also wait for the brilliance of the hour ineffable, when the universe shall be like a girdle for the midst of the ray of our love, extending beyond the permitted end of the endless One.*

The key to all this success can be found in the oft-neglected points 5 & 6 of the ritual:

5. And after each of these invocations thou shalt give the sign of silence, and afterward thou shalt perform the adoration that is taught thee by thy Superior. And then do thou compose Thyself to holy meditation.

6. Also it is better if in these adorations thou assume the God-form of Whom thou adorest, as if thou didst unite with Him in the adoration of That which is beyond Him.

Although "Liber Resh" is an official ritual of A∴A∴, 666 later gave instructions regarding the signs for those who

---

* Liber LXV, IV:64

have "no grade" in that Order.* He also insisted that the adorations be a universal practice in the profess-houses of O.T.O. It is clear therefore that aspirants should undertake this work whether or not they have been received into A∴A∴, and certainly it behooves clergy to avail themselves of the benefits afforded by this practice.

Like the Muslim *salāt* to which it is closely analogous, "Liber Resh" tightly regulates speech, thought and physical gesture, and yet affords room for variations based on traditional instruction and individual choice. The published ritual declines to provide important details in point 5, with respect to the "adoration" and "holy meditation."

The stanzas from the Stele of Revealing as paraphrased in chapter III of *Liber Legis* seem to have become the global default option for the "adoration" of point 5, which is, however, supposed to be "taught thee by thy Superior" among initiates. O.T.O. members at large may seem to lack a Superior for this purpose. Only members of at least the VIII° may approach the "Superior of the Order" (i.e. the Patriarch of the Church) as such. But the Abbot or Abbess of a profess-house would serve as a Superior to coordinate or vary the adorations of its residents, and E.G.C. clergy each have a Superior in the person of the bishop who provides them with supervision. Few—if any—bishops *require* a particular observance of the Adorations of the Sun from their clergy, but any of us should be willing to offer advice and direction if asked.

Crowley's later remark about "regularizing the practices" suggests that it might consist of one of the yoga exercises from Liber E, Liber Ru, Liber HHH, or Liber Yod. But the

---

* Specifically: L.V.X. signs at dawn, 4°=7□ at noon, 2°=9□ at sunset, 3°=8□ at midnight. Or, as indicated in correspondence from Crowley to Hymenaeus Alpha, full initiates of the Oasis Degrees of O.T.O. may (in private) use the signs appropriate to the symbolic times of day for those rituals. See *Magick,* p. 786.

precedent of *salāt* instead inclines towards the notion of reciting and reflecting upon memorized passages from the Holy Books of Thelema.* In my book *Thelema for the People* there is a more elaborate system of meditation based on the Ignatian Spiritual Exercises. It presumes the use of solar adorations to structure a fourfold daily practice.

All clergy should be familiar and proficient with the ritual of "Liber Resh" in its canonical form, so as to be able to serve as an *imam* or prayer-leader on those occasions where the adorations might be observed jointly by a group of Thelemites. However, as an individual practice it is possible to customize the ritual quite radically without diminishing its value. During a year's sojourn in Europe, my own personal observation of the Adorations of the Sun became very idiosyncratic. In fact, this variant (published in *Raise the Spell*) was the form of my practice when I was in Cairo for the centennial of the reception of *The Book of the Law*.

---

* See "Studying toward Sacerdotal Expertise," above.

Libellum de Pentalpha Flagranti

The revision of the Star Ruby in this section is intended to accurately expose my personal practice and includes details which help to reify and hypostasize formulæ and symbolism that I find implicit in the original ritual.

Although Ritual XXV was first published as "an official ritual of A∴A∴," it has also been prescribed for the general use of all Thelemites and practitioners of Magick in the New Æon, and it is relevant to the practice of individual O.T.O. initiates. With respect to this material, I write as a withdrawn Probationer of A∴A∴. I claim no imprimatur or official authority for my remarks. Readers must judge the contents on their theoretical and practical merits alone.

Unauthorized Revision of Ritual XXV

Facing East in the center of the space, the
ORGIAST *draws a deep breath, pressing his right*
forefinger against the lower lip of his closed mouth.
Then he dashes down the hand with a great sweep
back and out, crying:

ΑΠΟ ΠΑΝΤΟΣ ΚΑΚΟΔΑΙΜΟΝΟΣ.

He touches the same forefinger to his forehead:

ΣΟΙ

He touches the same finger to his member:

Ω ΦΑΛΛΗ

He touches the same finger to his right breast:

ΙΣΧΥΡΟΣ

To his left breast:

ΕΥΧΑΡΙΣΤΟΣ

Then he clasps his hands before him, interlocking
the fingers:

ΙΑΩ.

He advances to the East. He imagines a red
pentagram, aright, in his forehead. In the center of it is a
greenish yellow sigma. *Drawing his hands to his eyes, he*
flings it forth, roaring:

ΧΑΟΣ

He retires his hand in the Sign of Silence.

He goes round to the North. He flings forth a red pentagram with a greenish blue omicron *in its center, in the same manner, screaming:*

ΒΑΒΑΛΟΝ

He retires his hand in the Sign of Silence.

He goes round to the West. He flings forth a red pentagram with a violet alpha *in its center, in the same manner, saying:*

ΕΡΟΣ

He retires his hand in the Sign of Silence.

He goes round to the South. He flings forth a red pentagram with a red-orange chi *in its center, in the same manner, bellowing:*

ΨΥΧΗ

He retires his hand in the Sign of Silence.

He completes the circle widdershins and returns to the center, facing East. He raises both hands at his sides, palms forward, and recites:

Ρ.Λ.Ν.
Pi. Alpha. Nu.
Duality. Energy. Death.
The Pillars, Priapos, casting forth the seed.
The Pentagram, Hades, ruling the secret place.
The Scorpion, Nike, victorious over death and life.
Priapos, Hades, Nike: PAN!
ΙΟ ΠΑΝ!

He assumes the posture of the god Mentu, indicating pillars of arm and member.

N. The sign of the youth, fair and godly.

He takes the attitude of horned Bacchus, the averse pentagram.

O. The sign of the lord, dark and beastly.

He stands in the attitude of the Capitoline Venus.

The sign of the maiden, modest in desire.

He takes the stance of Babalon, alluding to Tiamat and Scorpio.

X. The sign of the lady, brazen in fulfillment.

He stands in the posture of Isis Rejoicing, the triumphant mother.

N.O.X. NOX, the Night of Pan! IO ΠΑΝ!

He extends his arms in the form of a Tau, and conjures the guardians:

ΠΡΟ ΜΟΥ ΙΥΓΓΕΣ ΟΠΙΣΟ ΜΟΥ ΤΕΛΕΤΑΡΧΑΙ ΕΠΙ ΔΕΞΙΑ ΣΥΝΟΧΕΣ ΕΠΑΡΙΣΤΕΡΑ ΔΑΙΜΟΝΕΣ ΦΛΕΓΕΙ ΓΑΡ ΠΕΡΙ ΜΟΥ Ο ΑΣΤΕΡ ΤΩΝ ΠΕΝΤΕ ΚΑΙ ΕΝ ΤΗΙ Ο ΣΤΗΛΗΙ Ο ΑΣΤΕΡ ΤΟΝ ΕΞ ΕΣΤΗΧΗ.

He repeats the Cross Qabalistic, with the gestures as before.

ΣΟΙ Ω ΦΑΛΛΗ ΙΣΧΥΡΟΣ ΕΥΧΑΡΙΣΤΟΣ ΙΑΩ.

He repeats the original apotropaic gesture and injunction.

ΑΠΟ ΠΑΝΤΟΣ ΚΑΚΟΔΑΙΜΟΝΟΣ.

Scholion on Sources and Structure

The ritual of the flaming star as here described takes as its basis the version published in *The Book of Lies, falsely so-called*, composed in a time near to the origins of the Gnostic Mass and using divine names which orient both to that Mass and to the Prophet's visions of the Thirty Aires. This original version is preferable to the one appended to *Magick in Theory & Practice*, for being more clearly linked to both the Creed of the Mass and *The Vision & the Voice*. It also more cleanly manifests the formula of Tetragrammaton. The later revision was an unperfected transitional form, the genuine virtues of which are more effectively implemented in the distinct Ritual of the Mark of the Beast (Liber V) composed at that time.

Chapter 25 of *Lies* ("The Star Ruby") provides the ritual, as a "new and more elaborate version of the Banishing Ritual of the Pentagram." One of the chief elaborations is the addition of opening and closing actions that emphasize and enhance the symmetrical quality of the original lesser pentagram ritual. For convenience, I will refer to these small sections as the apotropaisms. They consist of an injunction in Greek that is rhythmically similar to the formulae *hekas hekas este bebeloi* and *procul o procul este profani* used to dismiss the uninitiated before commencing a ceremony, and they serve essentially the same function: a general dismissal of irrelevant and impertinent "spirits."

The Cross Qabalistic is a Greek variation on the cabalistic cross used in the lesser pentagram ritual. The meaning of the original Hebrew *Ateh Malkuth ve-Geburah ve-Gedulah le-olahm Amen* is: "Unto Thee be the Kingdom, and the Power, and the Glory, for the ages. Amen." This text, familiar to Protestants (and some Eastern Christians) as the closing doxology for the Lord's Prayer, has its original source in Hebrew liturgy, which is in turn probably modeled on I Chronicles XXIX:11.

> Yours, O Lord, are the **glory**, and the **power**, and
> the **beauty**, and the **victory**, and the **splendor**, for
> all that is in the heavens and on the earth [is
> Yours]; Yours is the **kingdom** and [You are He]
> Who is exalted over everything as the Leader.

Magicians will note the qabalistic significance of the biblical
verse, which calls out six sephiroth: 4 (*glory*), 5 (*power*), 6
(*beauty*), 7 (*victory*), 8 (*splendor*) and 10 (*kingdom*). The
references to the sephiroth of Tiphareth, Netzach and Hod
are missing from the liturgical version and its magical
adaptation in the lesser pentagram ritual, both of which
substitute a cross for the simple descent of the sephiroth. In
addition, the Star Ruby version replaces the *kingdom*
(Malkuth) with the *phallus* (Yesod) and omits the liturgical
invocation of æonic time in favor of *IAO*, a formula of
Tiphareth.

The names with the pentagrams are entities corresponding to the components of Tetragrammaton, as
described in Chapter III of *Magick in Theory & Practice*. Chaos
is י the Father, Babalon ה the Mother, Eros ו the Son, and
Psyche ה the daughter. Each of them is represented
accordingly in the visions of Liber 418: Chaos in the 4th Aire,
Babalon in the 22nd, 15th and 2nd Aires, Eros in the 5th Aire,
and Psyche in the 9th and 4th. The Chaos-Babalon syzygy also
occurs in the Creed of Liber XV, and in Chapter 11 of *The
Book of Lies*. Although the identity is less than perfect, Chaos
and Babalon bear comparison to Phanes and Nyx in Orphic
cosmogony.

A *locus classicus* for Eros and Psyche is the fable that
stands as a centerpiece of the *Metamorphoses* (a.k.a. *The Golden
Ass*) of Apuleius. This couple has thus become subject
matter for a wide range of profane artworks and meditations.
An even earlier source, although with less vivid
personification, is the Platonic dialogue *Phaedrus,* doubtless
quite familiar to Frater Perdurabo inasmuch as his paper

"Energized Enthusiasm"—written at about the same time as the Star Ruby—is tacitly a commentary on it.

It is a curious fact that while the original lesser pentagram used four Hebrew names of four letters each, the Star Ruby violates this rule in precisely one instance: the name Babalon. Since it is a name of seven letters, it may be that there is a secret name of four (the four invisible to its seven visible), a name which may not be spoken among men, to which the magician indirectly appeals in this invocation.

The four differing styles of vocal production also reflect the formula of Tetragrammaton analyzed into the elemental kerubs, i.e. the "four living creatures" of Ezekiel and the Apocalypse, understood also as the fixed signs of the zodiac. The magician is to *roar* like a lion (י the fiery Leo), to *scream* like an eagle (ה the watery Scorpio), to *say* like a man (ו the airy Aquarius), and to *bellow* like a bull (ה the earthy Taurus). The later Commentary of Frater Perdurabo notes that "the Pentagram has the red colour of Geburah." I have added the letters in the center of the pentagrams, based on the substitution of ΧΑΟΣ for יהוה. They are individually colored based on the astrological correspondences for the voices and using the King Scale for their paths.

A Paian is merely a song of praise or tribute, and the simple Paian IO ΠΑΝ is one of the innovative elaborations that Frater Perdurabo added to the lesser pentagram ritual. In the present ritual, the Paian is fulfilled and amplified by the "analysis of the keyword P.A.N." derived from Chapter 1 of *The Book of Lies* ("The Sabbath of the Goat") and modeled on the analysis of I.N.R.I. in the lesser hexagram ritual. The sequence of the N.O.X. signs is taken from the Star Sapphire (Chapter 36 of *Lies*), which is also their order in the progression through the grades of A∴A∴ rather than the different sequence of the much later Liber V, where they are correlated to the names at the quarters of that ritual.

The long Greek passage that follows the Paian is an evocation of four orders of beings from the *Chaldaean Oracles*. Golden Dawn adept W. Wynn Westcott had edited a translation of this pseudo-Zoroastrian Neo-platonic mystery text. It also served as a source for several invocations in the Golden Dawn rituals. According to Westcott's "scheme" of the metaphysics of the *Oracles,* the three orders of Iynges, Synoches, and Teletarchai were "Intelligibles and Intellectuals in the Empyrean World" comprehended by the "Second Mind." The *Oracles* further points to a class of pure Daemons which are the divinized souls of men.* The concept is similar to the *augoeides,* or Holy Guardian Angel. And the Daemones are those humans who are in conscious possession of their particular genii.

These four orders—Iynges, Synoches, Teletarchae, and Daemones—are assigned by the Star Ruby to the four quarters, and thus this segment of the ritual parallels the establishment of the four pentagrams. However, the four pentagrams in the first half of the ritual are established in a counter-clockwise rotation (a circle), while the four "Chaldaean" orders are set out on latitudinal and longitudinal axes (a cross).

Following the evocation of the four orders, there is another Cross Qabalistic and a final apotropaism, so that the first half of the ritual is mirrored neatly in the second half. Thus from the outermost layer to the innermost, this ritual has a five-fold structure as follows:

1. Apotropaism
    2. Cross Qabalistic
        3. Pentagrams
            4. Paian
                (5. Analysis)
            4. Paian
        3. Evocation
    2. Cross Qabalistic
1. Apotropaism

---

* See number 91 in the Westcott edition.

Scholion on Performance

The symmetrical nature of the ritual permits the ready condensation of the ceremony. For an experienced practitioner, the initial apotropaism—identical with the final one—*includes* and thus subsumes all of the material that falls between the two. So in case of necessity, much of the effect of the entire ritual may be achieved through the apotropaism alone. A less radical abbreviation would take advantage of the manner in which the Cross Qabalistic surrounds and includes the work with the quarters and the Paian, and thus it would consist simply of the Cross Qabalistic preceded and followed by apotropaisms. This symmetry is also the justification for opening up the center of the central section, the Paian, to accommodate the added analysis of the keyword which is at the heart of the ritual in the present revision. The analysis may thus be omitted (as it always is by those to whom it is unknown) on the same principle as the condensations just described.

The first posture of the apotropaism is the Sign of Silence, which implies the assumption of the god-form of Harpocrates. Most importantly, this procedure involves imagining oneself as a child. Recollection of the sense of one's body in childhood is crucially helpful. All verbal thought and internal dialogue should be stilled while holding this sign, and the operator may luxuriate in it for a minute or more. Note that this initial Sign of Silence also sets a psychic baseline or point of calibration for the similar signs that conclude the projection of each pentagram.

When the words of the apotropaism are uttered, the god-form is released, but the magician's subtle body should then have acquired an enhanced coherence and plasticity for the actions that follow. The "great sweep" of the hand backward and outward may be conceived as an <u>arc</u>, a segment of a circle intended to complement symbolically the cruciform gesture which follows it.

The Cross Qabalistic may benefit from either of two sets of interesting practical considerations. The first is a particular form that may be assumed by the subtle body of the magician: the sacred gynander, as in the image of the Baphomet of Mendes according to Eliphas Levi's *Rituel de la Haute Magie*. With the word *Soi*, the magician identifies the pentagram as a seal or mark on his own forehead, the symbol of intelligence under the influence of the supernal triad represented by the torch and horns. *O Phalle* is directed to the caduceus rising from the loins of the figure. *Ischuros* and *Eucharistos* are the breasts, referring to the power and mercy with which the magician feeds his works. Finally, the two separated hands *Solve* and *Coagula* of the mystic androgyne are brought together, so that in the name of *IAO* the union of these two processes signals the ecstatic unfurling of the wings of the subtle body behind the *anahata* chakra.

Another approach to the Cross Qabalistic relies on color to help bring the sephirothic relationships into visual realization. With *Soi*, a silver-white light descends through the ajna chakra (attributed to Chokmah per *Liber 777*, column CXVIII). The colors of the other words follow from the Queen Scale, according to their sephirothic attributions. *O Phalle* is the purple Foundation of an equilateral triangle, where the upper corners, red *Ischuros* and blue *Eucharistos,* are the primary colors which blend into it. The triangle is thus super-imposed on a white cross, complementarily reminiscent of the altar implements in the Golden Dawn initiations, where the cross symbolizes mortality, and the triangle divinity. In this case, however, the triangle is point-downward, alluding to the deity Ra-hoor-khuit through his particular symbol. The three and four of the triangle and cross also evoke "Mysterious energy triform, mysterious matter in fourfold ... division": the alchemical *tria prima* and the four classical elements. Finally, with *LAO*, the third primary color is introduced, with a yellow Beauty as *centrum in centri trigono.*

To "imagine" the pentagrams may amount to a simplification of the lesser pentagram ritual, if they are visualized entire, rather than drawn in the air. However, it is possible that there is a distinct psychoactive value in the linear movement of the eyes that tends to accompany the manual inscription of a traditional *banishing earth pentagram,* which begins at the lower left point and proceeds clockwise. According to the "accessing cues" of some latter-day psychotechnicians, a typical person will rapidly access the following sequence of sensory channels as a result of the directions of the five lines of the pentagram: constructed visual imaging, kinesthetic feeling, recollected hearing, constructed interior hearing, and interior talking. This effect, if desired, can be retained by simply visualizing the process of drawing the pentagram in the forehead before projecting it in the Sign of the Enterer.

The establishment of the four pentagrams may be undertaken in light of the practical application of the formula of Tetragrammaton discussed in *Magick in Theory & Practice*. The pentagram for Chaos would then flame forth with a "swift and violent creative energy." The one for Babalon would emerge like "the irresistible force of a mighty river." The Eros pentagram would be expansive and penetrating, and the Psyche pentagram would form as "a crystallization resplendent with interior light." Each of these different modes of manifestation can be engaged after the individual pentagram is first imagined in the forehead, as the process by which it comes to occupy that quarter of space.

The Paian is a prayer to Pan, which Perdurabo's commentary to *The Book of Lies* calls "a generic name" for Truth. He is reflected in the inferior hebdomad and annihilated in the supernal triad (Chapter 11). That supernal annihilation is the "Night of Pan," which can also be understood as the mutual re-absorption of the creational syzygies in the apophatic ascent of the mystic. The reversed reflection of the Comedy of Pan is the Tragedy of Man. Where death and begetting (the letters N and X) are the supporters of the true cosmos (O!) in the supernals (Chapter 1), they are instead (as P and N) the oppressors of the ignorant microcosm (A) below the veil of the Abyss (Chapter 34).

In the analysis of the keyword P.A.N., the letters are identified with the initials of the Greek gods Priapos, Hades, and Nike, who correspond to the signs *puer, vir,* and *puella* which begin the N.O.X. sequence. That sequence is then executed in its full form, culminating in the sign *mater triumphans*. Thus it dramatizes the aspiration (or attainment) of the magician through the ranks of adeptship to the City of the Pyramids, as well as the trances of the mystic in an ascent to pleromatic annihilation. In the correct form of this sequence, the masculine desire for union/coition is transcended by the female desire for dissolution/parturition. (See

Lies, Chapter 3). Note too that a synthesis of the three gods in P.A.N. once more creates Baphomet, whom Eliphas Levi also identified with Pan: the phallus of Priapos, the horns of Hades, and the wings of Nike.

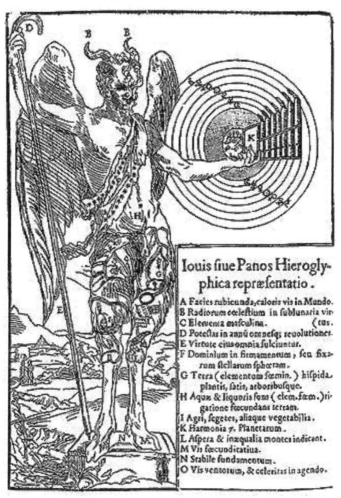

In the illustration above, an allegorical diagram of Pan from Athanasius Kircher's *Obeliscus Pamphilius* (1650), we also see the two implements peculiar to Pan: his crook and pipes, representing perhaps "Repulsion and attraction, will and love, right and left ... the forces, centrifugal and centripetal, male and female whereby God creates and redeems."[*]

An alternative to analyzing the keyword P.A.N. would be to recite the "Prologue of the Unborn" from Liber VII. This passage may certainly help to instill the ecstasy that is desirable for this keystone of the ceremonial arch. The N.O.X. signs can be deployed in it thus: *puer* for vv. 1-3; *vir* for vv. 4-8; *puella* for vv. 9-12; *mulier* for vv. 13-15; and *mater triumphans* for v. 16.

puer	Into my loneliness comes -- The sound of a flute in dim groves that haunt the uttermost hills. Even from the brave river they reach to the edge of the wilderness.
vir	And I behold Pan. The snows are eternal above, above -- And their perfume smokes upward into the nostrils of the stars. But what have I to do with these? To me only the distant flute, the abiding vision of Pan.
puella	On all sides Pan to the eye, to the ear; The perfume of Pan pervading, the taste of him utterly filling my mouth, so that the tongue breaks forth into a weird and monstrous speech. The embrace of him intense on every centre of pain and pleasure. The sixth interior sense aflame with the inmost self of Him,

---

[*] Anna Kingsford, "The Vision of Adonai," *Clothed with the Sun,* p. 181. See the discussion of Natural Sacraments, *supra.*

mulier	Myself flung down the precipice of being
	Even to the abyss, annihilation.
	An end to loneliness, as to all.
mater	Pan! Pan! Io Pan! Io Pan!
triumphans	

These suggestions for the pivot of the ceremony are entirely orthodox with respect to the ritual's goals and symbolic context, and they are effective in practice. They do also plainly exceed the instruction as written by Frater Perdurabo. As mentioned earlier, the telescoping symmetry of the ceremony permits such elaborations to be subsumed in any case, but it may be that the authorial intent was in keeping with the perspective and technique detailed in the fourteenth-century *Cloud of Unknowing* (chs. 38-39):

> A man who prays like this prays with all the height and depth and length of his spirit. His prayer is high, for he prays in the full power of his spirit; it is deep, for he has gathered all his understanding into this one little word; it is long, for if this feeling could endure he would go on crying out forever as he does now; it is wide, because with universal concern he desires for everyone what he desires for himself. ... We must pray, then, with all the intensity of our being in its height and depth and length and breadth. And not with many words but in a little word of one syllable.

The *Cloud* author goes on to suggest either "sin" or "God," but "Pan" covers both!

The long Greek evocation of the guardians has customarily presented great challenges to the imagination of practitioners of the Star Ruby. The *Chaldaean Oracles* themselves give very little detail on these entities, which are addressed in the fragmentary texts numbered 54 through 70 in the Westcott edition. There seems to have been no other attempt to employ them in modern magick. It may actually have been Frater Perdurabo's plan that this extended incantation in a dead language should serve as a "barbarous" passage, the incomprehensibility of which would arouse "the peculiar mental excitement required." But as in the case of the Cross Qabalistic, I offer two parallel ways of conceptualizing the evocation of the guardians, either of which can enrich the imagination in this phase of the ceremony.

The first approach relies on the straightforward identification of the Iynges, Synoches, and Teletarchae as the highest classes of metaphysical creatures in the Neoplatonic emanationism of the *Chaldaean Oracles*. It is simple enough to turn to the Neoplatonic *Hierarchies* of Pseudo-Dionysius, where the highest orders of angels are conveniently inventoried: the seraphim, kerubim, and ophanim. Like the Iynges, the seraphim are fiery beings. In fact, later revisions notwithstanding, the seraphim of ancient Hebrew lore were in fact *fiery serpents*, which can be identified with the radiant *Chnoubis* of the Gnostics, frequently referenced in Thelemic literature as the lion-serpent. The Synoches equate to the

kerubim, representatives of divine authority taking the form of great sphinx-like composite creatures with multiple pairs of wings. The Teletarchae are then the ophanim, interlocking systems of *wheels*, brilliant with countless eyes, most famously recounted in the vision of Ezekiel.[*] The Daemones, as discussed earlier, are those who are possessed of their genii,

---

[*] In G.R.S. Mead's treatment of the Chaldaean Oracles, the Ophanim are correlated to the *synoches* on account of the circular motion of the latter. See Mead, *Echoes from the Gnosis,* p. 350.

and thus as a transcendent class they are equivalent to "saints" as understood by Christian and Islamic Neoplatonists. In keeping with traditional representations, such saints might be imagined as white-robed and crowned with light, i.e. haloes or nimbuses. (Note that this visual convention predates Christianity and was common in classical paganism.)

In order to conceive the guardians as classes, rather than individuals, I picture *five* seraphic fire-serpents (the key-number of the pentagram ritual) for the Iynges. My Teletarchae are a group of *four* ophanim. For the Synoches, I imagine a *pair* of kerubim, as on the Ark of the Covenant. And my Daemones appear in a *triad*, like the triumvirate of the adepts. The particular Daemones that I visualize most often in this manner are Paschal Beverly Randolph, Anna Kingsford, and Aleister Crowley.

A different take on the guardians follows from the observation that the names of the orders seem to reflect offices or ceremonial roles in a classical mystery cult. The *Iynges* (from the name of a bird used in divination) might be oracles or soothsayers. The word *synoches* is sometimes read as "constraints," and these could be the officers in charge of marshalling candidates and attendees. *Teletarchae* has the literal meaning of "governors of initiatory rites," and these would be those who actually administered initiation. In this reading, the Daemones would necessarily be the *teletes*, the "perfected ones" who had received full initiation.

When I approach the ritual as an O.T.O. initiate in these terms, it is with an understanding of the four classes of guardians as initiatory functions rather than temple personnel. I picture the Iynges as the *words of the Holy Books* cascading down before me, like a shower of gems. (C.f. Liber LXV I:2-5) The Teletarchae behind me are my initiators, and their initiators, *et cetera*, reaching back in braided chains to TO MEGA THERION. The Synoches are emblematic personifications of my oaths on my right hand, and the Daemones at my left are the members of the Sanctuary of the Gnosis, both known and unknown to me, who "must veil their glory in a cloud of darkness."

The evocation of the guardians concludes with an affirmation of the persistence of the four pentagrams that were established in the first half of the ceremony. To these are added a pair of hexagrams, above and below the ritualist, completing the enclosure in the third dimension. Since the

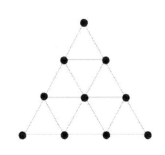

set of four elements were symbolized in Greek by the Pythagorean tetraktys (see the diagram on the left), in the form of a triangle, the combination of the four elemental pentagrams results in four equilateral triangles, one with a point in each cardinal direction. The east- and west-pointing triangles combine to form a hexagram underfoot, while the north- and south-pointing triangles combine to form one overhead.

The color of these hexagrams should be the solar gold of Tiphareth, just as the pentagrams have the martial red of Geburah. And I add a central letter, as I did for the pentagrams. The letters are midnight blue for Nuit above and emerald green for Hadit below, and each is a *tau,* as shown in the "Double Triangle of Solomon" represented in the second chapter of Eliphas Levi's *Dogme de la Haute Magie.* The earliest precedent for this *tau*-in-a-hexagram that I have located is the diagram which is fig. 155 of Crowley's *Goëtia.* Each *tau* has the value of 300, and their sum 600 is also the value for κοσμος (world or universe), η θεοτης (the godhead), and ευπραγια (success), among other terms. Note that the ritualist himself stands in the form of a tau, thus completing a set of three crosses "in the column": the hierophantic cross. The tripled *tau* value of 900 is the numerical value of the letter *rho*, which corresponds to the lineal figure of the Hexagram, thus confirming the attribution (see *Liber 777,* columns XLIX & LI). In addition, 900 is the value of το ζυγον (the union) and φοινος (bloody, c.f. *Liber Legis* III:11).

The ending Cross Qabalistic is identical to the beginning one. But the ending apotropaism's Sign of Silence has a somewhat different effect than the one in the opening. Instead of transitioning into the further mechanisms of imagining in the Cross Qabalistic, the release of the god-form of Harpocrates in this case results in the exciting sensation of being a child suddenly acquiring the gift of a fully-developed adult body with all of its physical powers, leaving the magician

> with mirth
> ... and with thanksgiving,
> To do [his] pleasure on the earth
> Among the legions of the living.   (*XLIV*)

Scholion on Gematria

The only comment provided by Frater Perdurabo to the original publication of the Star Ruby in *The Book of Lies* was a footnote to the phrase Ω ΦΑΛΛΕ, to the effect that "The secret sense of these words is to be sought in the numeration thereof." That remark is a clear invitation to the method of esoteric exegesis called *gematria*. It so happens that not only that phrase, but words and formulae throughout the ritual can be illuminated in this manner. Many contemporary magicians are accustomed to working with Hebrew gematria, but its application in Greek, while in fact older and more robust, is comparatively exotic.[*]

The Apotropaism

ΑΠΟ	151 ομμα (eye), κονια (dust, ashes)
ΠΑΝΤΟΣ	701 ταυ (T in full, mark), κελευσμα (command, shout)
ΚΑΚΟΔΑΙΜΟΝΟΣ	556 φημη (speech; oracle), ελασσον (lesser)
Total	1408 Ηχω (Echo, lament), Σωτηρ (Savior), ερμηνευω (translate, explain)

---

[*] Excellent material for study on this topic can be found in *The Greek Qabalah* by Kieren Barry and *Jesus Christ, Sun of God* by David Fideler.

The preceding table shows a full set of correspondences for the numeric values of the words in the apotropaism. For each word, a numerical value has been produced by summing the isopsephic values of the individual letters. Then other Greek terms with the same value are listed. The cumulative sense of these terms is surprisingly coherent. "You are dust to my eye," (i.e. irritating and negligible) "I mark the inferior ones with my commanding speech." The total value has the most interesting correspondences. The plaintive sense of the Greek *Echo* suits the dismissal of the "bad spirits" or *cacodaemons*, and alludes to the repetitive nature of this part of the ceremony. *Soter* was an epithet of Dionysos and other gods who presided over the antique mystery cults, long before it was co-opted by Christianity, and *hermeneou* suggests the "translation" from profane conditions to the sacred circumstance of the rite.

The Cross Qabalistic

ΣΟΙ	280 ιος (serpent venom, an arrow)
Ω ΦΑΛΛΕ	1366 η φωνη (the voice), κτεις + φαλλος (*kteis* + *phallos*)
ΙΣΧΥΡΟΣ	1580 ο ιχωρ (the ichor: godblood)
ΕΥΧΑΡΙΣΤΟΣ	1886 ρυπαρευω (make foul)
ΙΑΩ	811 αιω (to perceive, know, breathe), περιστεραι (doves), μαστος (breast, pap), αστερες (stars)

Total	5923
Arithmetic Mean	1185 τειχος (wall, fortress), ζωηρος (vivid, lively)
Geometric Mean	984 πατρια + λιθολογος (lineage + stonemason)
Harmonic Mean	746 εξουσια (free will, liberty), χαραγμα (mark, character)

In the Cross Qabalistic, the individual words do have some interesting values. Certainly, isopsephic significance is to be expected of an important formula like ΙΑΩ, where *aio* points to the action of the *ruach*, the "doves" are suggestive of central symbol of the O.T.O. lamen, and the *mastos/asteres* correspondences seem to invoke the "milk of the stars." The idea of ΣΟΙ as relating to "serpent venom" is especially appealing in light of the central theme of Liber LXV, thus helping to confirm the *augoeides* or personal genius (rather than a more general godhead) as the addressee of this invocation. Almost paradoxically, the secret sense of the vocative Ω ΦΑΛΛΕ includes the sum of the nominatives *kteis* and *phallos*.

The total value of the Cross Qabalistic is too high to permit easy correlations by means of standard references. But in this case, since the individual terms of the formula are deployed separately across the body of the magician, there are some further composite values that may be of use, as in any case where there are clearly distinct or separated components in a larger formula.

The arithmetic mean, or average, is simply the value most *common* to the set—if all of the excesses are cancelled against the lacks, each would adjust to the arithmetic mean. It is thus the common orientation of all the values. In the case of the Cross Qabalistic, we might conclude that each term serves to both "fortify" and "enliven" a sephirah within the magician's sphere of sensation.

According to Pythagorean tradition, the <u>geometric mean</u> relates to *space*, and thus its value suggests *where* the magician is placed by the formula. In this case, the speaker claims "descent" from a "mason," and thus the inherited power and authority to build fortifications!

The <u>harmonic mean</u> is associated with *time*, so its value characterizes the change worked by the formula. The correspondences here are quite lucid: by means of the Cross Qabalistic, the magician asserts his free will, and marks himself with a character (the cross, or cross and triangle per remarks above) by which that liberty is signified.

The Pentagrams

ΧΛΟΣ	871 σκοταιος (secret), φαρος (web), Φαρος (ancient lighthouse of Alexandria), αφρος (foam)
ΒΑΒΑΛΟΝ	156 γαρ αιμα (for blood), γαρ μαια (for mother), προγαστριδιον (apron), καλα + κακαι + ανα (beautiful + wicked women + on high)
ΕΡΩΣ	1105 φιλοπολεμος (combative), μετανατης (wanderer)

ΨΥΧΗ	1708 στυγεω (abhor)
Total	3840
Arithmetic Mean	960 συμμιξις (marriage), το κυκλον (the circle), Στυξ (Styx, detestation)
Geometric Mean	712 ραχια (surge), σφαγη (ritual slaughter), υβρις (*hubris*, wantonness), παντοιας (everything, universe), αγγελους (angels)
Harmonic Mean	442 εκϲαϲις (*sic*, ecstasy), μακαριος (blessed), οολβος (the bliss), θαλασσα (sea)

Through some simple addition of letter values, we discover that our "secret and ineffable Lord, in his name CHAOS," actually equates to *skotaios* or "secret." The "web" or weave that is *pharos* might relate to the Latin equivalent *textus,* in suggesting the distinctions and relationships inherent in the Word. *Pharos* was also an island near Alexandria that gave its name to the lighthouse built on it: one of the "seven wonders" of the ancient world.

The correspondences for ΒΑΒΑΛΟΝ speak strikingly for themselves. ΕΡΩΣ should be considered armed and unpredictable, according to gematria, as well as by general consensus. The sole gematria equivalence for ΨΥΧΗ seems at first a little off-key, but if these names are identified with the corresponding parts of the soul, then Psyche is the *nephesch* (see Revelation XII:11), and therefore the "animal soul" concerned with appetites and fears.

The arithmetic mean yields some very intelligible correspondences. Any neighboring pair of the names can be taken as linked to each other in a *symmixis* or "marriage." Each of the names is placed on "the circle" that the magician paces in order to establish them. That circle is identified with the river Styx: the boundary between the exterior world of the living and the hidden world of the dead that is Hades (the heart of P.A.N.). The interior of the circle is thus established as the world of the shades and spirits, an interworld of dream and vision.*

The geometric mean of the pentagram names characterizes the interworld in which the magician has placed himself. It is not a safe and drowsy retreat. Quite to the contrary, it involves a "surge" of divine presence to form a precinct fit for operations of "ritual slaughter!" It is a crowded "universe" where "angels" are at home, and where living humans venture at peril. Is it *hubris* that brings the magician here?

But the net effect of this change does not daunt the ritualist. The result of placing the pentagrams is that he experiences "ecstasy," he is "blessed," he receives "the bliss" from the great "sea" of Binah, through his own *neshemah* or intuitive faculty. Restriction be unto Choronzon in the name of BABALON!

---

* Valuable reading in this connection includes *Spiritual Body and Celestial Earth* by Henry Corbin, as well as *The Dream and the Underworld* by James Hillman.

The Syzygies

Higher Syzygy	
ΧΑΟΣ + ΒΑΒΑΛΟΝ	1027 ο μαγευτης (the magician)
Arithmetic Mean	512 τα ισα (the equalities), παυλα (rest, end), παναπλος (delicate), το μαννα (the manna), η υγρα (the waters)
Geometric Mean	367 εναργης (visible), ποσθη (penis, foreskin), Ηρακλης (Heracles)
Harmonic Mean	265 κλεις (key), απολογια (verbal defense)
Stooping Syzygy	
ΒΑΒΑΛΟΝ + ΕΡΩΣ	1261 τιμορια (vengeance)
Arithmetic Mean	630 παμφαγε (all-devourer), επιθειασμος (adjuration), τιμιος (precious)
Geometric Mean	415 αγυια (way, path), δεισιδαιμονια (religion, propitiation of spirits), παιδεραστης (lover of boys), παναγιος (all holy), αδοκιμος (rejected)

Harmonic Mean	273 εξης (next, serially), η κλεις (the key), βαξις (oracle, speech)
Lower Syzygy	
ΕΡΩΣ + ΨΥΧΗ	2813
Arithmetic Mean	1407 ζωτικος (vital, living), σκοτιζω (to be or become dark)
Geometric Mean	1374 το τεχνημα (the work), δουλοω (to enslave)
Harmonic Mean	1342
Rising Syzygy	
ΨΥΧΗ + ΧΑΟΣ	2579
Arithmetic Mean	1289 ο ιχθυς (the fish), Ηφαιστος (Hephaistos)
Geometric Mean	1220 τελειοω (to perfect), ευωδια (fragrance, sweet savor), κυω (to conceive), μωροις (by the fools)
Harmonic Mean	1154

The four names identified with the pentagrams and delivered with the Sign Horus are highly charged, and their interrelationships or "marriages" deserve further exploration. These are effectively *latent* features of the Star Ruby. They could be activated through the Star Sapphire, understanding ΧΑΟΣ as PATER, ΒΑΒΑΛΟΝ as MATER, ΕΡΩΣ as FILIUS, and ΨΥΧΗ as FILIA. Since these values are more potential than actual in the work of this ceremony, an exhaustive study of the correspondences would be out of place here. Still, there are a few that bear remark. The fact that the sum of Chaos and Babalon equals the Greek phrase for "the magician" is evocative of the declaration in Liber B that "the Magus is Love, and bindeth together That and This in His Conjuration." The sum of Babalon and Eros as *timoria* suggests the shedding of the blood of the saints into the cup of the "vengeance" of the Mother. In both the Higher and Stooping Syzygies, the harmonic means of the two terms create a correspondence with a Greek word or phrase for "key." For the Lower and Rising Syzygies, correspondences are in much shorter supply, but the values for the geometric means are still somewhat provocative.

The "marriages" just listed omit two further possible pairings. The masculine pentagram names are latitudinal, positioned towards the two horizons of the east and west. The longitudinal names are feminine, placed at the tropics where the circle turns from the south and north. As with the previous combinations, these are not emphasized by the course of the ritual, but the latitudinal names may be taken to inform the underfoot hexagram, while the longitudinal ones relate to the hexagram overhead.

Latitudinal Names	
ΧΑΟΣ + ΕΡΩΣ	1976 μεινωταυρος (Minotaur)
Arithmetic Mean	988
Geometric Mean	981 σοφιας (of wisdom), ο αξον (the axis), το στομα (the mouth)
Harmonic Mean	974 υποθεσις (foundation), μεταβολη ηλιον ("change of the sun," i.e. eclipse)

Longitudinal Names	
ΒΑΒΑΛΟΝ + ΨΥΧΗ	1864
Arithmetic Mean	932 καλμπτα (veil), φαρμακος (one who prepares poisons or medicines)
Geometric Mean	516 Εστια (*Hestia*, hearth)
Harmonic Mean	286 σκηνη (temple, house), μειλας (black)

The sum of the masculine names in the East and West is the value of "Minotaur," the child of Pasiphaë, often appreciated by the vulgar as a monstrous calamity visited on the house of Minos because of his refusal to sacrifice to Poseidon a bull—which then sired the Minotaur. The story of Pasiphaë is in fact one of the chief classical illustrations of the "formula called *The Beast conjoined with the Woman*" that pertains to the grade of Major Adept, and it is evoked in the Prophet's vision of the 16th Aire. In his Cefalu diaries, however, 666 alluded to the Minotaur as a figure for the result of male homoerotic magick:

> This truth learn thou, Genesthai, brother of mine!
> Learn this, thou Bull in my Pasiphae-pasture!
> Learn thou that I, worn out with wallowing
> though I be, or seem to be to thee, can breed thee
> Minotaur, while those meek calves that tempt thee
> with soft comeliness will but give birth to their
> base kind, to kine potential of no more than milk,
> veal, beef, and leather.[*]

The word *sophias* could suggest the qabalistic Chokmah. On the other hand, if understood as "of Sophia," the celestial mate of the adept according to the traditions of sophianic mysticism, then it could indicate Babalon as the Mother who alternately claims both the Father and the Son as her own. The original Greek word *hypothesis*—literally "set under"— meant "foundation," and might profitably be interpreted to reference the sephirah Yesod, and thus to have a phallic significance. It shares some of the ambivalence of the Minotaur on this count.

The geometric mean of the feminine names has the value of the goddess Hestia, which is also the Greek word for "hearth." Forlong Dux observes that the Indo-European etymology of the word is a root meaning "to shine" or "to

---

[*] Crowley (ed. Symonds and Grant), *The Magical Record of the Beast 666,* p. 296, diary entry of 12 December 1920.

burn," and that the cults of Hestia, Vesta, and cognate goddesses always involved the tending of an eternal flame. It is this sense of guarding the sacred energy that should govern the interpretation of this value, rather than a more pedestrian idea of domesticity. Likewise, *skene* meant "temple" as well as "house." Hestia was, in fact, typically represented as wearing a "veil."

The Paian

IO	80 Π (the letter P), βοη (war-cry), ηλαλια (the speech), Αθηναια (of Athens, Athena)
ΠΑΝ	131 αμοιβη (change), γονη (birth, womb, offspring), θαομαι (to suck), ιερεια (priestess), πελεια (dove)
Total	211 ισα (equilibrium), θεραπεια (healing), γης (of the earth)

The cry of rapture IO has the same value as the war-cry *boë,* and both are subsumed in the concept of *he lalia,* meaning not necessarily linguistic speech, but any vocal utterance. By means of the value of the letter *pi,* the number 80 corresponds to the various possible mean-ings of the 27th path of the Tree of Life (i.e. פ), which includes a large set of martial correspondences harmonizing with *boë.*

The value for ΠΑΝ suggests the "birth" of a Master of the Temple, and giving the Child "to suck" in the sign *mater triumphans.* This initiatory transformation is the ultimate "change" toward which the A∴A∴ guides aspirants. The qabalistic path of the "priestess" is the 13th, joining Kether to Tiphareth, the direct descent along which:

> Cast down through The Abyss is the Light, the Rosy Cross, the rapture of Union that destroys, that is The Way. The Rosy Cross is the Ambassador of Pan.[*]

This descending Rosy Cross might also be compared to the cruciform dove that descends in the center of the lamen of O.T.O.

The total value of the phrase IO ΠAN identifies it as the point of "equilibrium" inserted by Frater Perdurabo to serve the fulcrum of the ritual. Equilibrium is marked as an essential condition of attainment throughout the literature of Thelema.[†] Indeed, the initials O.T.O. and A∴A∴ alike are equilibrated combinations of letters, with each letter equilibrated on its own axis.

In Liber CD, the fifth column gives the methods of equilibrium suited to the different stages of attainment. The neophyte setting out seeks balance "among the Shells." As we read in *Magick*, "… any idea not … equilibrated is below the Abyss, contains in itself unmitigated duality or falsehood, and is to that extent qliphothic and dangerous."[‡] The graphic emblem of this discipline among the *qliphoth* is the Moon Trump of the Tarot, with a running stream (a *cursus,* "course" or "curse") flanked by the hounds Love and Death, which are the letters P and N of P.A.N., with the aspirant's own microcosm figured as the A.[§]

---

[*] Crowley, *The Book of Lies,* ch. 11.
[†] Direct instruction of a general sort on this topic is given in Libri XXX, XLI, and XC, and Liber IV, Pt. III, cap. VIII, among others.
[‡] *Magick,* p. 182.
[§] See *The Book of Lies,* ch. 34.

The Adepts of the Magick of Light must exercise equilibrium "on the path," as represented in the Adjustment Trump. In contrast to the open area filled with drops of blood in the Moon Trump, the middle field of Adjustment shows a woman or goddess with a sword along her central axis. The design is structured around that of the Masonic jewel of a Prince of Jerusalem (figure at left): a diamond enclosing a sword and balances, another modification of which appears as a lamen in *Magick* (at right). In the Masonic jewel, the letters D and Z (for Darius and Zerubbabel) appear over the cups of the balances. In both redesigns, the lamen and the trump, the letters are *alpha* and *omega*, as the first and the last. Adding the letters of the Thelemic design to those in the Masonic jewel yields the Hebrew words אל and עז, signifying insubstantiality and solidity.

The cups of the balances are the testes and the sword is the phallus. Thus the testes contain the extremes of human experience *in potentia*, from beginning (A) to end (Ω). They hold the vital principle of the dyad, the chromosomal division into two types to be realized through their subsequent union. The context of that union is represented by the enclosing diamond—or vesica. Being "on the path," the adepts have grasped ideas that are both "positive and negative, active and passive, male and female," and thus "fit

207

to exist above the Abyss" in the Night of Pan.* Ultimately, the Adjustment trump, with its phallus-bearing goddess, can be seen as yet another form of the Baphometic gynander.

The corresponding values for "healing" and "of the earth" are together suggestive of *Liber Legis* I:53. Equilibrated initiation not only serves to redeem the individual, but to regenerate the world. It is the kiss toward Hadit (I) from Nuit (O), passing through and reconstituting the universe (ΠΑΝ) which lies between the asymptotes of all-encompassing continuity and atomic individuality.

Analysis of P.A.N.

ΠΡΙΑΠΟΣ	541 βλαστη (bud), το καλον (the beautiful), πραγματεια (operation, work), ιπποτα (knight, horseman), το αορ (the sword), ταλις (maiden)
ΑΔΗΣ	213 ααγης (unbroken), ακαρπια (barrenness)
ΝΙΚΗ	88 πη (how, whence)
Total	842 φοβος (fear), τραυμα (wound), χασμα (chasm, pit)
Arithmetic Mean	281 μας (whole, entire), οσια (divine law), στερνον (heart), κοπρια (filth), γοης (howling; wizard)

---

* Again, see *Magick,* p. 182.

Geometric Mean	216 επιμιξια (intercourse), η πνοη (the breath)
Harmonic Mean	168 η παλαμη (the force), μονη (abode), νομη (pasture), δηλεομαι (to devastate)

Although these three names were not part of the original Star Ruby, I have provided their correspondences because of their importance to the present revision. The words corresponding to the value for ΠΡΙΑΠΟΣ (duality, or conception), include terms fitting the god of gardens, such as "bud," which should be read with reference to Chapter 86 of *Liber Aleph*, as well as "the beautiful," and the "work" of the gardener which is the task of a Master of the Temple. A second set of terms brings to mind an armed "knight" and his relations with a "maiden." The god ΑΔΗΣ (energy, or preservation) is characterized by his invisibility, his "unbroken" grasp on his treasures which include human souls, and the "barrenness" of the winter earth after his rape of Kore. His realm is the fatal interiority of persons and events, the timeless world of the ancestors. The sole correspondence listed for ΝΙΚΗ (death, or birth) is, admittedly, not very illuminating.

The total of these values, an expanded form of ΠΑΝ, corresponds to the *panic* or "fear" that the god instills in mortals. (Note also the translation of φοβος as פחד, a title of Geburah with the value of 93.) The value of *chasma* suggests the Abyss which is known as "Consciousness" and "The Universe" (*Lies,* chapter 10), and which is a "wound" in the unity of the Real.

The arithmetic mean indicates that each of the component gods is "whole," and an integral expression of "divine law." Although it appears by position that Hades is the "heart" of the formula, each of them are entitled to the center in a sort of holographic arrangement. Each of these constituents of the demonized shepherd-god Pan is equally a sort of forbidden "wizardry" (*goes* is the root of *goetia*) or "filth" that has been abominated by the worshippers of the slave-gods. These are the Idol, the Devil, and the Goddess: a most sacred Trinity, the principal theological operators of the unconscious. In this aspect, they even correspond to the Great Ones of *Liber Legis*: the "visible object of worship" Ra-hoor-khuit, the "secret Serpent" Hadit, and the "Queen of Space" Nuit.

The geometric mean suggests the "intercourse" between the magician and his genius which empowers this ritual, and to which the practitioner aspires in the Paian. "The breath" is *spirit, pneuma, ruach, ruh, nefesh, nafs* &c. Just as Tetragrammaton-Elohim first "breathed into his nostrils the breath of life" and limitation (Genesis II:7), so the Holy Guardian Angel breathes the dissolving breath of the infinite into the spirit of the magician. As Adonai speaks in Liber LXV (I:15), "I breathe, and there is infinite dis-ease in the spirit," glossed by 666 as: "Life disturbs the placidity of the mind's acceptance of dead symbols as reality."

The correspondences for the harmonic mean suggest that the result is a paradox: "the force" capable of "devastation" creates a "pasture" (suited to pastoral Pan) for the "abode" of the magician.

The Guardians

ΙΥΓΓΕΣ	621 ο φιλια (the love), σαρκικος (fleshly), ρυομαι (to rescue)
ΤΕΛΕΤΑΡΧΑΙ	1352 αφωνα (consonants), χαμψαι (sacred Egyptian crocodiles)
ΣΥΝΟΧΕΣ	1525 = 61 × 25
ΔΑΙΜΟΝΕΣ	380 κοπις (dagger), τοι (truly)
Total	3878
Arithmetic Mean	969 ειδωλον (image), πληροφορια (abundance, full assurance), μεγας ειρευς (high priest), αρχιποιμην (chief shepherd, cf. II Peter V.4)
Geometric Mean	835 φαιδιμος (shining, glorious), εικο (to retire, go home)
Harmonic Mean	710 ψι (the letter Ψ in full), πιστον (faithful, true), προθυμια (willingness, desire), Πνευμα Αγιον (Holy Spirit)

The individual values of the guardian classes yield correspondences that are difficult to interpret. The mean values are another story.

The corresponding terms *eidolon* and *plerophoria* for the arithmetic mean indicate that each quarter's guardians should indeed appear visually as an "image" to give the magician "full assurance" of the efficacy of the ceremony. As 666 remarked to his Agapé Lodge pupils regarding the archangels in the lesser pentagram ritual: "note well that they should appear and if the ritual is properly performed do appear." Nor does this remark prohibit the active application of the imaginative faculty; in the same memo he wrote, "You can figure out for yourself the forms of the Angels, or rather the Archangels," proceeding to outline the customary Golden Dawn procedure for building up the image of an angel from the correspondences of the letters of its name in Hebrew. The further correspondence of *megas hiereus* indicate that the guardians are all invested with the æonic power of the Priest of the Princes, whose initiative made them a part of this ritual. And while *archipoimen* could metaphorically refer to the same hierophantic office, it also serves to denote the power and position of the "chief shepherd" Pan.

The correspondences for the geometric mean indicate that when the magician has been enclosed in his "consecrated box," as Perdurabo called the outcome of the pentagram ritual in a 1914 EV letter to *The Occult Review*, the lineal figures should be gloriously "shining." He is then in a position to be fully "at home" in his astral circumstances.

The letter *psi* indicated by the value of the harmonic mean was traditionally used as an abbreviation for *psyche* or "soul." This phase of the ceremony has confirmed and consummated the soul's "willingness" to be "true" to its genius, integrating its powers through the formulae of the New Law. If the "cloven tongues like as of fire"— qabalistically ש—on each of the faithful in the Pentecost legend were a sign of the indwelling of the "Holy Spirit,"

212

how much more so are the complete array of six stars (four pentagrams and two hexagrams) with their total of thirty-two points, corresponding to the complete thirty-two Paths of Wisdom. In the *Sepher Yetzirah,* these thirty-two paths are correlated to the thirty-two teeth of a human mouth, and שׁ is verily a single tooth!

Parting Caution and Blessing

In Aleister Crowley's first rewriting of the lesser pentagram ritual, a verse paraphrase entitled "The Palace of the World," he added a note to the effect that

> Those who regard this ritual as a mere device to invoke or banish spirits, are unworthy to possess it. Properly understood, it is the Medicine of Metals and the Stone of the Wise.

Certainly, such a judgment pertains even more strongly to this ritual of blazing star, reformulated for the use of the adherents of Θελημα. But whether or not the practitioner appreciates its true value, repeated practice of the ceremony has the effect of organizing and strengthening the personal aura of the magician until it becomes perfectly equilibrated and adamantine.

The Benediction of the All-Begetter, All-Devourer be upon thee.

ΑΠΟ ΠΑΝΤΟΣ ΚΑΚΟΔΑΙΜΟΝΟΣ.

Angelic Phoenix

This is an Enochian-language version of the Mass of the Phoenix, intended for the private celebration of a Thelemite. He or she begins at sunset, standing bare-breasted before an altar on which are the Burin, Bell, Thurible, and two Cakes of Light. These represent the five senses (as in the Eucharist of the G.D. Neophyte): touch, sound, sight, taste and smell.

———————

Make sign of Horus directed to the West.

> Ils RA, ds tas aqlo elzap
> G tabges ors!

Make sign of Harpocrates.

Take up Bell in right hand, Thurible in left.

> Ol harg lvsdi Raasi siaion
> Erm olprit od nidali g zien!

Strike battery 333-55555-333 on bell; place Fire in Thurible.

> Oali Lviahe, ol iolci Lvciftias,
> Gohvs nonasci cicles:
> ABRAHADABRA

Strike battery 333-55555-333 on Bell.

Light Thurible, replacing the vanished sunlight with the light of Magick.

> Emna ol ecrin Iad: Noromi,
> A dooain ovof peripsol!
> Vls sonf, vls geh lansh.
> Emna i vgear, emna i cnila.
> Iolcam nothoa ors vi ror!
> Obelisong qting od avavox!
> Ar L de gon momao
> Emna ti saamir zimz. AMEN

Place first Cake on Thurible.

> Ol ialpon obloc,
> Oecrin de dooain:
>
> Ol sonf vorsag goho Iad balt lonsh
> Calz vonpho sobra z-ol ror i ta nazps
> Od graa ta malprg ds hol-q
> Qaa nothoa zimz od commah
> Ta nobloh zien soba thil gnonp prge
> Aldi ds vrbs obleh g rsam
> Casarm ohorela taba Pir ds zonrensg
> Cab erm Iadnah pilah farzm
> Znrza adna gono Iadpil ds hom od
> Toh soba ipam lu ipamis ds
> Loholo vep zomd poamal od bogpa
> Aai ta piap piamol od vaoan zacare
> E ca od zamran odo cicle
> Qaa zorge lap zirdo noco
> Mad hoath Iaida.

Strike battery 333-55555-333 on Bell.

Make sign on breast with Burin: an inverted Tau.

> Micma zir cnila saanir
> vrbs a cormf siaion

Touch wound with second Cake.

> Ol prdzar cnila, vgear i ednas,
> Sapa olora siaion!

Eat second Cake, and take Oath as follows:.

> Abramg vgear, ol zvrza
> Ta zirdo vep oecrini.
> Ge rit, ge oalim,
> Ohorela: THELEMA

Strike battery 333-55555-333 on Bell.

ABRAHADABRA
Ol zimii a ohio,
A moz zir tas,
Ar ol fisis qvasahi caosgi
Aaf tom ds hom.

Exit the temple.

Threefold Eucharist

This solo Eucharist of Three Elements uses texts derived from point 15 of Liber Turris and Crowley's Rite of Jupiter.

A double-cube altar is clothed in purple. It is set with a lit candle; filled cup of water; paten bearing a single grape, a morsel of chocolate, and a roasted, salted nut; a dagger; a scourge; and a chain. The dagger is on the far side of the altar, towards the Boleskine kiblah. (If desired, a copy of the Stele of Revealing may be set up apart from the altar in the direction of the kiblah as well.) These are arranged on the altar so that they take the following places in a qabalistic scheme (see diagram):

- The dagger (1) has its handle to the right, and represents the path of *daleth*, crossed by the path of *gimel*.
- The cup (3) represents the sephirah *Chesed*.
- The candle (2) represents the sephirah *Geburah*.
- The paten (4) represents the sephirah *Tiphareth*.
- The chain (6) represents the path of *nun*.
- The scourge (5) represents the path of *ayin*.

The celebrant is shirtless in black pants and a black skull-cap or brimless hat.

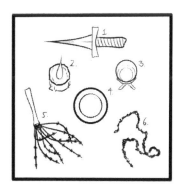

I. OPENING

Do what thou wilt shall be the whole of the Law.

I have at hand the Mystery
Of triform primal energy.

It is my will that these be wrought
Into my every deed and thought.

Love is the law, love under will.

II. INVOCATIONS

Fercula nostra Deum sapiant,
Horus et influat in pateras;
seria, ludicra, verba, iocos,
denique quod sumus aut agimus,
trina superne regat pietas.

*("May our dishes savor of God, and Horus be poured into
our bowls; may all things grave or light, our talk, our cheer,
all that we are or do, be governed by the threefold love from on
high.")*

Sulphur, Salt, and Mercury:
Which is master of the three?

Salt is Lady of the Sea;
Lord of Air is Mercury.

Now by God's grace here is salt
Fixed beneath the violet vault.

Place chain around neck.

Now by God's love purge it through
With our right Hermetic dew.

Cut breast with dagger.

218

Now by God wherein we trust
Be our sophic salt combust.

Scourge self eleven times.

Circumambulate the altar once deosil.

Then at last the Eye shall see
Three in One and One in Three,

Sulphur, Salt, and Mercury,
Crowned by Heavenly Alchemy!

To the One who sent the Seven
Glory in the Highest Heaven!

To the Seven who are the Ten
Glory on the Earth, Amen!

III. CONSECRATIONS

Place right hand over water.

Aqua est, que occidit et vivificat.

("It is water that kills and makes alive.")

Place right hand over paten.

Dicunt sapientes: Tria et Tria sunt unum.
Deinde dixerunt: in uno sunt tria.

("Therefore the wise say: Three and Three are one. Further they said: in one there are three.")

There is no law beyond Do what thou wilt.

IV. CONSUMMATIONS

Drink water.

How should I cease from lethargy?

Eat nut, drink again.

How should I quench activity?

Eat chocolate, drink again.

How should I give up ecstasy?

Eat grape, drink again.

Let this Royal Alchemy
Work upon itself in me.

Sulphur, Salt, and Mercury:
I am master of the three!

Hic sancto satiatus
ex propheta iustorum
capiet cibos virorum,
qui fructum Domino metunt perenni.

*("Then will he receive from the holy prophet the food of
righteous men who reap the harvest for their everlasting
Master, and will be satisfied.")*

V. Closing

Move to the far side of the altar, and turn around to face it.

Do what thou wilt shall be the whole of the Law.

I have within the Mystery
Of triform primal energy.

My word is said, my will is done,
Mine is the glory of the Sun.

Love is the law, love under will.

Features and Formulæ of the Gnostic Mass

There is little mistaking the fact that Aleister Crowley's Gnostic Mass is the chief sacramental activity of Ecclesia Gnostica Catholica. So much is this the case that in many areas there seems to be nothing to the Church itself other than the repeated, little-varying enactment of the Mass, and E.G.C. clergy as such are often viewed (and encouraged to view themselves) primarily as ritualists specializing in this single, uniform operation. The consolidation of the church hierarchy in the U.S. and increased intercommunication among local groups has led to greater consistency in the presentation of the Mass. At the same time, the Mass itself allows for a certain measure of variation in performance, and it practically demands a wide range of interpretive strategies. The following essays and papers are dedicated to examining many of these practical and theoretical issues and offering them for the use and contemplation of clergy.

Conditions for Eucharistic Magick

> With regard to the preparations for such Sacraments, the Catholic Church has maintained well enough the traditions of the true Gnostic Church in whose keeping the secrets are.
>
> **Chastity** is a condition; **fasting** for some hours previous is a condition; an earnest and continual **aspiration** is a condition. Without these antecedents even the Eucharist of the One and Seven is partially—though such is its intrinsic virtue that it can never be wholly—baulked of its effect.
>
> —Aleister Crowley, *Magick in Theory & Practice**
> (emphases added)

These conditions are given as applicable to any Eucharistic magick whatsoever. They would be pertinent to the lay communicant in the Gnostic Mass, just as well as the priest. They would also apply to the Mass of the Phoenix and other magical operations in which the procedure "consists in taking common things, transmuting them into things divine, and consuming them."†

Note that when Crowley writes of "the Catholic Church," he is indicating the Roman Catholic Church in the early years of the first Thelemic century. He is therefore referencing the centuries-old procedures of the Tridentine Mass maintained prior to the Second Vatican Council, which weakened many of the ritual traditions supporting that church's Eucharist. In a footnote to the text above, Crowley also instructs the student to consult "the Roman Missal, the Canon of the Mass, and the chapter of 'defects.'" The latter document specified appears to be the Roman Papal bull *De*

---

* Crowley, *Magick,* p. 269.
† *Op. cit.,* p. 267.

Defectibus, which itemizes defects in the performance of the Roman Mass along with their consequences and remedies, if any.

So, with reference to those (now antiquated) Roman Catholic sources and to Crowley's various writings, we should be able to get a fairly detailed idea of these three central prerequisites for Eucharistic magick.

The first condition is **chastity**. We are immediately warned:

> The Word Chastity is used by initiates to signify a certain state of soul and of mind determinant of a certain habit of body which is nowise identical with what is commonly understood. Chastity in the true magical sense of the word is inconceivable to those who are not wholly emancipated from the obsession of sex.[*]

Since Crowley is emphasizing the special sense of the term in its use "by initiates," we may safely disregard the Roman Church's published resources on this particular count. It is certainly not a matter of priestly celibacy.

In the chapter "On Chastity" in *Liber Aleph*, Crowley advises that "Love is an Expression of the Will of the Body," and that chastity consists in maintaining the purity of that expression, through fervency, firmness, and stability.[†] Further, in *Little Essays Toward Truth* he writes that "Chastity may be defined as the strict observance of the Magical Oath; that is, in the Light of the Law of Thelema, absolute and perfected devotion to the Holy Guardian Angel, and exclusive pursuit of the Way of True Will."[‡]

In our Gnostic and Catholic Church, clergy have taken magical oaths under the sacrament of our holy orders, our

---

[*] *Op. cit.,* p. 269 *n.*
[†] Crowley, *Liber Aleph,* p. 112.
[‡] Crowley, *Little Essays Toward Truth*, p. 71.

ordination being an initiatory passage into the chastity of the Church's Eucharistic mystery. But members of the laity, and even skilled magicians who are not formally affiliated with the Church, can cultivate the required chastity in the context of the Gnostic Mass—by observing and applying their own obligations and consciousness of the Great Work as communicants.

Insofar as chastity "is connected only by obscure links with the sexual function,"* it depends on the free erotic vitality of the individual. The libidinal condition of the Eucharistic operator should not be weakened by either denial or sateity. In this respect, it is important to consider the preeminent idiosyncrasy of sexual appetite. Only the operator can judge what sexual situation best facilitates his or her own chastity. The idea of *sublimating* the erotic force into the ceremonies, as implicity advanced by those sacramentary bodies that require celibacy of their priests, is actually incorrect by an angle of 90°. The strength of the sexual charge *induces* a Eucharistic current perpendicular to the libidinal circulation.

Taken as a whole, the magical concept of chastity may be summarized by the opening of Psalm CXIX: *Beati quorum via integra est: qui ambulant in lege domini.* "Blessed are those who are whole in the Way, who walk in the law of the Lord." The chaste magician has *integrity*, in the literal sense of "wholeness." The magician's entire being is dedicated to the work. This commitment is a dynamic walking of the Way, not a static position of timid "purity." The Lord is the personal genius or Holy Guardian Angel of the magician, and his law is Do what thou wilt.

On the topic of **fasting**, we have no guidance from Crowley and perhaps too much from the Roman Catholic Church. Rules and standards for the Eucharistic fast have been changed over time in Roman Catholicism, with some

---

* *Op. cit.,* p. 69.

224

traditions and customs particular to certain countries or orders within the church. In *De Defectibus* the stipulations for fasting are classed under "Defects of the disposition of body":

28. If a priest has not been fasting for at least one hour before Communion, he may not celebrate. The drinking of water, however, does not break the fast.

29. The sick, even though they are not bed-ridden, may take non-alcoholic liquids as well as true and proper medicine, whether liquid or solid, before the celebration of Mass, without any time limit.

30. Priests who can do so are earnestly invited to observe the ancient and venerable form of the Eucharistic fast before Mass.

The "ancient and venerable form" dictates that fasting would commence on the midnight before the celebration of Mass. During the last century, the Roman Church has shown an inclination to lessen the severity of requirements for fasting, particularly with respect to evening Masses. Pope Paul VI is said to have reduced the fasting requirement for priests to a mere fifteen minutes under some circumstances.

In my own practice, I have found that a fast of about four waking hours is optimal. Such a rule should be adjusted for the health and metabolism of the individual magician, through trial and experience. The fast should permit a full digestion of prior meals, so that the Eucharist is consumed on an empty stomach. A slight conscious hunger can be an asset in the execution of Eucharistic magick. The fast should not be taken to the point that weakness ensues, or that a deficiency of blood sugar creates irritability or loss of concentration.

For Christians the fast is colored by a notion of a penitential observance which does not apply to the Thelemic magician. Moralistic arguments regarding the subjugation of concupiscence are also quite irrelevant to our Eucharists. Instead, the essence of the fast is informed by the idea presented in the creed of Liber XV, which equates the Miracle of the Mass with the metabolic transformation of food and drink into human activity and experience, i.e. "spiritual substance." By observing a Eucharistic fast, the food and drink of the ceremony is distinguished as its own meal, a sacred feast set apart and specially devoted to conscious prosecution of the individual's spiritual work. The fast promotes an awareness of both the sacramental substances and the magician's own body as vehicles of the divine force.

The condition of earnest and continual **aspiration** is in some measure addressed by the section on "Defect of intention" in *De Defectibus*:

> 23. The intention of consecrating is required. Therefore there is no consecration in the following cases: when a priest does not intend to consecrate but only to make a pretense; when some hosts remain on the altar forgotten by the priest, or when some part of the wine or some host is hidden, since the priest intends to consecrate only what is on the corporal; when a priest has eleven hosts before him and intends to consecrate only ten, without determining which ten he means to consecrate. On the other hand, if he thinks there are ten, but intends to consecrate all that he has before him, then all will be consecrated. For that reason every priest should always have such an intention, namely the intention of consecrating all the hosts that have been

> placed on the corporal before him for
> consecration.

This passage is especially pertinent with respect to the issue of "earnestness." A mere pretense of enacting the ritual, whether to impress others, to provide for their instruction, or as a deliberate deception, will not suffice to effect consecration. Note also that for clergy to reduce Eucharistic ceremony to pretense is a violation of sacerdotal chastity as defined above.

Continuity of aspiration is closely related to its earnestness. Continual aspiration must be an inherent development of the ongoing spiritual condition of the magician. It cannot be a provisional or experimental attitude. It cannot be feigned or temporarily posited. Many questions in a Eucharistic ritual may be resolved on a provisional basis, but not the central aspiration of the magician.

The "Defect of intention" passage contains a further point which merits discussion:

> 26. It may be that the intention is not actual at
>   the time of the Consecration because the
>   priest lets his mind wander, yet is still
>   virtual, since he has come to the altar
>   intending to do what the Church does. In
>   this case the Sacrament is valid. A priest
>   should be careful, however, to make his
>   intention actual also.

This loophole of "virtual intention" would certainly not apply to a solo Eucharist like the Mass of the Phoenix. Nor would it apply to the priest's own communion in the Gnostic Mass, since our magick does depend on the practitioner's puissance, rather than an alleged transmission of god-given authority embodied in "what the Church does." But this possibility of "virtual intention" suggests, and appropriately so, that the efficacy of the Eucharist for a congregation may be somewhat independent of a failed (and thus "virtual") intention of the priest. A magician communicating as a member of the congregation could receive a full Eucharistic benefit as long as his or her own actual intention were fully formed and maintained. Thus, for the individual communicant, the communicant's intention can be taken to "override" that of the Mass officers. This consideration becomes especially apt when considering the need for aspiration appropriate to the individual's state of attainment, inasmuch as the aspiration of the officiating clergy may either surpass or lag behind that of a given communicant.

Crowley distinguishes between aspiration on the one hand, and mere spiritual ambition on the other.* Ambition may be directed to further attainment by development of the magician's knowledge and abilities. Aspiration requires an orientation to something which is other and beyond the aspirant. The first aspiration of the true magician is to the Knowledge and Conversation of the Holy Guardian Angel. The aspiration of the adept who has attained to that Knowledge and Conversation will then be to the interior church, the illuminated brotherhood which Thelemic scriptures figure under the image of the City of the Pyramids. Those who have taken their places in the City of the Pyramids aspire to the magick progress and transformation of humanity as a whole. These stages are the aspirational sequence described in Crowley's theories of magick. Precocious operators may aspire beyond their grade, and other aspirations may be the basis for the work of magicians laboring outside of the categories defined by those theories.

The fulfillment of the three foregoing conditions do not guarantee the efficacy of Eucharistic ceremony, but they provide the magician with an essential foundation for that work. They can be figured under the formula of the masculine trinity of Father, Son, and Interior Spirit, where:

---

* In his discussion of the Holy Oil in *Magick,* p. 60.

228

- The Father is the Sun, the Egyptian *Ra*, the central aspiration of the magician, the radiant heart fueling the magick.
- The Son is Mars, the Egyptian *Hoor*, the chastity of the magician, the vigilant and fervent limbs defending the magick.
- The Spirit, *Khuit* in Egyptian, is the Eucharistic fast, the balanced appetite of the magician, the warm and eager blood circulating the magick.

Ο ΠΑΤΗΡ
ΕΣΤΙΝ Ο ΥΙΟΣ
ΔΙΑ ΤΟ ΠΝΕΥΜΑ ΑΓΙΟΝ.
ΑΥΜΓΝ. ΑΥΜΓΝ. ΑΥΜΓΝ.

May the observance of these conditions inspire, fortify, and fructify our magicks, in the name of IAO.

Biological Allegory

First Disclaimer: This essay was written some years ago, when I was a Priest of *Ecclesia Gnostica Catholica*. It is offered here as a provocative example of ritual interpretation. The symbolism and significance of the Mass as proposed here have no guaranteed accuracy and are binding on no one, including me. THIS PAPER DOES NOT REPRESENT AUTHORITATIVE DOCTRINE.

Second Disclaimer: This essay includes an accounting of biological facts which were probably unknown to Past Patriarch Baphomet XI° when he composed the Gnostic Mass. It is therefore unlikely that the complete set of ideas presented here could be traced to conscious authorial design in the symbolism of that ritual. Some related sentiments of a more general nature, however, may be found in his commentary to *Liber Legis* I:52.*

> Now is the Pillar established in the Void;
> now is Asi fulfilled of Asar; now is Hoor let
> down into the Animal Soul of Things like a
> fiery star that falleth upon the darkness of
> the earth.
>
> —*Liber Cordis Cincti Serpente* V:5

The Gnostic Mass is a Eucharist based on and expressive of the formula of the Aeon of Horus, that of the Crowned and Conquering Child. The Priest and Priestess must both participate to prepare the sacramental feast, and their co-operation is in many respects suggestive of sexual congress. If there is symbolic coitus, the "Formula of the Child"

---

* *The Law Is for All,* pp. 59-74.

implies that there is also symbolic conception. As human conception occurs though the union of ovum and spermatazoon, so it would appear that the magick act of conception in the Mass occurs in the *commixtio*, the moment in the ceremony of the Mystic Marriage when the *particula* is introduced to the wine in the Graal.

The Cake of Light, or host, is essentially feminine. The Priest identifies it three times as "life." In Latin and kindred Romance languages with irrational gender, 'life' is feminine (*viva* or *vita*). The substance of the Cake is attributable to Demeter, the goddess of grain and terrestrial life. Demeter and Dionysus were the focal deities of the classical Eleusinia, the archetypal Western mystery cult.

The substance of the wine is attributable to the ecstatic god Dionysus, who was also the principal god of the Orphic mysteries. The wine is essentially masculine. The Priest identifies it three times as "joy." In Latin, 'joy' is the masculine *laetatio*—or possibly *juvius*, or even *felix*, all masculine. The contents of the Cup of the Scarlet Woman are the blood of the Saints, who are masculine under the rubric of Liber XV.

So the wine is the semen, "the blood that is thy life,"[*] that flows from the grapes of the testes. And the host divided into two signifies the ovaries. The *particula*, which is taken as a fragment from half of the host, is an ovum. It is introduced to the seminal vintage in the womb represented by the Graal. The *commixtio* thus demonstrates the "covenant" (agreement) between the generative substances from the male and female, through which the recurrent resurrection of the human race is effected.

There is no need to be confused by the false cognate in the Priest's incantation over the particula: ΤΟΤΥΟ ΕΣΤΙ ΤΟ ΣΠΕΡΜΑ ΜΟΥ. The word *sperma* means 'seed,' like

---

[*] Liber CLVI, v. 2.

plant seed. And it is the ovum or 'egg' that is the seed of the human. The so-called 'spermatazoa' are mere pollen. We owe the confusion of terms to a time when neither plant nor human procreation was well understood.

Nor does a problem arise from the delivery of the *particula* by the Lance. While often perceived as a uniformly phallic symbol, the Lance can represent channels other than the male urethra. It often appears to allude to the *sushumna*, or central energy passage in the human subtle body. When the Priestess takes the Lance for the Mystic Marriage, it is possible for it to assume the role of the fallopian tube that delivers the ovum to the "waiting womb." And, indeed, contemporary biological studies reveal that the womb waits for the ovum after the semen. Spermatazoa are capable of surviving for several days in the uterine environment. The typical sequence of conception involves the fashionably late arrival of the guest of honor, the egg.

When approached on this plane of interpretation, the "shrill scream of orgasm" that is HRILIU refers not so much to the coital ecstasy, but rather to the rapture of union between the generative substances. The sexual congress of the mother and father is the *dedication* of those substances, as enacted during the Office of the Collects and the Ceremony of the Consecration of the Elements. That sequence is bracketed by the first tersanctus at the Opening of the Veil and the second one at the Elevation of the Host.

Of course, these elaborate ceremonial mechanics are only applied to the elements consumed by the Priest. Communicants from the People do not perform a *fractio* of their Cakes, nor a *commixtio* in their goblets. Does that mean that there is no magical conception in their communion, no realization of the Formula of the Child? On the contrary, that process may be understood to be hidden within each communicant. The seventh article of the creed identifies "the miracle of the Mass" with the process of human metabolism, through which our spirits are renewed from the matter of meat and drink. We may conclude then, that the magick that the Priest performs in outward ceremony may be reenacted through the interior transmutations of each magician who partakes of the Eucharistic substances.

Offerimus tibi donum corpus dei.

One Mass, Four Worlds

There has been some discourse to date regarding the "proper" assignment of the Tree of Life pattern to the physical design and layout of the temple in the Gnostic Mass of *Ecclesia Gnostica Catholica*. But any persistence in the study of the Mass quickly reveals that there are many different methods of drawing such correspondences. Nor is it obvious that any one design of this type should invalidate the others. In what follows, I propose several different sets of assignments, with the object of realizing the Four Worlds of the Qabalah as reflected in four Trees in the blueprint of the Gnostic Mass temple.*

The Atziluthic Tree, representing the primordial **World of Emanation**, is traced in the Ceremony of the Introit. It is upon and above the High Altar, within the eastern shrine. This Tree has Kether at the Stele, Tiphareth at the Book, Yesod at the Graal, and Malkuth at the Paten. The top rank of candles are Chokmah and Binah, the lower rank of candles are Chesed and Pachad, and the roses are Netzach and Hod.

In Lurianic Kabbalah, the World of Atziluth is the first derivation from the primordial cosmos that *is* Adam Kadmon. Thus for this view of the temple, the Stele is the crown, the Book is the heart, the Graal is the sex, and the Paten is the foot of the Tree. The Atziluthic Tree is a map of the mechanism which underlies the homologous patterns of all that follows in the Mass, just as human morphogenesis adumbrates the experience and processes of human life. This arrangement in the Mass is the first and 'brightest' of the

---

* Readers unfamiliar with the essential qabalistic doctrines of the Tree of Life and the Four Worlds are referred to Br. John Bonner's *Qabalah: A Primer,* Archbishop DuQuette's *Chicken Qabalah of Rabbi Lamed ben Clifford*, and Dion Fortune's perennial classic *The Mystical Qabalah.*

various Trees. Only the Priestess as virgin Sophia comes into contact with it. (It is effaced or obscured upon her return to the shrine with the Priest.)

Atziluth is the world of archetypes free from any descent into phenomena. Its Tree centers on *The Book of the Law* as an artifact of intelligible, i.e. *noumenal*, sublimity. Atziluth is the very body of God, shadowed forth in the cakes and wine, the body which can only be perceived by the Chiah or pure life-force.

The Creative World of Briah is represented by a Tree which centers its Tiphareth on the High Altar, decorated with a "fleur-de-lys in gold, a sunblaze, or other suitable emblem." So the Stele is still Kether, and the Book on the super-altar is Daath, i.e. Knowledge. The great candles are the pillars of Mercy and Severity, represented in Chesed and Geburah. Yesod is the top of the dais within the veil, and the temple floor below the steps is Malkuth. The Gnostic Mass Veil represents the outer Veil of Initiation in this scheme, crossing the path of *tau* and concealing the higher Tree from the profanum of Malkuth.

This Briatic Tree is especially evident during the first part of the Ceremony of the Opening of the Veil, i.e. before the Veil is closed. The Priest is then on the path of *samekh*, serving as the alchemical angel who lustrates and censes the priestess. The enthroned Priestess is on the path of *gimel* overshadowed by *teth*, thus taking on the potency of Mau or Sekhmet.

Briah is the World most associated with the divine Throne. So its Tree centers on the High Altar as the throne of the Priestess. The World of Creation is apprehended by the intuition, or Neschemah.

The least evident of the four Trees in the Mass is the one for **the World of Yetzirah, or Formation**, in which the Veil of the shrine represents the Veil of Paroketh. This Tree is particularly appropriate to the later part of the Ceremony

of the Opening of the Veil, after the Priest's circumambulations. In this World, Malkuth is the altar of incense
and Yesod is the three steps of the dais. The space between
the veil and the High Altar, where the Priestess stands for
her great invocation, is Tiphareth. Geburah and Gedulah are
the pillars. The superaltar with the Stele of Revealing is
Daath.

The supernal triad for Yetzirah remains metaphysical
and must be hypothesized *beyond* the phenomena of the
physical temple: Babalon/Binah, Chaos/Chokmah, and
Aion/Kether. Compare this arrangement to the Neophyte
ceremony of the Hermetic Order of the Golden Dawn. In
that temple, Malkuth is attributed to the central double cube.
The pillars of the Neophyte Temple are below the dais, and
they represent Netzach and Hod. In this view of the Gnostic
Mass they are on the dais and stand for Geburah and
Chesed.

During the Ceremony of the Consecration of the
Elements, the Priest occupies the path of *samekh,* while the
Children are on the paths of *ayin* and *nun* in this Tree.

Yetzirah is the world of the angels: the *imaginal* world, in
the terminology of Henry Corbin. The Tree of this world
centers on the space before the High Altar. The Priestess
and the Priest draw on the supernal entities that resist
concrete location, despite the vivid **presence** of those
entities when invoked. Yetzirah is perceived through the
Ruach, the mediating spirit or breath of reflective consciousness.

The Tree that comprehends the entire Gnostic Mass
temple represents **the World of Assiah, or Manifestation**.
It has Malkuth at the Tomb, Yesod at the Font, Tiphareth at
the small altar, Kether at the super-altar/Stele, Binah at the
north pillar, and Chokmah at the south. The Veil (of the
shrine) represents the Veil of the Abyss in this scheme. The
veil of the Tomb corresponds to the Outer Veil of Initiation

that was represented by the Veil of the shrine in Briah. The Tree of Assiah is especially pertinent to the Office of the Collects and to popular communion.

In the World of Manifestation, the enthroned Priestess is at the juncture of *gimel* and *daleth*. The Deacon intones the Collects from the intersection of *samekh* and *peh*. The Children offering the elements of the Eucharist are on the paths of *vau* (cake) and *cheth* (goblet of wine).

The World of Manifestation is sometimes characterized as the World of 'Action.' It is the World in which entities become material or concrete. Its Tree centers on the altar of incense in its form of a *double cube*. The double cube has a surface of ten square units, representing the Sephiroth, and it is itself generally a symbol of the Tenth Sephirah, which is the Kingdom of terrestrial phenomena, the Sphere of the Elements. Assiah is the object of the perceiving faculties of the Nephesch or 'animal soul.' It is the World that has been pulled over one's senses, or as Crowley calls it in *Magick*, "the world of material illusion." *

So each of the Trees descending through the Four Worlds is apparently "larger" than the one before it, expanding towards the western Tomb in the progression of the ceremonies through the course of the Mass. They all begin with and reflect the pure and universal pattern of the original emanations, so that as each Tree dissolves into its grosser counterpart, we offer in sacrifice the body of God.

---

* Crowley, *Magick,* p. 163. See also *The Book of Lies,* ch. 10.

Apocalyptic Symbolism

It is not the aim of this paper to represent the Gnostic Mass as a dramatization of the Christian Apocalypse, attributed to John. On the contrary, as an adherent of the Law of Thelema I view the Johannine Apocalypse as a text which contains a murky presentiment of the Gnostic Mass and of the arcana which our Mass adumbrates. Consider these reflections from our Past Patriarch:

> The seers in the early days of the Aeon of Osiris foresaw the Manifestation of this coming Æon in which we now live, and they regarded it with intense horror and fear, not understanding the precession of the Aeons, and regarding every change as catastrophe. This is the real interpretation of, and the reason for, the diatribes against the Beast and the Scarlet Woman in the XIII, XVII and XVIIIth chapters of the Apocalypse.
>
> Further study of this card [Atu XI. Lust] may be made by close examination of Liber XV.*

ଓଃ

> All I get is that the Apocalypse was the recension of a dozen or so totally disconnected allegories, that were pieced together, and ruthlessly planed down to make them into a connected account; and that recension was re-written and edited in the interests of Christianity, because people were complaining that Christianity could show no true spiritual knowledge, or any food for the best minds: nothing but miracles, which only deceived the most ignorant, and Theology, which only suited pedants.
>
> So a man got hold of this recension, and turned it Christian, and imitated the style of John. (Note:

---

* Crowley, *The Book of Thoth,* pp. 93-5.

There is no question in my mind that this explanation is correct from the viewpoint of profane scholarship. "Angels" who offer absurd theories about material affairs are false elementals who amuse themselves at the expense of the naivete of the would-be-Magician.) And this explains why the end of the world does not happen every few years, as advertised.*

Here then are some notes on correspondences that may be rooted in the presentiment of Osirian seers, or in the archaic Christian hijacking of true spiritual knowledge.

The twenty-two candles of the shrine may be taken to correspond to the twenty-two chapters of the Apocalypse, both of which suggest the twenty-two letters of the Hebrew alphabet and the twenty-two Trumps Major of the Tarot. The myriad septenaries of the Apocalypse have no obvious counterpart in the Gnostic Mass, but magically educated clergy will be aware of the sevenfold powers conventionally represented by the planets and other patterns of seven as well.

The saints are described as wearing white robes in Apocalypse VII, just as all of the Mass officers have white robes as the basis of their regalia, and our laity wear white robes for confirmation.

The Book of the Law corresponds to the "little book" of Apocalypse X. Upon placing the Book in the east, the Deacon assumes the visionary form described in the Apocalypse X:1, i.e. a "mighty angel come down from heaven, clothed with a cloud: and a rainbow upon his head, and his face as it were the sun, and his feet as pillars of fire." This form pertains to the Deacon while addressing the congregation. He speaks while standing on the black and

---

* Crowley, *The Vision & The Voice,* ARN (2nd Æthyr), p. 222.

white squares of the dais, suggesting "his right foot upon the sea, and his left foot on the earth." (X:2)

The Virgin at her entrance is constituted spiritually as described in the Apocalypse XII:1, i.e. "a woman clothed with the sun, and the moon under her feet, and upon her head a crown of twelve stars." Her three-and-a-half circumambulations of the temple correspond to the 1,260 days (i.e. forty-two months, or three-and-a-half years) for which the woman retreats into the wilderness (XII:6).

The Priest's outer robe is scarlet, as though it were "dipped in blood" (XIX:13). It should have gold trim, and it might also bear insignia or an inscription in gold, e.g. ΒΑΣΙΛΕΥΣ ΒΑΣΙΛΕΩΝ ΚΑΙ ΚΥΡΙΟΣ ΚΥΡΙΩΝ (XIX:16). But see also XVII:3.

On the Priest's recitation at the opening of the veil: "And I heard a voice from heaven, as the voice of many waters, and as the voice of a great thunder" (XIV:2).

ΑΓΙΟΣ ΑΓΙΟΣ ΑΓΙΟΣ
ΚΥΡΙΟΣ Ο ΘΕΟΣ Ο ΠΑΝΤΟΚΡΑΤΩΡ
Ο ΗΝ ΚΑΙ Ο ΩΝ ΚΑΙ Ο ΕΡΧΟΜΕΝΟΣ.

Holy, holy, holy,
Lord God Almighty,
which was, and is, and is to come. (IV:8)

In my astral appraisal, the Priest's brow bears the word BLASPHEMY or ΒΛΑΣΦΗΜΙΑΣ (XIII:1, XVII:3). On the brow of the Priestess is the word MYSTERY or ΜΥΣΤΗΡΙΟΝ (XVII:5). She is seated on the scarlet altar-cloth which is "arrayed" about her (XVII:4).

The Cup contains the blood of the Saints (XVII:6): "thou hast given them blood to drink, for they are worthy" (XVI:6) says the third angel of judgment.

The hosts are "the flesh of kings, and the flesh of captains, and the flesh of mighty men, and the flesh of horses, and of them that sit on them, and the flesh of all men, both free and bond, both small and great," (XIX:18) since *there is no god but man.*

In the Priest's communion the host makes a cross on the circular face of the paten so that the cross is encircled. The circular opening of the goblet is moved in a cross so that the circle is crucified. In both cases, the cross is motion or energy, and the circle is matter or space, consistent with the pervasive symbolism of the Rosy Cross in the work of 666. If we take the cross-and-circle as (one of the several forms of) the Mark of the Beast, the first is on the hand of the priestess, the second over her heart. Earlier, at the beginning of the Mystic Marriage, the Priest elevates the paten toward the Stele for the "Lord most secret" invocation, and then makes a cross (a Mark) with it toward the forehead of the priestess. In connection with all of this, note that the Beast of the Apocalypse "causeth all, both small and great, rich and poor, free and bond, to receive the mark in their right hand, or in their foreheads" (XIII:16). We see this trope also rehearsed in *The Vision & the Voice*, where it is exhibited by Aiwass[*] and the Crowned and Conquering Child.[†]

The summary of the Law issues from the mouth of the Priest like "a sharp sword," and the Lance in his hand is as "a rod of iron" (XIX:15).

> He that is unjust, let him be unjust still: and he which is filthy, let him be filthy still: and he that is righteous, let him be righteous still: and he that is holy, let him be holy still. And, behold, I come quickly; and my reward is with me, to give every man according as his work shall be. (XXII:11-12)

---

[*] LEA (16th Æthyr), p. 128.
[†] LIL (1st Æthyr), p. 247.

Vegetation of the Gnosis

In the invocation pronounced by the Priest on the first step of the dais in the Ceremony of the Introit, a specific formula of magick is declared under the figure of vegetable growth:

> ...not unto Thee may we attain, unless Thine image be Love. Therefore by seed and root and stem and bud and leaf and flower and fruit do we invoke Thee.

The Priest indicates that the infinite can only be invoked as Love. The plant anatomy which follows must then be a diagram of the creative will, since "Love is the law, love under will." It is described in seven stages, which—like all creation—naturally progress from a hidden condition to a manifested one. These seven stages can be referred to the seven horizontal planes indicated by the emanations of the qabalistic Tree of Life, and, in turn, to the psychological model advanced in the qabalah.

I.   The creative process begins with the **SEED** or Hidden Master. Work proceeds from an inscrutable source, whose name is "Mystery of Mystery." It is buried in the dark substrate of reality (the "Night of Pan" beyond the Abyss), just as the seed is buried in the earth.

II. The seed sends forth a **ROOT**, a still-subterranean extension that begins its orientation towards the world of events, i.e. the Universe of Contraries. It engages—on the Chokmah/Binah plane—the dual polarity which characterizes all phenomena below the Abyss.

III. This archetypal plant, which symbolizes the will, breaks into light by shooting forth a **STEM**, a distinct impulse towards change which has been determined by the seed and provided for by the root.

IV.   Of these seven segments, the one of greatest interest
        to the magician is the **BUD**, which is at the mid-
        point of the series and attributable to Sol. In the
        process of the passage of the will from its hidden
        origin to its manifested accomplishment, the BUD is
        the point of balance at which magick force can be
        brought to bear with the greatest effect. In *Liber
        Aleph* (Chapter 86), Crowley specifically references
        the "bud-will" and its importance in the Work of
        the Sovereign Sanctuary of the Gnosis. A
        transliteration of BUD reveals the principal officers
        of the Mass in the guise of Tarot trumps: B = The
        Magician (Deacon), U = The Hierophant (Priest),
        and D = The Empress (Priestess). The astrological
        glyphs which correspond to these trumps likewise
        are of note, since Taurus (U) and Venus (D) com-
        bine in the figure of Mercury (B).

V.   The bud opens into a **LEAF**, the visible surface
        which is the characteristic expression of the plant.

VI.   The leaves support the **FLOWER**, which brings the
        plant into communication with other creatures
        through sight and scent and provides for pollination
        with other plants.

VII.   The pollination of the flower culminates in the
        FRUIT, the finally manifested product of the
        process, which conceals within itself new seeds to
        perpetuate the creative pattern. The journey of the
        fruit in returning the seeds to the dark earth is
        emblematic of a different formula complementary to
        the one under discussion.

A couple of illustrations may help to elucidate the
application of this formula. One example is the creative work
of O.T.O. through *Mysteria Mystica Maxima* as an initiatory
institution. In this case, the SEED is Baphomet or the Secret
Master, possibly considered as the esoteric instruction

244

concealed in the depths of the rituals themselves. The ROOT is the Grand Master who authorizes the enactment of the initiations and is the custodian of their form. The STEM is the presiding ritual officer (initiator) who organizes and implements the ceremony. The BUD is the candidate who enters into the Mysteries. The LEAF is the Lodge (or Chapter, or other body) that results from the collaboration of initiates. The FLOWER is the Order as a whole, visible to the initiate and the profane. And the FRUIT is the totality of human society to which the Order offers the Law and the message of Universal Brotherhood.

Another instance is the production of literature. Here, the SEED is the secret muse of the author, the inspiration which brings him or her into the process of writing. The author as the original container of the idea issuing from the muse is the ROOT. The author's work of writing is the STEM by which literature raises itself into view. The BUD is the text itself. The text shows its LEAF in its publication. The reader savors it like the appreciation of a FLOWER. And the FRUIT is its passage into the world of discourse in literary posterity.

The vegetation formula could be applied to nearly any human enterprise, since "Every willed act is a magical act." But the text of Liber XV directs our attention particularly toward its use in the *invocation of Love as an image of the divine.* We might profitably consider what Liber Nu calls the "first practice of Intelligence": the appreciation of the rim of the Stele of Revealing as described in the stanza of *Liber Legis* I:14.

> Above, the gemmed azure is
> The naked splendour of Nuit;
> She bends in ecstasy to kiss
> The secret ardours of Hadit.

The growing plant, from its hidden seed to its full fruition, desires the unattainable: union with the heavens. It expresses its nature as a centrifugal striving, outwards towards Infinite Space. And yet every growth of the plant is already *in space*. Nuit is "above you and in you" (*CCXX* I:13). The Infinite curves itself in love around every point-of-view, and the Priest's acknowledgement of love as the divine image, of *love as the law,* is an invocation that transports him to the embrace of heaven.

	Sephiroth	Psychology	Will	M.M.M.	Literary Endeavor
Seed	Kether	Self (Yechidah)	The Hidden Master, "source and seed of life, love, liberty and light."	Baphomet	Muse
Root	Chokmah/ Binah	Life Force (Chiah), Intuition (Neschemah)	Emergence of the Master's design into the Universe of Contraries	Grand Master	Idea
Stem	Chesed/ Geburah		Realization of the design in a particular impulse toward change	Initiator	Writing
Bud	Tiphareth	Consciousness (Ruach)	Formulation of the impulse as intention, balanced between the Hidden and the Manifested	Candidate	Text
Leaf	Netzach/ Hod		Expression of the intention	Body of Initiates	Publication
Flower	Yesod	Animal Soul (Nephesch)	Perception of the expression	Order	Reading
Fruit	Malkuth	Body (G'uph)	The Manifested Result	Humanity	Posterity

The Tersanctus

ΑΓΙΟΣ ΑΓΙΟΣ ΑΓΙΟΣ ΙΑΩ

This Tersanctus ("thrice holy") is a formula that occurs twice in the Gnostic Mass, as it also occurs twice in the Bible. In the Bible it is found first in Isaiah VI:3.

> And one cried unto another, and said, **Holy, holy, holy,** [is] the LORD of hosts: the whole earth [is] full of his glory.

The "crier" in the verse from Isaiah is one of the *seraphim*, angels supporting the divine throne or chariot, the *merkabah*. It is these who are again related as calling out the formula in Apocalypse IV:8.

> And the four beasts had each of them six wings about [him]; and [they were] full of eyes within: and they rest not day and night, saying, **Holy, holy, holy,** Lord God Almighty, which was, and is, and is to come.

Note that in the instance from the Apocalypse, the Tersanctus is juxtaposed with a related formula which occurs at the conclusion of the creed of the Gnostic Mass: "which was, and is, and is to come." The Greek gematria of the Tersanctus is suggestive of the relationship between the two formulae. The sum value of αγιος αγιος αγιος is 852, which is also the value of ο στιβος, meaning "the path." The symbol of the path leads naturally to the conception of transcending time and to the threefold division of past, present, and future.* Thus the thrice-holiness of this formula can be read as "holy as it was, holy as it is, holy as it is to come," or "holy from the beginning, holy in the middle, holy unto the end."

In a liturgical context, the "Tersanctus" (or simply "Sanctus") is a term used with reference to the "holy, holy,

---

* A brief exploration of this line of thought is Crowley's "Pilgrim-Talk," Chapter 13 of *The Book of Lies*.

holy" formula as it occurs in Latin and Roman-derived liturgies. In Greek liturgies, the verbally analogous term *Trishagion* does **not** refer to that prayer but rather to an entirely distinct one, which is more similar to the *Kyrie Eleison*. The Tersanctus formula in Greek liturgies forms a part of the *Epinikion* or "victory prayer." The Hebrew text from Isaiah has also been incorporated into Jewish cere- mony, where *Adonai* is substituted for the Tetragrammaton in "*Qadosh, Qadosh, Qadosh l'IHVH Tzabaoth.*"

In traditions of the Piscean era, interpretations are broadly consistent that the Tersanctus in ritual use is intended to express a chorus among the terrestrial speakers and an angelic choir—with the latter emblemized by the seraphim and indicated by the "hosts" or armies of the Lord in the divine title from Isaiah. Interestingly for the purposes of the Thelemic Gnostic Mass, Liberal Catholic Bishop C.W. Leadbeater observed that "Though the Church now most appropriately interprets [the Hebrew word *Sabaoth*] as referring to the Angels, there is little doubt that the Jews originally took it as signifying the host of the stars."* In Thelemic parlance we might say, "the company of heaven." The Tersanctus' Greek numeric value of 852 is also that of πανηγυρις, meaning a "festive assembly," which emphasizes this dimension of the formula.

Christian explicators of the Tersanctus often insist that its presence in liturgy is an elliptical reference to the triune godhead: "Holy [Father], Holy [Son], Holy [Spirit]." There is no reason to consider that reading as obsolete in the Gnostic Mass, considering the presence of that "masculine trinity" in the prayer of the *fractio* as well as its explication in Chapter 87 of *Liber Aleph*. (Crowley does note elsewhere, however, that "Considerations of the Christian Trinity are of a nature

---

* C.W. Leadbeater, *The Science of the Sacraments*, p. 179.

248

suited only to initiates of the IX° of O.T.O., as they enclose the final secret of all practical Magick."*)

Alternatively, or in addition to the Christian Trinity, we may note the trinities invoked through the name or formula IAO which crowns the Thelemic Tersanctus. The most common reading of Isis-Apophis-Osiris could be certainly considered in this case, even as Crowley affirms its identity with the Christian Trinity in the Rosicrucian formula:

> *Ex Deo nascimur.*
> *In Jesu Morimur.*
> *Per Spiritum Sanctum reviviscimus.*[†]

Crowley also suggests analyses of IAO as Father-Child-Mother, Virgin-Babe-Beast, Hermes-Dionysos-Pan, and still others, any of which might inform the operation of the Tersanctus.

In the Mass of the Roman Church, the Tersanctus traditionally falls between the preface and the set of sacrificial prayers that precede the Eucharistic consecration. This placement corresponds precisely to the first instance of ΑΓΙΟΣ ΑΓΙΟΣ ΑΓΙΟΣ ΙΑΩ in the Gnostic Mass, which is at the end of the Ceremony of the Introit, just before the eleven prayers or Collects. The Gnostic Mass does not have a bell for our first Tersanctus, but the Roman rite generally does.

> The ringing of a bell at the Sanctus is a development from the Elevation bell; this began in the Middle Ages. ... It was rung to call people to church that they might see the Elevation. The Sanctus bell is an earlier warning that the Canon is about to begin. ... The hand-bell was only a warning to the ringers in the tower.[‡]

---

* Aleister Crowley, *Magick in Theory & Practice*, p. 138, *n.*
† *Op. cit.*, p. 28.
‡ Adrian Fortescue, "Sanctus" in *The Catholic Encyclopedia*.

Our second Tersanctus occurs with the Elevation that concludes the Ceremony of the Consecration of the Elements. The Roman Mass does not have a Tersanctus at that juncture, but—as indicated in the above quote—it does have a bell. Without being reduced to this function, it is evident that the Tersanctus of the Gnostic Mass has taken on the previous role of the bell, as demarcating the point of the initial approach to the Consecration of the Elements on the one hand and its accomplishment on the other. To illustrate this process, the Priest may elevate the Lance during the first Tersanctus, to presage the elevation of the Eucharistic elements and to further illustrate the transfer of the divine force from the thrice-holy rod to the thrice-holy bread and wine.

Taking the word ΑΓΙΟΣ on its own, a quick analysis reveals its pertinence to the Gnostic Mass. In fact, its five letters are a complete illustration of the ritual officers of the ceremony:

- *Alpha* corresponds to א and the Fool trump of the Tarot. He is wand-waving Iacchus. This Pure Fool is Parsival, the bearer of the Holy Lance and seeker of the Graal. He is the simplest and most direct depiction of the Priest among the Major Arcana of the Tarot.

- *Gamma* is ג and the High Priestess. There is no ambiguity about her identity with the Priestess of the Gnostic Mass. She is the Initiatrix Kundry in *Parsival.*

- *Iota* is י and the Hermit. As Crowley notes in *The Book of Thoth*, the Hermit is that form of Mercury (ruling Virgo, to which *iota* corresponds) known as Hermes Psychopompos, the guide of souls; this reflects the Deacon's role as leader of the People. The Hermit is also an occulted form of the Magician (Mercury proper), another Trump suitable to represent the Deacon. In *Parsival*, The Hermit is Gurnemanz.

- **Omicron** corresponds to ע and The Devil. This letter is paired with **sigma**, which could be either שׁ or ס in Hebrew. In either case, *sigma* would be The Angel. The letter שׁ is the Aeon, a card formerly known as Judgment or The Angel. The letter ס is Art, formerly Temperance, and the Rebis figure central to that card is evolved from simpler depictions of angels, usually reminiscent of the one described in Apocalypse X. This pair, the Devil and Angel, are the Negative and Positive Children, in the role of the *kakodaimon* and *eudaimon*, the evil genius and the good genius. These are the Demon and the Angel, of which Liber Tzaddi instructs "Unite yourself with both!":

  > My adepts stand upright; their head above the heavens, their feet below the hells. But since one is naturally attracted to the Angel, another to the Demon, let the first strengthen the lower link, the last attach more firmly to the higher. (vv. 40-41)

  In terms of the paths of ע and שׁ, the *kakodaimon* and *eudaimon* may be represented as the Egyptian gods Set and Horus according to the early conception under which each ruled half of the divided Egypt.

Note how the letters of the word are all in alphabetical order; thus they fall on paths descending the Tree. The idea communicated is one of an unhindered influx of blessing from a higher source. The tripling of the word emphasizes this quality, as Crowley indicates that the number three is "the receptive as 2 is the assertive self." [*]

---

* Aleister Crowley, "An Essay on Number," in *Equinox* I:5, p. 98.

Letter	Trump	Symbolism	Mass Officer
A	O - Fool	Parsival, Iacchus	Priest
Γ	II - High Priestess	Kundry, Hecate	Priestess
I	IX - Hermit	Gurnemanz, Hermes Psychopompos	Deacon
O	XV - Devil	*kakodaimon*, Set	Negative Child
Σ	XX - Angel	*eudaimon*, Horus	Positive Child

In addition, the word αγιος taken on its own has the sum value of 284, equating it with θεος or "god," and with αγαθος, "good" in its purest sense.

In Hebrew, *Qadosh* (קדוש) enumerates to 410, which is also the value of מצרף. Pronounced in one manner, the latter word means "crucible" or "melting pot." With another pronunciation it means "joined" or "purified." The word הרהר, meaning "thought," and used in Daniel IV:2 to signify an oracular vision, also sums to 410 as does משכן, the Tabernacle.

קדוש קדוש קדוש

αγιος αγιος αγιος

Holy, Holy, Holy
are these Truths that I utter,
knowing them to be but falsehoods,
broken mirrors, troubled waters;
hide me, O Lady, in Thy Womb!
for I may not endure the rapture.*

---

* *The Book of Lies,* ch. 11.

Reflections on "Thou Who Art"

My own understanding of the Office of the Anthem in the Gnostic Mass has changed over time and with the course of initiation. The Liber XV Anthem text is in some sense the kernel from which the Gnostic Mass was germinated. In his *Confessions*, Crowley writes:

> During this period [1913 EV] the full interpretation of the central mystery of freemasonry became clear in consciousness, and I expressed it in dramatic form in 'The Ship.' The lyrical climax is in some respects my supreme achievement in invocation; in fact, the chorus beginning:
>
> > Thou who art I beyond all I am...
>
> seemed to me worthy to be introduced as the anthem into the Ritual of the Gnostic Catholic Church, which, later in the year, I prepared for the use of the O.T.O., the central ceremony of its public and private celebration.[*]

Crowley often referred to that invocation as the *Tu Qui Es* ("Thou who art"), and he referenced it as a component in his *Grimorium Sanctissimum*—his most powerful private ritual, incorporating both A∴A∴ and O.T.O. techniques in a single idiosyncratic canon.[†]

The "Priest's part" of the *Tu Qui Es* has two different versions. Some editions give: "Appear most awful and most mild, / As it is lawful, to thy child!" Others give "... in thy child!" (Crowley started with "to" in *The Ship* and the original edition of Liber XV in *The International*, and changed to "in" in some later editions.)

---

[*] Aleister Crowley, *Confessions* (abridged by Symonds & Grant), p. 417.

[†] *Ibid.*, *Magick,* pp. 566-8.

Who or what is the entity invoked, the "Thou" addressed? Perhaps it is a function shared by every individual personal genius or holy guardian angel; perhaps it is the genius of humanity as a whole; perhaps it is the "carrier signal" of phenomenal reality. It seems to be an ultimate One, penultimate to the None. Is it the "particle of dust" which the Priest "gives"? Is it the particula from the host that is the *seed* (ΣΠΕΡΜΑ) of the Priest? Is it the Lord of the Æon, Ra-Hoor-Khuit? Is it Baphomet? Lucifer? Demeter? Jehovah? Satan? Osiris? Jesus? I assert none of these things, but I consider them all. I would not rebuke a Thelemite for choosing among them, or for rejecting them all. There is no formal doctrine explaining this mystery to the People of our Church; and in any case, our doctrines (e.g. the Creed) are those profound ideas that we must think **about**, not pre-fabricated notions to which we must conform without reflection. A Priest who invokes by means of the anthem is not, however, entitled to omit these considerations.

Who is the child, within whom or to whom the invoked "Thou" is to appear? Perhaps that "Thou" is to appear within the Priest himself, appearing to the Priestess. Perhaps vice versa, or both reciprocally. Perhaps it is to appear in the graal after the commixtio of the particula and the wine. Perhaps the child is the congregation, the Church as a whole, or humanity, or the Terrestrial System, or the Solar System, or the Galactic System. I assert none of these things, but I consider them all.

This sort of indeterminacy has value. At its ritual best, traditional Christianity could include this sort of well-formed, yet unassigned sanctity. At a Latin Mass in centuries gone by, it was impossible to know, on the basis of mere participation, whether a Roman Catholic devotee was principally worshipping Jesus, Jehovah, Mary, some saint or other, personal ancestors, or what have you. The mechanism of metaphysical ambiguity permits different individuals to approach the ceremony in their own spiritual perspective and allows passage to other perspectives as well.

On the other hand, it is not helpful for a ritual officer to be wondering about such indeterminacy during the ceremony. An unresolved intellectual preoccupation is an obstacle to ritual puissance. In order to be reconciled to the work while enacting it, it is necessary either to make a provisional choice, or to permit a void to open within the question so that there is "no difference" between the alternatives.

A provisional choice would impose a temporary resolution, in order to facilitate the work, with the idea that the ritualist could then evaluate the choice based on the results. ("Today, I'm going to direct the anthem to Eros. Let's see how that goes.") This is an *experimental* approach, in keeping with our aspiration to *scientific religion*.

In one sense, finding the void within the question suggests that the indeterminate object of the anthem is not essential to its function of adoration. The ritualist could simply *let go* of that conundrum. A more elaborate way of finding the void would be to perform a synthesis on all of the objects considered feasible, so that the ritualist comes to understand, e.g. Jesus, Hadit, Satan, human sperm, and the axial orientation of the Solar System all as different perspectives on the same essence.

In addition to these considerations, the functional components of the Mass look very different from the various ritual roles. A Deacon, for example, might consider the Anthem to be a point at which the congregation is brought to identify with the Priest, in preparation for the Mystic Marriage. A Priestess, on the other hand, might see it as a stage in which she aligns subtle currents in herself and the Priest. A Priest might look at it as a period of "ripening" in which the charged elements of the Eucharist grow ready for consummation.

The Rhapsody of Chrysippus

Here follows an alternate anthem for the Gnostic Mass, written by Aleister Crowley, originally adapted by Dionysos Thriambos, and annotated by T Polyphilus according to his correspondence with T Apiryon.

PRIEST: Hear then! By Abrasax! The bar
Of the unshifting star
Is broken—Io Asar!
My spirit is wrapt in the wind of light;
It is whirled away on the wings of night.

WOMEN: Sable-plumed are the wonderful wings,
But the silver of moonlight subtly springs
Into the feathers that flash with the pace
Of our flight through the violate bounds of space.

MEN: Time is dropt like a stone from the stars:
Space is a chaos of broken bars:
Being is merged in a furious flood
That rages and hisses and foams in the blood.

PRIEST: See! I am dead! I am passed, I am passed
Out of the sensible world at last.
I am not. Yet I am, as I never was,
A drop in the sphere of molten glass
Whose radiance changes and shifts and drapes
The infinite soul in finite shapes.
There is light, there is life, there is love beyond sense,
Beyond speech, beyond song, beyond evidence.
There is wonder intense, a miraculous sun,
As the many are molten and mixed into one.

PEOPLE: With the heat of its passion, the one hath invaded
The heights of its soul, and its laughter is braided
With comets whose plumes are the galaxies,
Like wind on the night's inaccessible seas.

The text of this anthem is from Crowley's *The World's Tragedy*. It consists of the bulk of a speech of the character Chrysippus in the prologue of that work.* The passage is neither padded nor abridged; it is simply divided into antiphonal sections along the model of the original Anthem in Liber XV.

It was first performed experimentally in AL IV ii at Scarlet Woman Camp. It was authorized by the Patriarch as an alternate in AL IV iv and subsequently performed at Mass at Circle of Stars Sanctuary. In late AL IV vi I first set it to music, using a modification of the hymn tune "Fortunatus," in a Mass I performed with Sister Ananda as the Priestess and Brother Apollo as the Deacon. I have been unsatisfied with that tune, however, and remain interested in other musical settings of the text.

When first contemplating the use of this anthem and some other experiments, I sought the guidance of Bishop T Apiryon. He offered a set of criteria for evaluating the proposed anthem. The criteria are reproduced here as they provide the structure for analyzing this alternate, and they could provide clergy with a frame of reference for proposing other alternates in the future.

1. How did you gauge [experimental] success [of the alternate anthem]?

Besides evidence of the fulfillment of the other specified criteria, I gauged the "success" of the anthem in performance by the demonstrated involvement of the People during the anthem and by their later conscious reactions to it. The Office of the Anthem is second only to the recital of the Creed in the amount of attention and verbal activity that

---

* See pp. 14-15 of the New Falcon edition.

it demands from the People,* and any effective anthem must be able to engage the People. One of the functions of the Anthem appears to be that it breaks the trance of the People established during the Collects and maintained through the Consecration of the Elements—and replaces it with another trance more fitted to the Work of Communication. (Note that I do not use the word 'trance' in any will-negating coercive sense. For present purposes, various trances are merely *focusings of awareness* on an individual or group level.) This alteration of trance is also a "magical function," though one that operates on a fairly accessible theatrical basis.

2. **How does your alternative fulfill the magical function of the Anthem? What aspect of Deity is invoked? How does it transform the Priest? Into what does it transform him? What effect does it have on the Priestess? What effect does it have on the Host?**

The magical functions of the *Tu Qui Es* of Liber XV are clear in its original context, Crowley's mystery-play *The Ship*, where it appears as a celebration of the death-and-resurrection drama of the Lesser or Infernal Mysteries and as the announcement of a sacrament. *The World's Tragedy* likewise sheds light, though less obviously, on this variant drawn from it. The entire passage is spoken by Chrysippus, the disciple of the philosopher Heracleitus, and is occasioned by a command from his mentor to distill mystical ecstasy from his attraction to a scene of innocent debauch. The magical operation is very Gnostic in its essence, as Chrysippus aspires to the *pleroma*, metaphorically ascending through various heavenly phenomena.

---

* At least in those cases where—as is most commonly practiced— the people all join in the choruses and semi-choruses. There is no explicit instruction in Liber XV, however, that the "chorus" is a *chorus of the whole people.*

The passage begins with an invocation with the name Abrasax. Abrasax is a Gnostic name for the demiurge having a value in Greek of 365, the number of days in a solar year. The breaking of "the bar of the unshifting star," points to the movement of the pole star, a phenomenon intimately associated with the precession of the Equinoxes and the change of astrological ages. In *The World's Tragedy,* the implication is that the Osirian age of Pisces is imminent, but in a Gnostic Mass, the allusion would be to the new Æon of Horus and the Age of Aquarius.[*]

"Io Asar!" would have been a greeting to Osiris in the context postulated by *The World's Tragedy.* The Priest can use it as a cry of recognition to the old forces as he is overcome by the new, so that by the end of the anthem he adores the "miraculous sun" associated with Ra-Hoor-Khuit. 'Io' is a cry of aspiration; in *The World's Tragedy* it would signify aspiration to Asar, but in the Mass it indicates aspiration *as* Asar, the slain-and-resurrected Osiris. As the Manifesto of the Church indicates, only those who have "fulfilled [the] formulæ" of previous æons are "capable of comprehension" of the new formula and its sacraments. In the *Tu Qui Es*, the Men imply their fulfillment of the formula of Osiris when they say, "Glory to thee from gilded tomb!"

As with the *Tu Qui Es*, the Priest strives through image and symbol to identify with THAT which informs his essence. The Liber XV Anthem describes THAT as "beyond speech and beyond sight," just as the Rhapsody of Chrysippus asserts that it is "beyond speech, beyond song, beyond evidence." In the *Tu Qui Es*, the success of this operation is heralded by the chorus proclaiming the trinity. The trinity may refer to the supernal triad to which the Priest aspires across the Abyss. Similarly, it is the final chorus of

---

[*] The correspondence between Thelemic/Gnostic æons and astrological ages is rough and debatable, but it is also popular and accessible.

the People in the Rhapsody of Chrysippus that declares that the invasion of the heights of the soul is accomplished.

The Rhapsody of Chrysippus seems to have some significant relevance to the work of the Priestess. The concluding sections particularly relate to the formula of *solve et coagula* as presented in *The Book of Lies*.* The anthem proclaims *coagula*—the many longing for the one in coition/dissolution—as the work of the Priest; the Priestess performs the complementary work of the one longing for the many in creation/parturition (*solve*).

The later portions of Chrysippus' soliloquy are not included in this anthem, not only out of consideration for performance length, but because they exceed the mandate of the Office of the Anthem as a magical mechanism. The final lines of that passage push beyond Chrysippus' exaltation to the One and into his annihilation in the None, a stage that I perceive as more suited to the Consummation of the Elements than the Office of the Anthem.

3. **How does your alternative fulfill the devotional function of the Anthem? How does it transmit the adoration of the Priest and the People to the aspect of Divinity being invoked?**

Devotionally, the Rhapsody of Chrysippus finds its culmination in the praise of the "wonder intense, a miraculous sun" to which the Priest directs his adoration. One of the relevant senses of the many being "molten and mixed into one" is the sacerdotal function of the Priest so that he expresses both his own devotion and that of the People.

The imagery of the alternate anthem focuses on the cosmic and celestial rather than the vegetative and organic

---

* See especially Chapters 3 & 12: "The Oyster" and "The Dragon-Flies."

orientation of the *Tu Qui Es*. But both make elaborate reference to the passage of time and come to a final focus on the sun as a representation of the principle adored.

4. How does your alternative fulfill the teaching function of the Anthem? How does it assist to symbolically convey the Central Mysteries of the Order?

While I will not break certain bounds of confidentiality regarding the Central Mysteries of the Order, the explanations of the previous points do in many cases relate both to our principal doctrines and to the secret work of initiates. The Rhapsody of Chrysippus furthermore itemizes Light, Life, Love, and Liberty, as does the *Tu Qui Es*, as a way of emphasizing the Emanations of that Law which it is the Order's purpose to promulgate.

There seems to be little chance that any other text could ever match the suitability of the *Tu Qui Es* to the Office of the Anthem in Liber XV. It was, after all, the germ of the composition of the liturgy of the Mass as a whole, it was even incorporated by 666 into the *Grimoirium Sanctissimum*. Still, it was the direction of Past Patriarch Baphomet that this one passage of the Mass be the point of liturgical variation. Such variation demonstrates that the liturgy is only the clothing of the living body of our ecclesiastical Magick.

Music Program

Liber XV frequently calls for music to accompany the action of the ceremonies, and sometimes for music of a particular character. The optimal fulfillment of these instructions is by means of live musicians who may work with any number of different instruments. I have attended beautifully accompanied Masses where the principal music was hand drumming, others where it was an electric or acoustic guitar, violin, flute, or a gong. I have been known to play whistles (usually in concert with drumming) or keyboards myself.

In the absence of musicians who are educated on the particular demands of the ritual, however, it can be tempting to use recorded music. In fact, it can also be very effective to use recorded music. But I do not recommend just turning the music on and letting it play throughout the Mass. Such an approach assumes that the music should be ambient and continuous, and the instructions in Liber XV directly contradict that assumption. Instead, a program or playlist should be carefully constructed. Playback should be entrusted to an assistant who can adjust the volume as needed, and who will make sure that each track begins and ends according to its proper use in the ceremonies.

N.B. I strongly discourage the practice of lowering the volume of the music (live or recorded) when individual communicants say, "There is no part of me that is not of the gods." The music volume should be kept at a level where each may easily speak over it, or not, as they will. Adjusting the volume for this proclamation tends to provide a direction or demand to the communicant and falsely implies that it is necessary for the congregation to hear the declaration.

I have constructed many such scores in the past. Rather than rehearsing the details of any particular playlist, the following table shows the standard sequence of tracks that I use in putting together a Gnostic Mass accompaniment recording, along with the cues for each track.

TRACK	CEREMONY
1	Entry and seating of people *Cue before admission of people;* *End when all people are seated.*
2	Entry of Priestess *Cue after final AUMGN of Creed;* *End after Priestess adores in shrine.*
3	Priestess' Circumambulations
4	Priest's Penitence *Cue after Priestess' "...to the Brethren"* *End when Priestess goes to font.*
5	Triumph *Cue on Priest's "...of the lifted Lance!"* *End when Priest kisses Book.*
6	Priest's Circumambulations *MUST end when all kneel.*
7	Consecration of Elements *Cue when all sit after collects;* *End when Priestess kisses Lance.*
8	Fractio *Cue when Priest kisses paten;* *End during Greek invocation of Trinity.*
9	Popular Communion *Cue after Priest proclaims "not of the gods";* *End when Priest closes veil.*
10	Exeunt Omnes *Cue after closing benediction.*

Waves of Æthyr, Houses of the Sun

The creed of Liber XV declares belief in the *Miracle* of the Mass, thus affirming a thaumaturgical character of the ritual. The miracle in question is identified with the transformation of meat and drink into spiritual substance, but the nature of the spiritual substance and its effect on the experience of the participants are not specified in the Creed. The effects are more explicit in the blessing of the elements at the commencement of the Mystic Marriage: "health and wealth and strength and joy and peace, and that fulfillment of will and of love under will that is perpetual happiness." These consequences are intended to flow from any and every enactment of the Mass.

But there are enactments of the Gnostic Mass intended to have more specific effects on the communicants. Some of these are itemized in the exceptions to the communion protocol in Liber XV: the ceremony of marriage, the ceremony of baptism, and of Confirmation. Besides the limitation of communion, there are other aspects or features of the Mass that might be deliberately varied for these (and other) especially miraculous intentions.

Let us return to the question of the nature of the spiritual substance produced by the miracle. In his communion, the Priest declares, "In my mouth be the essence of the Life of the **Sun**," and, "In my mouth be the essence of the Joy of the **Earth**." The solar-terrestrial relationship is clearly a defining feature of the sacrament in the Gnostic Mass. The Priestess operates from the summit of the Earth. The Priest offers the sacrifice of the Eucharistic elements to our Lord and Father the Sun, that travelleth over the Heavens in his name ON. As noted during the first Collect, the spatial dimension of the solar-terrestrial relationship varies in both a diurnal and annual fashion. For the purposes of these remarks, discussion will be restricted to the diurnal cycle, although many of these considerations could be applied analogically to the annual one.

Traditional astrological work has determined the qualitative sense of the diurnal cycles that relate the Greeting of Earth and Heaven to one another and has expressed them in a system of twelve houses. Given the solar emphasis in the Gnostic Mass, we can view the progression of the sun through the houses as an indicator of the auspicious times for various intentions exercised in the Gnostic Mass. Since the sequence of the twelve houses is always the same in the never-retreating passage of the sun, they may be defined by pairs of hours. It must be kept in mind that these are not mundane *clock-hours* of a regular, mechanical duration, but rather magick *sky-hours*, dependent on the latitude and time of year for their particular lengths. Daylight hours grow longer in the summer and shorter in the winter, with the night hours complementing their fluctuation. The hours nearest to dawn and dusk exhibit the least change in length, while those nearest to noon and midnight have the greatest.

The present article, then, proposes associating the time of day or night at which a Gnostic Mass takes place as having a direct bearing on its thaumaturgical quality, as determined by the astrological house in which the sun may be found at the time. Although it is constructed on the basis of traditional correspondences, that is no grounds for dismissing such a scheme as merely symbolic. As discussed in the "Conditions" essay above, Crowley identifies fasting as a prerequisite of Eucharistic Magick. If we presume a three-to-four-hour fast to precede communion in the Gnostic Mass, then the fast will enhance and transform the already marked effect that diurnal biological cycles are likely to have on ritualists and communicants.

Another technical issue worth considering is the point in time at which the Gnostic Mass may be said to happen. Certainly, the ceremonies of the Mass may extend over more than a single hour. In keeping with the premises discussed above, let us take the time of the Mass for thaumaturgical purposes as the time of communion by the individual communicant.

The following explorations reference the hours of the night and day by their magical names, which are found in a corrupted form in Francis Barett's *Magus, or Celestial Intelligencer* (1801 EV), where they have often been referenced by Anglophone occultists. The names in this essay are from an early German edition (c. 1680) and a late nineteenth/early twentieth century French facsimile reprint of Pietre d'Abano's *Heptameron*, with the spelling of the names rectified from later English sources.

YAYN & JANOR

The first two hours of the day are when the sun is passing through the 12th house. Although the houses are now typically referenced by their numbers alone, each has a traditional Latin name. The 12th is *CARCER*, which means 'prison.' This dawn period might be used for a Mass with the specific intention of consecrating cakes for later administration to the shut-in and sick members of the Church community.

NANIA & SALLA

The midmorning hours see the passage of the sun through the 11th house, or *BENEFACTA*. The time is very suited to a Gnostic Mass intended to affirm a spiritual order or association and might be chosen for a Mass with attendance restricted to initiates of a particular degree.

SADEDALI & THAMUR

The hours preceding noon are when the sun is in the 10th house, named *REGNUM*, or 'kingship.' These are appropriate hours to conduct a Gnostic Mass in recognition of an august visitor or perhaps for a Gnostic Mass at a large gathering where high initiates will be presiding.

OURER & THAMIE

Following noon are the hours which have the sun in the 9th house, or *PIETAS* ('duty'). These hours are therefore especially auspicious for a Gnostic Mass celebrating the conferral of Holy Orders, whether sacerdotal or diaconal. This astrological house is the one most concerned with aspiration and instruction in a religious body.

NERON & JAYON

The sun crosses through the 8th house during the mid-afternoon hours. The great luminary is then in the house of *MORS*, i.e. 'death,' and a requiem Mass is the special operation of the Church most suited to this time of day.

ABAI & NATALON

In the last two hours of daylight, the sun passes through *UXOR* ('wife'), the 7th house, making these hours most conducive to a wedding Mass.

BERON & BAREL

The initial evening hours have the sun in *VALETUDO*, or 'health.' These 6th house hours of the sun are best for a Mass in which catechumens are confirmed to full membership in the Church as servants of Ra-hoor-khuit. Crowley notes in *The General Principles of Astrology* that the 6th house "has also a very secret and peculiar reference to the occult development of [the astrological native's] Ego," and Patriarch Hymenæus Beta cites further writing by Crowley which ties the 6th house to personal prowess in Magick:

> It is for him to link his lower to his higher Will, to set the latter to drive the former ruthlessly forward, and as soon as this resolution becomes operative the concatenation of circumstance will bring unexpected success.[*]

---

[*] Crowley, *The General Principles of Astrology,* p. 57.

THAMI & ATHIR

During mid-evening, the sun travels through *NATI*, the 5th house. *NATI* means 'children.' These hours are the optimal time for a Baptismal Mass, when the Church turns her attention to childhood and children.

MATHON & RANA

The pre-midnight hours have the sun in the 4th house. This house *GENITOR* relates to the home and means 'father.' The midnight Mass, then, is one in which we may especially affirm the origins of our Church, commemorating the Feast days of saints of old time and honoring our Past Patriarch Baphomet, the Prophet of the Æon.

NETOS & TAFRAC

After midnight come the hours during which the sun occupies the 3rd house. Its name *FRATRES* means 'brothers,' and signifies local community. This time is good for a private Mass enacted among those with personal, working relationships to each other, with only invitees in attendance. The 3rd house also relates to intellect and study, in the more practical and immediate sense, and thus its hours are very suited to private Mass practice by novices and Low Masses generally.

SASSUR & AGLO

These hours fall midway between midnight and dawn, and they witness the sun's progress through *LUCRUM* ('money'), the 2nd house, referring to personal possessions. This inconvenient period could be the magically auspicious time to conduct Mass with the particular intention of consecrating the sacred weapons and regalia used in the ceremony.

CALERVA & SALAM

The pre-dawn hours have the sun passing through *VITA* or 'life,' the first of the astrological houses. This house is concerned strictly with the individual life. Thus it tends to confine the effect of the Gnostic Mass to a contribution to the health, wealth, strength, joy, peace, and fulfillment of the individual communicant, blessing that one uniquely in his or her way towards the Summum Bonum, True Wisdom, and Perfect Happiness.

IMPORTANT NOTE

The ideas presented here are not for the purpose of restricting the scheduling of Gnostic Mass. They will possibly to motivate greater variety in scheduling. Chiefly the intention is to inspire conscious reflection on the significance of the times at which we conduct these sacred feasts. May those times be free and glorious, regular and enduring, as is our Father the Sun.

5. Benediction

> Flowers and fruits I bring to bless you,
> Cakes of corn, and wealth of wine;
> With my crown will I caress you,
> With my music make you mine.
> Though I perish, I preserve you;
> Through my fall, ye rise above:
> Ruling you, your priest, I serve you,
> Being life, and being love.[*]

May all readers of this book attain to their True Wills, the Great Work, the Summum Bonum, True Wisdom, and Perfect Happiness.

And may every minister of Thelema promulgate, celebrate, and sustain the Law by means of the authentic teachings and sacraments of the rites through which we are called and ordained.

And may Ecclesia Gnostica Catholica faithfully shadow forth the glory that is veiled in that darkness that clouds the threshold of the Sovereign Sanctuary.

And may the virtues of the clergy and the integrity of the Church serve to redeem the Earth as the perfect Kingdom of the Crowned and Conquering Child.

AUMGN. AUMGN. AUMGN.

---

[*] Aleister Crowley, *The Ship*, in *The Equinox* I(10), p. 77.

Ecclesiastical Terminology

There are sacred dimensions of the Western dramaturgical tradition, reaching back into the theater of Hellenistic antiquity and the Passion Plays of medieval Christianity. It is important to realize, however, that what we do in E.G.C. is dramatic ritual rather than ritual theater. The distinction may seem fine, but it's a significant one. (For Crowley's basic theory of dramatic ritual, see Chapter 19 of *Magick in Theory & Practice*.)

Because of the overlap in technical requirements, it is all too easy and far too common for E.G.C. clergy to use the language of the profane theater (where the implicit goal is entertainment) instead of the language of liturgy (where the implicit goal is spiritual fulfillment). The technical language of liturgy is an arcane specialty in our society, whereas the mass media have acquainted us all with the language of theatrical entertainment. But the more familiar terms are often a poor fit. The rubrics of Liber XV are not "stage directions," because *there is no stage*. The attendees at a Gnostic Mass are not an "audience," because they are themselves speakers and actors (i.e. *agents*, not players of pretended characters) at various points in the ceremony.

The following page offers a quick table of "translations," showing both customary theatrical language that can creep into our discussions of ceremonial technique in the Church and the corresponding liturgical and magical terms that more accurately indicate our sources and goals. If clergy adopt the technical language that is native to our undertaking, it should also provide the benefit of feeling a greater sense of propriety and effectiveness in our work.

Vulgar Theater	Ritual (Liturgy or Magick)
Scene, Act, or Play	Ceremony
Audience	Congregation, Attendees
Part, or Character	Office
Player, or Actor	Ritualist, or Officer
Playing	Serving As, or Enacting
Script	Ritual
Stage Directions	Rubric
Lines	Speeches (or Invocations, Exhortations, Prayers, etc.)
Costume	Vestments, or Regalia
Props (Properties)	Implements, or Weapons
Onstage	In Temple

A further note: In live theatrical production, there is a useful technical term with no obvious parallel in liturgical discourse. That term is "blocking," which is the directorial/rehearsal process of adapting the demands of the script (in our case, *ritual*) to the physical constraints of a specific space and set of performers. Given the strong identification of this term with theater, I have been loathe to use it in the process of ritual production. Two possible candidates have been suggested to me as terms for "liturgical blocking." The first was from Br. Taren, who proposed "floor work," a phrase for a comparable notion in the Masonic ritual tradition. The second was in the post-Vatican-II Catholic liturgical study *Sacred Mysteries* by Dennis Smolarski, who recommends "choreography." While I consider either of these terms to be improvements over "blocking" in a liturgical context, neither is a perfect fit for the ecclesiastical lexicon. The optimal language remains a conundrum.

Glossary

The terminology covered in this glossary includes both recondite words of esoteric, ecclesiastical and liturgical provenance and more common words that are used with particular technical significance in the context of our rite.

Article—The E.G.C. **Creed** is made up of eight brief articles, each of which addresses a distinct topic of Church doctrine. The eight articles are complemented by the triple **pranava** at the end, to form the magick eleven.

Adoration—A gesture signifying reverence and affection, usually performed by kissing the object revered or kissing one's hand towards it.

Affusion—The baptismal procedure of pouring water on the head, as contrasted with the preference of some traditions for *immersion* of the entire body below the surface of the water.

Antependium—The decorative face suspended on the forward side of the **High Altar**. Liber XV prescribes "a sun-blaze or other suitable emblem in gold" to adorn the antependium. Alternatives include the Mark of the Beast, ankh, unicursal hexagram with five-petalled rose, fleur-de-lys, heraldic bee, and Jerusalem Cross.

Anthem—1. A hymn in which the congregation participate. 2. The fifth ceremony within the Gnostic Mass, which celebrates the divine power informing the sacrament. 3. The **Tu Qui Es**.

Antimension—A consecrated cloth that may lie on top of the **High Altar**. It may also be used to provide temporary consecrated altar status to unconsecrated tables. It might be embroidered with an image of a double eagle or of Babalon and the Beast conjoined, with suitable versicles or mottos around the outside edge. Suitable dimensions are 2' × 6'.

Aspiration—A precondition for performing any ecclesiastical magick whatsoever. Aspiration is distinguished from mere spiritual ambition by the aspirant's desire to *unite with that which is beyond him.*

Benediction—A ceremonial blessing of those present, usually at the close of a Mass or service.

Canon—Authoritative text, particularly with respect to Eucharistic ritual. Liber XV is the canon of the Gnostic Mass. In Western Christianity, this term drifted over time from its original meaning of simply the "rule of the Mass," or a ritual standard for the Mass. It featured as a heading over the fixed speeches and rubrics for the Eucharist set within texts for the "Mass of the Faithful," and thus it eventually came to denote that component liturgy focused on the consecration of the Eucharistic bread and wine. In this sense it corresponds roughly to Section VI "Of the Consecration of the Elements" in the Gnostic Mass. However, the Gnostic Mass ritual text Liber XV also has for its full title *O.T.O. Ecclesiae Gnosticae Catholicae Canon Missae.* In this case, the Latin phrase *canon missae* clearly carries its original meaning and not the acquired sense that is common in Roman Catholic usage. Liber XV provides the rule or standard for an entire Mass, and not a 'canon' component within one. It is interesting to note, however, that other Thelemic Gnostic verbiage has already begun to undergo a degeneration comparable to the one by which 'canon' acquired its more specific meaning in Roman Catholicism. Gnostic Mass participants can sometimes be heard or observed referring to "Liber Fifteen" as a thing done, an event or activity—which is properly speaking The Gnostic Mass— rather than as a document, as the word Liber ('book') plainly indicates. Just so, Roman Catholic liturgists often refer to the 'canon' as a performative component of their mass, rather than simply a section within their missal.

Cakes of Light—The sacrament prescribed in *Liber Legis*, used as the **hosts** in the Gnostic Mass.

Celebrate—This word is sometimes offered as a general-purpose verb for the enactment of the Mass, using "celebration" to displace "performance." While the English word has many merits in this context, including long ecclesiastical precedent, it suffers from a constraint imposed by its use in Liber XV, where Baphomet XI° writes: "The exceptions to this part of the ceremony are when it is of the nature of a <u>celebration</u>, in which case none but the PRIEST communicate...." Thus, a "celebratory" Mass is one at which there is no popular communion. This latter usage is a technical one peculiar to the Gnostic Mass.

Ciborium—A lidded vessel to hold **Hosts**. Some E.G.C. clergy have discovered Christian ciboria and mistaken them for ecclesiastical chalices. A ciborium can be distinguished from a cup by virtue of its flat, rather than bowl-shaped, interior bottom.

Chastity—An indispensable precondition for performing any Eucharistic magick, such as the Gnostic Mass. Chastity is a *condition of pure will* and in no wise to be confused with *celibacy*, a mere rule of sexual abstinence. "Chastity in the true magical sense of the word is inconceivable to those who are not wholly emancipated from the obsession of sex."[*]

Chiah—The Life Force, a qabalistic "part of the soul" corresponding to the super-personal emanation of Wisdom.

Chierotonia—The sacramental imposition of hands, particularly as used in ceremonies of confirmation and ordination.

Collects—The eleven petitionary prayers which constitute the third ceremony within the Gnostic Mass.

Commixtio—The introduction of the **particula** to the cup in the ceremony of the **Mystic Marriage**.

Confirmand—An aspirant undergoing confirmation to lay membership in the Church.

Congregation—Literally, those "gathered together." The non-officer participants in a ceremony of the Church.

Consecration—1. Ordination to the episcopate. 2. The dedication of an implement, article of furniture, or location to the use of the Church and her ceremonies. Consecration

---

[*] Aleister Crowley, *Magick,* p. 269 *n.*

increases the magical puissance of the object consecrated and of the rituals in which the object is used. It is possible to work with unconsecrated spaces and materials, but a regularly operating sanctuary will be best served by undertaking and maintaining the consecration of its properties. 3. The fourth ceremony within the Gnostic Mass, in which the material elements of the Eucharist are magically dedicated.

Creed—A profession of faith. In an ecclesiastical environment, recitation of the Creed serves to facilitate dramatic ritual by ensuring that the congregants are "initiates of the same mysteries, bound by the same oaths, and filled with the same aspirations."*

Discourse—A sermon or lecture delivered to the congregation. The more generic-seeming term "discourse" may be preferred to avoid the negative connotations associated with "preaching" and "sermonizing."

Doxology—A short hymn of praise. One doxology conspicuous in Thelemic liturgies is that of Liber XXXVI (The Star Sapphire), which begins: *Gloria Patri et Matri et Filio et Filiæ* &c. It is based on the traditional "lesser doxology" of Western Christianity.

Enact—When taking a ceremony for its object, this verb shares the virtues and shortcomings of "to do," (see entry for **Say**) but it is less informal.

Eucharist—"One of the simplest and most complete of Magick ceremonies is the Eucharist. It consists in taking common things, transmuting them into things divine, and consuming them. ... With regard to the preparations for such Sacraments, the Catholic Church has maintained well enough the traditions of the true Gnostic Church in whose keeping the secrets are. **Chastity** is a condition; fasting for some hours previous is a condition; an earnest and continual **aspiration** is a condition."†

---

* Crowley, *Magick*, p. (from *MiT&P* ch. XX)
† Crowley, *Magick,* p. 269.

Extreme Unction—A blessing with holy oil for the benefit of the dying.

Fasting—A traditional discipline of religion and mysticism, enlisting the regulation of eating in the hypostasis of desire. This practice is specified by the Master Therion as a condition of Eucharistic magick.

Feast—"The difference between 'rituals' and 'feasts' is this: by the one a particular form of energy is generated, while there is a general discharge of one's superfluous force in the other. Yet a feast implies periodical nourishment." (*Extenuation* II:36*) A set of sacred days or "feasts" is specified in the calendar passage of *Liber Legis* (II:36-43). Some dates may also be recognized as feasts of particular individuals revered, especially saints of the Church and inductees of the Orders of the Lion and Eagle. The appropriate feast date of an individual is the anniversary of his or her death or a date traditionally held to be that anniversary if it is unknown. The feasts of living individuals are held on the anniversaries of their births.

Fractio—The breaking of the host during the ceremony of the **Mystic Marriage**.

General Exordium—An incantation used to preface a lection. The standard General Exordium for Thelemic use is the one from the Golden Dawn neophyte ritual, which has been variously rewritten and modified in Libri LXIV, DCLXXI, and others.

Gnostic Mass Temple—A space containing the arrangement of furniture described in Liber XV, section I. As a general rule, ceremonies that do not include cardinal sacraments of E.G.C. should not be held in an unmodified Gnostic Mass temple.

G'uph—Typically omitted from "parts of the soul" in hermetic qabalistic inventories, the *g'uph* is the physical body, distinct from consciousness and animation.

---

* Crowley, *The Law Is for All* (ed. Regardie), p. 209.

Hallows—The principal ritual weapons or implements in the Gnostic Mass. The "lesser" hallows are the Sword and Paten, which fall under the formula of Dionysos. The "greater" hallows are the Lance and Cup, under the formula of Iacchus. The fifth hallow is the Stele of Revealing, under the formula of Pan.

Holy Days—The period from March 20 through April 10, comprehending the Feast for the Supreme Ritual and the Feast for the Three Days of the Writing of the Book of the Law. These are more properly called the *Vernal* Holy Days, since all days have the holiness indicated by *CCXX* II:42.

Host—The prepared solid element in a Eucharist of two elements, both before and after **consecration**. Etymologically, the Latin term *hostia* ('sacrifice') has been explained by Ovid to come from *hostis,* 'enemy,' and to refer to the ancient practice of sacrificing vanquished foes (cf. *CCXX* III:11). For many centuries, traditional Christianity has used specially prepared unleavened crackers for hosts. We use **Cakes of Light**. Although Epiphanius observed *hoc est enim rotundae formae* of the Christian host, ours may take various shapes. In addition to circles, triangles, stars, and little humans all have symbolic merits.

Hymn—A sacred song.

Iconoclasm—Detestation and deprecation of religious images.

Idolatry—Rreligious veneration of images. (See *LXV* I:7-9 and *CCXX* III:21-22.)

Introit—The first ceremony within the Gnostic Mass, in which the congregation and officers are introduced to the sanctuary of the temple.

Low Mass—The descriptor 'High Mass' does not appear in Liber XV, nor in the regulations of our Church. I have noticed it deployed variously, to mean Masses at which a full saints list is recited, to ones where attendance is restricted to members of higher grades, to other things besides. The significance of the term in Roman Catholic parlance, where it first appears, is also somewhat fuzzy, sometimes referencing the addition of a musical setting or the presence of additional clergy. However, my reading seems to suggest that it was originally coined by reverse formation from the invention of the suitably-designated 'Low Mass,' i.e. one performed by a priest with minimal assistance, and in the absence of a congregation. I would be happy to see the term 'High Mass' dismissed from any sort of E.G.C. usage, while in contrast 'Low Mass' seems particularly helpful as a label to distinguish those operations founded in Liber XV which are undertaken in the absence of the people and therefore primarily for the benefit of the officers.

Magisterium—The teaching function of the Church generally and the clergy particularly: promulgation of the Law and adumbration of the Supreme Secret.

***Mysteria Mystica Maxima* (M∴M∴M∴)** —The "preliminary degrees" of O.T.O., from Minerval (O°) through VII°.

Mystic Marriage—The beginning of the sixth ceremony of the Gnostic Mass, in which the elements of the Eucharist are perfected prior to their consummation.

Narthex—An anteroom or area just outside of the ritual space. The narthex is where the congregation assembles before and after Church ceremonies.

Nephesch—The Animal Soul, a qabalistic "part of the soul" embracing perception and subconscious reflex.

Nepios—(Greek, 'child') A prayer addressed to Ra-Hoor-Khuit as the Child, based on the Christian Pater Noster. Two principal versions exist, both from *The Book of Lies* (chapters 2 and 44).

Neschemah—The Intuition, a qabalistic "part of the soul" corresponding to the super-personal emanation of Understanding.

Novice—A member of the Church undergoing a novitiate, or period of training and preparation prior to **ordination**.

Novitiate—1. The period of training undergone by a **novice**. 2. The entire class of **novices**, considered collectively.

The adjectival construction 'novitiate clergy' is incorrect; they are **novice clergy**.

Office—1. An arrangement of prayers and worship for a specific time of day or time of year. Vespers is a diurnal office (for evening time) and there are annual offices for the spring Holy Days. An office as such does not generally include the administration of the Eucharist or any other sacrament. 2. The work undertaken by an officer.

Officer—A ritualist with a designated role (or **office**) in a given ceremony. The chief officer of a ceremony is the *presiding* officer; those who lead the congregation and recite significant invocations are *principal* officers; those other than principal officers are *assisting officers*. In the Gnostic Mass, the priest and priestess are presiding officers. They along with the deacon are principal officers, and the children are assisting officers.

Officiant—A generic term for a presiding officer, irrespective of clergy status.

Order of the Eagle—An honor assigned to historical women who have been formally recognized by the U.S. Grand Lodge of O.T.O. as having "contributed in diverse but important ways to the development and advancement of the great principles of our Order."

Order of the Lion—An honor assigned to historical men who have been formally recognized by the U.S. Grand Lodge of O.T.O. as having "contributed in diverse but important ways to the development and advancement of the great principles of our Order."

Orders—1. Classes of clergy within the hierarchy of the Church. 2. The obligations of congregational service and hierarchical obedience peculiar to clergy status. In E.G.C. there are five orders of clergy. In ascending rank, they are the diaconate, priesthood, episcopate, primacy, and patriarchate. The novitiate is a further subclass of clergy, but since they lack ordination, and they are not properly an "order."

Ordination—The conferral of diaconal and priestly **orders**. Ordination to the episcopate is usually called **consecration**. Clergy working under the sanction of the Church without the benefit of orders are **novices**.

Ordinand—One undergoing the process of ordination.

Paleognosticism—The ancient Hellenistic religious culture mixing Near Eastern mythology and Neoplatonic soteriology. Paleognosticism was quite diverse, and disparate groups such as the Naassenes and the Valentinians each held different positions that might be seen in resonance with Thelemic Gnostic ideas.

Particula—The fragment from the broken host used in the **commixtio**.

People—The **Congregation**. A usage established in Liber XV.

Perform—Some people find this verb troubling because of its modern association with theatrical and musical entertainment. It is indeed worth pointing out that the Mass is not a "performance" *in that sense*. Attendees at the Mass are participants, not mere spectators. But the general denotations of performance, including the application of a skill and work according to a plan, are all pertinent to the Gnostic Mass.

Nor is the idea of theatrical performance completely alien to our work as Mass ritualists. While no level of theatrical technique will *by itself* consummate a work of Eucharistic Magick, it is still the case that a certain amount of theatrical skill is needed in order to make the dramatic ritual of the Gnostic Mass effective. Also, the denigration earned by some contemporary shows should not obscure the ancient traditions of sacred theater, which emerged from the cult of Dionysos and in turn contributed to the mystery religions of late antiquity. If we can be said to "perform the Gnostic Mass" with the enthusiasm and ecstasy reported for performances of these ancient religious rites, then we are fulfilling our Church and ourselves.

What is more, we have the highest relevant sanction for this usage, in *Liber Legis* II:35, "Let the rituals be rightly performed with joy and beauty!"

Practice—I prefer "practice" to "rehearsal" when referencing enactments of the Mass. The difference in connotation is that "rehearsal" is merely preparatory, while "practice" has a larger sense: the one indicated in "medical practice" or "*Magick in Theory & Practice*." The idea of "rehearsal" suggests an attempt to execute the ritual without a resulting effect on attendees. But the effect on attendees is not the sole or even principal purpose of the Gnostic Mass from the perspective of a practicing officer—whether attendees are present or not. In general, I recommend dispensing with preparatory walk-throughs and neutered quasi-ritual in favor of actual magick to whatever degree the ritualists are capable. (See also **Low Mass**.)

Pranava—Orignally the Hindu AUM or OM. In Thelemic ecclesiastical practice, this mantric syllable is identified with the Christian "Amen," and often revised as AUMGN (or AΥMΓN), for symbolic, phonetic, and numerical reasons.

Primitive Cake—A **Cake of Light** that has been bloodied in accordance with *CCXX* III:23-24, and not yet burned in keeping with III:25.

Private Ceremony—A ritual of the Church attended only by initiates of *Mysteria Mystica Maxima*.

Prunikos—(Greek, "lewd one") An incantation in the Bathyllic language from *The Vision and the Voice*, starting with "Omari tessala marax." The English translation begins, "I am the harlot that shaketh death." *Prunikos* is a Greek word meaning "lewd one," which was used by early Gnostics as a title for Barbelo. The Prunikos may be sung to sound effect using the tune "Zavorka" (originally from *Kancional*, 1602 EV).

Public Ceremony—A formal operation of the Church open to profane visitors and/or laity who have not been initiated in *Mysteria Mystica Maxima*.

Rite—1. An institution comprehending a ceremonial tradition expressed in functional ritual. *Ecclesia Gnostica Catholica* is one rite within O.T.O. and *Mysteria Mystica Maxima* is another. Traditional Christianity includes a variety of rites, as does Freemasonry. 2. (*in sensu lato*) A ceremony.

Ritual—1. The authoritative text describing a ceremony and instructing its officers. 2. The ceremony itself.

Ruach—The Intellect, a qabalistic "part of the soul" embracing conscious reflection and reason, and corresponding to the emanation of Beauty.

Rubric—The instructions for actions, or other details excluding recitations and speeches, represented in a ritual. In dramatic literature for the theater, such text components are called "stage directions." The rubrics in the rituals of this book, like those in most editions of Liber XV, are frequently *italicized*. (In old Christian sacramentaries they were in *red*, thus the word "rubric.")

Sacerdotal—Priestly.

Sacerdotalism—A doctrine (foreign to E.G.C.) requiring the intervention of a priesthood for the salvation of a believer.

Sacrament—A sacred ritual.

Sacramentary—A book of rituals for Church use.

Sacristy—A space set aside for the preparation of ritual **officers** or clergy for Church ceremonies. In E.G.C., particularly the place to which the Priestess and Children retire before their entrance in the Gnostic Mass.

Saint—A person considered to be holy. See the extended discussion in "Secret Chiefs and the Invisible Church" in this book, along with pp. 54-62 of *Thelema for the People*.

Sanctuary—1. An informal institution comprehending the work of a local community within the Church, i.e. a group of collaborating clergy and their associated laity. 2. The ritual space proper within a physical temple facility, as distinguished from the **narthex**, **sacristy**, and other areas.

Sanctuary, Sovereign—The single global body of the highest initiates of O.T.O. The doctrines and practices of the Gnostic Catholic Church are intended to promulgate the Law of Thelema and to adumbrate the secrets of the Sovereign Sanctuary.

Say—This usage follows a longstanding custom in Roman Catholicism, where Priests "say" Mass routinely. It exhibits two difficulties. First, it implies the Roman Catholic theory of sacramental efficacy, in which practically incompetent ritualists are considered to be effective merely by virtue of their institutional status and having "come to the altar intending to do what the Church does" (*De Defectibus* 26). In contrast, "the Gnostic Mass is a magical rite, depending for its efficacy on the knowledge, power and talent of the celebrants. The effectiveness of the rite is directly proportional to the magical skill of the officers" (Sabazius, "The Role and Function of Thelemic Clergy in Ecclesia Gnostica Catholica"). Second, "to say the Mass" prioritizes the verbal over the gestural, the word over the deed. In the *Faust* of E.G.C. Saint Wolfgang von Goethe, the magician protagonist declares: "The spirit speaks! And lo the way is freed, / I calmly write: 'In the beginning was the Deed!'" (I, ll. 1236-7). In this same spirit, I and other Gnostic Mass participants often colloquially refer to "doing Mass." However, the best formulation is that of Liber XXX (v. 13): "True ritual is as much action as word; it is Will."

Shrine—The space in the East of the Gnostic Mass temple which is enclosed by the veil: i.e. the High Altar and its appurtenances, the super-altar, the pillars, and the dais—except for the steps.

Temple—1. A space for ceremonial operations, particularly one configured according to the instructions in Liber XV. 2. A facility housing such a space. 3. Mystic Temple: a body of VI° initiates of *Mysteria Mystica Maxima.*

Tersanctus—The incantation ΑΓΙΟΣ ΑΓΙΟΣ ΑΓΙΟΣ ΙΑΩ corresponding to the "*Sanctus, Sanctus Sanctus Dominus Deus Sabaoth*" of the Roman liturgy, and the "*Qadosh, Qadosh, Qadosh l'Adonai Tzabaoth*" of the Hebrew liturgy.

(The term "Trishagion," while reflecting the actual Greek of the Gnostic Mass, refers to a very different prayer in the Greek Orthodox liturgy.) Biblical precedents can be found in Isaiah VI:3 and Revelation VI:8.

Tabernacle—An ornate cabinet designed to hold the Cup and the Paten, a **ciborium** and a bottle of wine, and *The Book of the Law*.

Tu Qui Es—(Latin "Thou Who Art") The original or "father" anthem of the Gnostic Mass, first composed for Crowley's Masonic mystery-play *The Ship*.

Work—This verb has a rich magical heritage and evokes the idea of the Gnostic Mass as a magical "working." It does, however, suffer from the ill connotations associated with backlash from the Protestant ethic. All work and no "play" (performance?) might represent the Mass as a pious chore rather than the holy exuberance suggested by "to **celebrate**."

Yechidah—The Self, a qabalistic "part of the soul" corresponding to the emanation of the Crown.

Bibliographies

Volumes Containing Approved Texts of Liber XV

The International, March 1918, ed. Aleister Crowley.
The Blue Equinox (Equinox III:1), ed. Baphomet XI°.
Equinox III:10, ed. Hymenaeus Beta with Frater HaLayL.
Magick: Book 4 (revised one-volume edition), ed. Hymenæus Beta.
Mystery of Mystery (*Red Flame* #2), ed. T Apiryon.

Other Key Works of Aleister Crowley

Little Essays toward Truth.
Jesus (a.k.a. *The Gospel According to St. Bernard Shaw,*
        a.k.a. *Crowley on Christ*).
777 and Other Qabalistic Writings of Aleister Crowley.
The Book of Lies.
The Holy Books of Thelema (Equinox III:9).
The Law Is for All.
The Vision & the Voice, and other papers (Equinox IV:2).

Contemporary Works Regarding E.G.C.

These books and articles have all been published by and for initiates since the 1970s revival of O.T.O. and E.G.C. under Hymenæus Alpha.

Mystery of Mystery, by T Apriyon and Helena.
Rites of Public Celebration, edited by Fr. Mesniu.
Thelema for the People, by M. Dionysius Rogers.
Advice for Deacons, by Dionysus Soter.
"On the Gnostic Catholic Church," by Hymenæus Beta, *The
        Magical Link* III:4 (Winter 1990 EV).
"New E.G.C.-O.T.O. Policy," by Hymenæus Beta, *The Magical
        Link* V:3 (Fall 1991 EV).
Gnostic Gnews, Vol. I, Nos. 1-4 (1988–1989 EV).
Liber XV with "Additional Stage Directions and Commentary" by
        Soror Meral, *In the Continuum* II:4 (1979 EV).
To Perfect This Feast, by James and Nancy Wasserman.

Non-E.G.C. Neo-Gnostic Texts

Gnosticism: New Light on the Ancient Tradition of Inner Knowing, by Stephan A. Hoeller. A popularizing primer of Christian Neo-Gnosticism.

The Gnostic Jung and the Seven Sermons to the Dead, by Stephan A. Hoeller.

Clothed with the Sun, by Anna (Bonus) Kingsford. Includes all of the visionary writings of the founder of the Hermetic Society, who was also an influence on founding patriarch Jules Doinel of the French Gnostic Church.

Astral Projection, Ritual Magic, and Alchemy by "S.L. Mathers and others." Interesting for the Cromlech Temple material in part 8.

The Serpent's Gift: Gnostic Reflections on the Study of Religion, by Jeffrey Kripal. Insightful explorations of "eroticism, humanism, comparative mysticism, and esotericism" in religion as approached through academic research.

Initiatic Eroticism, by Maria de Naglowska. See especially the essays "White Masses, Black Masses, Golden Masses," "The Priestesses of the Future," and "Masculine Satanism, Feminine Satanism."

Pertinent Histories, Theory of Religion, Liturgical Studies

This list is intended as a supplement to the "Book List for E.G.C. Priests and Priestesses" by Sabazius (*Mystery of Mystery,* p. 326). All O.T.O. initiates are urged to consult the fuller curricula published by Hymenaeus Beta in the revised edition of *Magick: Book Four* (pp. 476-485).

The Unknown God: W.T. Smith and the Thelemites, by Martin P. Starr. History of the Thelemic movement in North America during the lifetime of the Prophet.

The Chalice of Ecstasy, by Frater Achad. Charles Stansfeld Jones' qabalistic exegesis of Wagner's *Parsifal.*

Devil-Worship in France, by Arthur Edward Waite. A contemporary history of the "Leo Taxil" hoax, notable relative to the E.G.C. forebear rite *Église Gnostique.*

Église Gnostique: History, Sacraments and Teachings, by Jules Doinel (ed. Rune Ødegaard). A popular (i.e. not scholarly) edition of these historical documents.

Beyond Enlightenment, by David Allen Harvey. A historical study of Martinism and related French movements in the period of O.T.O. origins.

The Essence of Christianity, by Ludwig Feuerbach. There is no god but man.

The Theosophical Enlightenment, by Joscelyn Godwin. History of the origins of modern occultism, along with solar and phallic theories of religion.

Do What You Will: A History of Anti-Morality, by Geoffrey Ashe. Historical study of the tradition of paleo-thelemic libertinism, from Rabelais to Crowley.

The Mass: A Liturgical Commentary (2 vols.), by A. Croegaert. A highly detailed and informative study of the Roman Catholic ritual of the Tridentine Mass.

The Origins of European Dissent, by R.I. Moore. History of resistence to Roman Catholic hegemony prior to the Protestant movement, with fascinating details on numerous individual heretics, and sects including Catharism. (See also *Heresies of the High Middle Ages,* by Wakefield and Evans.)

The Grail: From Celtic Myth to Christian Symbol, by Roger Sherman Loomis. A conservative, literature-based study of the origins of the Grail story. Includes translations of the principal early Grail narratives.

A Short History of the Western Liturgy, by Theodor Klauser. A primer.

The Ecclesiastical Hierarchy, by Pseudo-Dionysius. This key text of medieval angelology also includes Neoplatonic reflections on the Christian sacramental system.

Drudgery Divine, by Jonathan Z. Smith. Explains how scholars fail to come to terms with the origins of Christianity.

To Take Place, by Jonathan Z. Smith. A provocative (and locative) theory of ritual.

Holy Terrors: Thinking about Religion after September 11, by Bruce Lincoln. Provides a comprehensive definition of religion that does not rely on "belief" or "god," and insightfully discusses the potentials of religion in twenty-first-century society.

Apocalypse, by D.H. Lawrence. A stunning and highly Thelemic reading of the biblical book of Revelation.

The Apocalypse Unsealed, by James M. Pryse. A valuable esoteric study of Revelation, as glowingly reviewed by Crowley and Yarker.

The Mysteries of the Qabalah, or Occult Agreement of the Two Testaments, by Eliphas Levi. An occultist comparison of the visions of Ezekiel and John.

Jesus Christ, Sun of God: Ancient Cosmology and Early Christian Symbolism, by David Fideler. A penetrating look at heliolatry in the origins of Christian scripture, related to the Pythagorean tradition.

Egyptian Magic, by Florence Farr. Includes paleognostic materials from the Bruce Codex, edited by an adept of Mathers' Golden Dawn.

The Mystery-Religions, by S. Angus. An older study that does not benefit from the latest archaeological or theoretical materials, but one that actively and usefully attends to comparisons between pagan mystery cults and early Christianity.

The Gnostics, by Jacques Lacarrière. An accessible and imaginative description of Gnosticism in antiquity and its relevance to modernity.

History of Gnosticism, by Giovanni Filoramo. A more detailed and scholarly treatment of ancient Gnosticism, also tying it to later movements.

Images of the Feminine in Gnosticism, edited by Karen L. King. A diverse collection of valuable papers.

Hermetica, edited by Brian Coepenhaver. Religious and philosophical texts from the pagan Neoplatonist milieu of late antiquity.

The Mass and Its Mysteries Compared to the Ancient Mysteries, by Jean-Marie Ragon. Recommended by Crowley as "a complete demonstration of the incorporation of the Solar and Phallic mysteries in Christianity."

Lunar and Sex Worship, by Ida Craddock. Esoteric comparative religion, drawing extensively on the works of prior theorists of phallicism.

The Symbolical Language of Ancient Art and Mythology, by Richard Payne Knight.

"Section 2" Reading List for E.G.C.

Crowley complemented the instructional matter in his A∴A∴ reading list with an inventory of "Other books, principally fiction, of a generally suggestive and helpful kind." The present document is intended to supply that service for aspirants to holy orders in E.G.C.

Parsifal, by Richard Wagner. An important source of symbolism in the Gnostic Mass. The Englished version by Oliver Huckel (*Wagner's Parsifal,* 1904) is helpful.

Golden Twigs, by Aleister Crowley. Short stories that illustrate principles of religious theory.

Seraphita, by Honoré de Balzac. An influential esoteric novel by an author recommended by Crowley.

Ancient Evenings, by Norman Mailer. A compelling re-creation of the magical perspective of the pharaohs.

The Bacchae, by Euripides. A classical dramatic exposition of the Mysteries of Dionysus. See especially the James M. Pryse translation with commentary, *Adorers of Dionysos: Bakchai.*

The Scroll of Thoth, by Richard L. Tierney. Pulp adventure stories set in antiquity, with the Gnostic heresiarch Simon Magus as the protagonist.

The Golden Ass, by Apuleius. Crowley says, "Valuable for those who have wit to understand it."

Antichrist, by Cecilia Holland. A story of Saint Frederick von Hohenstaufen.

Memoirs of a Gnostic Dwarf, by David Madsen. A novel about a Gnostic sect in sixteenth-century Italy.

The War Hound and the World's Pain, by Michael Moorcock. An inventive Graal story.

La-Bas, by J. K. Huysmans. Crowley says, "An account of the extravagances caused by the Sin-complex."

En Route, by J. K. Huysmans. Crowley says, "An account of the follies of Christian mysticism."

With the Adepts, by Franz Hartmann. A Rosicrucian fantasy by a founding member of the Sanctuary of the Gnosis.

Jurgen, by James Branch Cabell. A picaresque fantasy. Chapter 22 "As to a Veil They Broke" is an artful rewrite of the Gnostic Mass, which got this novel banned.

Something about Eve, by James Branch Cabell. Explores themes such as the diabolical pact and solar-phallic religion.

The Baphomet, by Pierre Klossowski. It has been said of the author that "he never failed to keep one foot in the seminary and the other in the brothel."

The Sea Priestess, by Dion Fortune. A leisurely novel about the visionary aspects of magical practice, as well as their effects on artistic creativity and interaction with libidinal expression.

Many Dimensions, by Charles Williams. A parable regarding the magical will, set in an extended scrimmage over the Stone of the Wise from King Solomon's Crown.

The Theater and Its Double, by Antonin Artaud. Includes avant-garde application of alchemy to dramatic arts.

294

Heaven and Hell, by Aldous Huxley. Further develops some ideas about religion and visionary experience along lines inaugurated in the same author's *Doors of Perception.*

"Tlön, uqbar, orbis tertius," "The Aleph," and other short stories by Jorge Luis Borges.

The Erotic Comedies, by Marco Vassi. Profound and hilarious short stories. "The Land of the Sperm King" is indispensable.

Godbody, by Theodore Sturgeon. The final novel by a perceptive storyteller.

Stranger in a Strange Land, by Robert Heinlein. This tale about a Gnostic sect in the near future was influenced by Thelema, and has been a major influence on American counter-culture.

VALIS, by Phillip K. Dick. A consummate neo-gnostic novel, written after the author's own spontaneous mystical experience.

Ubik, by Phillip K. Dick, and also *The Three Stigmata of Palmer Eldritch,* by the same author. Science-fiction parables of Eucharistic magick.

Promethea, by Alan Moore. A hermetic-qabalistic superheroine saga in five graphic novels.

Hypnerotomachia Poliphili, by Francesco Colonna. The so-called "pagan bible of the Renaissance."

The Works of Francois Rabelais. Crowley says, "Invaluable for Wisdom."

The Expulsion of the Triumphant Beast, by Giordano Bruno. An Hermetic fable of universal reformation.

The Marriage of Heaven and Hell, by William Blake. Along with his other works.

The Bible, by various authors unknown. Crowley says, "The Hebrew and Greek Originals are of Qabalistic value. It contains also many magical apologues, and recounts many tales of folk-lore and magical rites.

Also by M. Dionysius Rogers:

Mysteries of the Great Beast Aleister Crowley

A Liturgical Cycle for Thelemites

Full texts and rubrics for a set of five original
ceremonies celebrating the accomplishments of the
most consequential magician of our age:

- Initiation of the Prophet
- The Prophet and His Bride
- The Supreme Ritual
- Annihilation of the Prophet
- Greater Feast of the Prophet

Thelema for the People

Exploring New Æon Gnosticism

The people who join as the congregation in the
Gnostic Mass of Aleister Crowley's magical religion
are not passive spectators. Aspirants and laity in the
Gnostic Catholic Church are Thelemites participating in a modern mystery rite. *Thelema for the People*
supplies in-depth discussions of issues important for
such participation:

- Our Law of Do what thou wilt
- Our Gnostic Mass of
  Light, Life, Love and Liberty
- Our Creed and its arcana
- Our Prayer to the Crowned and Conquering Child
- Our Prophet of the New Law
- Our Æon of Force and Fire

In addition, the book offers useful histories of Gnosticism and Thelema,
and outlines an original program of contemplative practice for those who
embrace the Law of Thelema and seek to manifest it in daily living and
lifelong attainment.

Available in paperback and e-book formats on Amazon.com.

Raise the Spell

An Arsenal of Thelemic Ceremony

Collects ceremonies oriented to the Thelemic liturgical year, original work along the fundamental lines of magick as laid down in traditional canons of Thelemic ritual, and domestic rituals for Thelemic households. Over a dozen rituals with full texts and rubrics, including:

- A Short Eucharist
- Liturgy of the Word of the Law
- Feasts of the Cross-Quarters
- Daimonic Vespers
- Vernal Holy Days: Office of Readings
- Renunciation of Slave Religion
- And Others

Available in paperback and e-book formats on Amazon.com.

Forthcoming from M. Dionysius Rogers:

Erotopharmakohymnia Onorio

A Ludibrium of Initiation

Recounts a dream-vision in which the protagonist Lucius Onorio is inducted into the mysteries of a fabulous realm.

A Bishop's Advice

For Gnostic Mass Officers

Practical instruction regarding the performance of the Gnostic Mass by Thelemic magicians.

Made in United States
Orlando, FL
24 June 2022